Contrarian Ripple Trading

Contrarian Ripple Trading

A Low-Risk Strategy to Profiting from Short-Term Stock Trades

AIDAN J. McNAMARA

MARTHA A. BROŻYNA

Foreword by
ROBERT TEITELMAN

John Wiley & Sons, Inc.

Published by John Wiley & Sons, Inc., Hoboken, New Jersey.

Published simultaneously in Canada.

Wiley Bicentennial Logo: Richard J. Pacifico

For general information on our other products and services or for technical support, please contact our Customer Care Department within the United States at (800) 762-2974, outside the United States at (317) 572-3993 or fax (317) 572-4002.

Wiley also publishes its books in a variety of electronic formats. Some content that appears in print may not be available in electronic formats. For more information about Wiley products, visit our Web site at www.wiley.com.

Library of Congress Cataloging-in-Publication Data:

McNamara, Aidan J., 1957–
    Contrarian ripple trading : a low-risk strategy to profiting from short-term stock trades / Aidan J. McNamara and Martha A. Brożyna.
      p. cm.
    "Published simultaneously in Canada."
    Includes bibliographical references.
    ISBN 978-0-470-13976-9 (cloth)
  1. Speculation.   2. Stocks.   3. Investments.   I. Brozyna, Martha A., 1973–   II. Title.
    HG6041.M386 2008
    332.63'22–dc22   2007016901

Printed in the United States of America.

10 9 8 7 6 5 4 3 2 1

For our children,
Jonathan, Justine, and Liam

Contents

Foreword

There are few things in contemporary American life more ubiquitous, and more replete with contradictions, than personal investing. Over the last half century, ordinary adults have been expected not only to intelligently invest in stocks as a sort of recreational pastime—a rite of adulthood, an aspect of manhood, particularly when markets are rising and money appears to be there for the plucking—but increasingly, with the spread of self-directed pension plans, as a necessary source of retirement funds. Speculation, as opposed to investing, has become something of a right, like legalized gambling.

At the same time, the myth arose with the advent of personal computers and the Internet that amateurs had access to the same financial information and the same tools as professionals. This produced the shimmering mirage of the "level playing field" upon which amateur investors could compete effectively with the pros. Personal investing thus became wrapped in a sort of Emersonian optimism: Investing had been democratized. The failure to play the market successfully suggested some deficiency in the individual, a personal failure to seize the day with real, particularly postretirement, repercussions.

Around these potent myths about personal investing has grown a tangled mass of magazines, books, Web sites, TV shows, motivational speakers, conferences, even cruises, which paper over or simply ignore the underlying reality of investing. The reality, backed by decades of academic studies, is that amateurs will not beat pros, not to mention the market as a whole, (which study after study suggests that even pros have difficulty doing), particularly when you factor in transaction and opportunity costs. There is no level playing field unless regulators artificially create one. Amateurs can do decently well by investing for the long-term, dollar-cost averaging, or putting money into intelligently balanced low-cost indexing—the solution long preached by Vanguard founder John Bogle.

But speculation is a fool's errand. We know that and yet we're also aware that Boglesesque strategies are about as interesting as watching paint dry. The precepts of intelligent investing for the long run can be printed on the back of a postcard. They are not complex. They do not require special expertise. Investing, in short, is dull. Speculation is exciting. Investing should be relatively low cost. Speculation generates flocks of fees. Investing produces modest but real returns over the long run. Speculation holds the promise of Vegas-type riches.

The brutal fact is that you can't make lots of money selling magazines, books, brokerage services, or attracting a large television audience by simply mumbling the spare catechism of "intelligent investing." You have to wave your arms and offer hot stocks. You have to sell the dream.

Enter Aidan McNamara and Martha Brożyna who actually have the nerve to begin their introduction to *Contrarian Ripple Trading* with the warning, "This book will not make you rich." This is enough to jolt any bewildered devotee of the personal investing literature. The pair is not saying that this book will not make you money, just that it won't make you rich, which is a subtle, if important, distinction. And quickly enough there are other signs that this book is something of a fascinating outlier in the investing genre. The authors accept many of the realities that make speculation, particularly for amateurs, so difficult. They know most working adults have neither the time nor the skill necessary to conduct the kind of investment research of professionals. They recognize the daunting odds against long-term success. They point out the duplicities and irrationalities of many investing "systems." Then they do something that's really eye-opening: they open up their books and show their trading records.

Although the title evokes the kind of technical trading that has long been one of the more seductive come-ons in personal investing, their technique is based on a pragmatic empiricism developed over a number of years. ("Ripple" in this context comes from the developers of Dow Theory, who had a penchant for ocean metaphors.) They are less interested in the metaphysics of market cycles and trends and more into the regularity of certain short-term market tendencies. *Contrarian Ripple Trading* rather modestly combines aspects of "investing," notably the need for safety and decent returns, with the short-termism and quick turns of "speculation." They are not value investors. They are also not day traders. Yet their technique, which hinges on discipline, a basic knowledge of their stocks, and a relatively modest set of metrics, can be mastered and practiced by any reasonably intelligent person.

The key to their approach is that word *contrarian*. Investment and market commentators, from John Maynard Keynes to Warren Buffett and George Soros, have noted that market success often hinges on trading against the moblike currents that determine a market price at any given moment. But acting in the market as a true contrarian is extremely difficult, not to mention, lonely. You are always fighting accepted wisdom. You are always battling the current. As Keynes once noted so famously, the market is a beauty pageant in which judges are not attempting to arrive at any objective measure of beauty, but rather trying desperately to guess how the other judges are voting. Value investors, of course, argue that over the long run a general consensus will emerge that distinguishes "beauty" from, well, nonbeauty. In other words, a rational objectivity asserts itself over the long term. McNamara and Brożyna acknowledge the difficulties of the value investors' craft and the patience, fortitude, and sheer expertise necessary to make it work—virtues only the extremely rare amateur masters. (In fact, those are virtues few professionals possess, Buffett being such an extraordinary anomaly that some financial economists once attributed his success to luck.) Nevertheless, the authors identify another kind of contrarianism that is better suited to the nonprofessional. Their ripple technique employs a routinized contrarianism that Soros calls *reflexivity*, grounded not in murky, mysterious market patterns, but in the comprehensible behavior of that dominant force in markets—ironically, professional investors. They offer a mechanism. Playing the "ripples" can occur because of the tendency of professionals to mirror the overall market and to regularly overshoot some ideal price on both the upside and downside. Their contrarianism is both short-term and prudent, tailored to the realities of the ordinary retail investor.

If Buffett's school of value investment can be translated into a rough-and-ready market Platonism—there is something called *value* that only manifests itself over time—the trading technique presented in *Contrarian Ripple Trading* offers a different, far more practical, if less idealistic world view. Value investing is an excruciatingly difficult discipline to do well. The stock market as a whole might be more efficient if everyone tried their hardest to discover real, long-term value, but for individuals that project would involve both an unreasonable expenditure of effort and more often than not produce extremely ugly losses. A world in which everyone is a value investor would generate even greater disparities between winners and losers than today's highly diverse markets. Value investing is an ideal; ripple trading, like indexing, is a practical compromise with market reality.

Let's not get carried away. Ripple trading is not the answer to all the contradictions raised by mass investing—nor is it the magic carpet ride to megawealth. We do not know what would happen if millions suddenly embraced it; but it might not be good (except for the authors, of course). This book does suggest, and this is heartening, that you can combine some form of short-term speculation with prudence and cost-effectiveness in a variety of market conditions. It also suggests that you don't have to be a cowboy to survive in the Wild West, and it's not "immoral" in the Buffettian sense to engage in short-term trading. As long as we continue to believe in some variation of what George W. Bush called "an ownership society"—and there are no signs of a retreat from that concept even as the Bush era fades away—the ripple trading technique described by McNamara and Brożyna belongs in every stock player's diversified bag of tricks. If you doubt it, check their results.

Robert Teitelman

Preface

O ur mission in writing this book is very simple. We wish to outline a method with which regular, middle-class families across America can earn an extra income through short-term trading in stocks over and above what they earn from their regular jobs. Our straightforward technique is based on an easy-to-understand, yet effective equities trading strategy using predominantly well-known, large-capitalization company stocks.

Many of those books crowding the investing section shelves in bookstores claim that they can help you make fast money by investing in the stock market. However, they are a little deceptive in the promises they make and the actual results they deliver. When we pick up a book written by some big name who controls investment pools containing hundreds of millions of dollars, yet promises he can help the Average Joe replicate his success, our finely tuned BS antennae activate immediately. After all, investing is this expert's day job. It involves constant attention to and copious research on the business and financial worlds, something that the average person cannot realistically do. The average person does not have the capital to invest or the time to devote to study of huge amounts of research material, which would also include reading and absorbing research done by others. The amount of information on individual stocks and on market trends available today from many different sources, delivered both on paper and electronically, is staggering. Moreover, many of these big name traders and investors also have a natural gift for picking stocks. It is for this reason that we cannot help but shake our heads as to how they can claim that they can virtually wave a magic wand and effortlessly transfer their investing or trading talents and skills in a way that lets regular folks with limited resources imitate their success. This is like the world-famous Luciano Pavarotti promising to give away the secrets that allow anyone to be a successful opera singer, which, if feasible, would soon lead to a worldwide glut of tenors!

Promised successes that really can't be delivered are not the only problems with the big name books. We are always bemused by academic and oftentimes pseudo-academic investing books that come complete with complex charts, ratios, and arcane jargon of those who approach investing from a scientific approach. (Stochastic oscillators anyone?) Clearly, whatever the value of these well-researched and thoughtfully presented tracts, their relevance and value to the Average Joe is probably close to zero, except possibly for those out there suffering from acute insomnia.

So who are we and what on earth possessed us to think that we have something to offer to others on the subject of making money through short-term stock market trading? We are a married couple, both regular people who work outside of the investment world, but who happen to be active traders. We have developed a method that consistently generates short-term profits on trades in large capitalization stocks regardless of whether the market has gone up, down, or sideways. We have learned this skill through direct trading experience and, in the case of Aidan, over 13 years of successful trading using precisely this technique. Our most recent track record, a listing of all of our 2005, 2006, and January and February 2007 trades, speaks for itself and can be found in Appendixes A through D at the end of this book. (As an aside, we have yet to find any stock trading or investing guru willing to publish a book in which his or her own recent trading record is revealed in its entirety for all to see.) We believe strongly that we have something of value to offer based on the proven success of our technique. We also believe that it can help many readers who would be very happy to achieve what can be essentially considered an additional income through the disciplined short-term trading of stocks. We call our approach *contrarian ripple trading.*

The difference between us and the high profile experts is setting a goal that has not only been in our own reach, but we believe is within the reach of most regular Americans. Our method of earning income from trading is done in such a way that it should put at ease even the most conservative and fearful.

We use a low-risk approach that essentially focuses on the trading of stocks of well-known, large-capitalization companies, the kind that also typically pay out reasonable dividends. We trade stocks that do not fall into this category only to a relatively small extent and only in cases where our own personal knowledge of the company's business and prospects make us comfortable regarding the company's stability and future growth potential. It is precisely because we approach the subject of short-term trading as "regular folks" that we are qualified to help those people who would like to make money from trading stocks, but feel that the high-risk/reward strategy that goes along with making a "killing" on the stock market, an almost unattainable ambition, is not for them.

Because we consider our method of trading to be an essentially simple one, we are not going to dazzle our readers with pseudo-science. In our explanations, we attempt to avoid talking down to our audience or wrapping them up in confusing market theories, jargon, ratios, and assorted gobbledygook that fill most of the tomes penned by the majority of those whose writing on investing and trading strategies is aimed at Joe—and Jane—Public. We avoid passing on to our readers the kind of immersion in irrelevant complexities that plague most investing and trading books precisely because of their irrelevance. It is in any case our contention that most how-to books of this genre try to teach their audience relatively simple techniques, some of which are useful, others wrong-headed. Indeed, we have read more than one investing book that takes over 300 pages to educate its readers that the long-term strategy of buying and holding stocks is the best way to earn money in the stock market. This is not necessarily an unworthy lesson if the subject of the book is investing rather than trading. However, if this is the author's basic message, and it is one that actually can be adequately covered in one chapter, what are the other eleven chapters about? These books tend to cover the simple basics of the stock market to a ludicrous degree of detail based on an assumption that their readers lack the most basic knowledge of the stock market, investing, or personal finance at all.

But there are other problems we perceive with these books. Even those that start with the assumption that their readers have zero knowledge on the subject, will often try to cover ground of what should really be territory reserved for the more sophisticated or professional reader, including areas such as futures and options. These books provide detailed information on how these instruments work, but often warn the average investor or trader off using them (and rightfully so). In general, we feel that the inherent simplicity of what is offered to the general public as investment "how-to" writing does not lend itself to producing books that pass the "weight test" that many authors feel establish credibility. As a result, we are convinced that much of the additional content of these books is included as a form of padding to ensure that a book is perceived as having "gravitas." We endeavor not to fall into this trap of adding quantity at the expense of quality.

Aidan McNamara works in advertising sales for a New York based business and financial weekly magazine, *The Deal*, a publication that covers the world of mergers & acquisitions, private equity, bankruptcy and restructuring, and other topics touching on what the publication calls "the deal economy." Note, he is not a financial journalist. He works on the business side of the publication, and his advertising clients are mostly marketing professionals at investment banks and corporate law firms that look to *The Deal* as a relevant platform for the placement of their advertising targeted narrowly at "deal professionals." He has worked in financial publishing, and specifically in financial advertising sales, for the last eleven years. For the fourteen years prior to that, he worked for a London-based international bank in a number of commercial banking positions including both long-term and short-term assignments in dozens of countries spanning four continents. He was posted to the New York branch of the bank in 1992 and has worked in Manhattan since then.

UK native Aidan has had professional involvement with Wall Street as well as its London equivalent "The City," and the financial and investing community for all his working life. This has offered him keen insights into the ways in which this world works, but he has himself never worked as an investing professional or anything similar. From an academic background, he is far removed from the position of a financially qualified individual. His master's degree is in area studies from the University of London (London School of Economics/School of Slavonic & East European Studies)—a political science degree with a focus on the politics and economics of Eastern Europe. His bachelor's degree is in German from the University of Manchester, England.

Martha Brożyna holds a Ph.D. in history from the University of Southern California, and a bachelor's degree in history and political science from Rutgers University. Her educational background is even further removed from the financial world than Aidan's. Martha has taught courses on ancient and medieval gender and sexuality at Rutgers and has edited one published book related to her specialty.[1] Since marrying Aidan in 2002, she has become a strong devotee of the short-term trading technique that Aidan has used for many years. Presently, both Martha and Aidan use this technique together as a part of running their own finances, and Martha also successfully manages a significant amount of money for family members (informally and unpaid) using the same trading principles.[2]

We are not Peter Lynch, John Templeton, Jeremy Siegel—or even Jim Cramer. Yet this is precisely the reason that we feel eminently qualified to advise people who, just like us, do not have the professional investing track record or business studies academic background that usually mark out an investing or trading guru. We believe that approaching this subject as nonexperts, we have nonetheless developed a simple yet successful technique through personal experience that addresses the real needs and realities of our audience. This approach sets us apart from those whose writings on this subject imply they can create a nation of Warren Buffetts.

The target audience for this book comprises those people who make up the majority of the U.S. adult population—working couples, couples in one-income families, or single households, male or female. Moreover, it is generally directed at those individuals economically placed in the broad middle class because these are people who have some savings that they want to multiply whether for long-term goals such as saving for their retirement or paying for their children's college to more immediate wants and needs such as purchasing a home or being able to afford an exotic vacation. They may be interested in doing this by making regular and consistent income rather than through the capital appreciation that comes with longer-term strategies. More importantly, our readers do not need to be in the business or financial world to understand our technique. People from all occupational backgrounds can easily apply fully the trading techniques espoused in this book.

For you to answer the key question of whether this book holds value for you, you need to check out our Appendixes A through D. If you look at our trading record from the beginning of 2005 to the end of February 2007 and tell yourself you would like to replicate such results in your own finances, then this book and its techniques will be useful to you.

Who can benefit from an extra income generated in this fashion? Turning that question around, if you are a middle-class couple currently earning salaries of $70,000 and $30,000 annually and you are offered the chance to have a third job involving very little sacrifice of either partner's time but paying out say $15,000 to $50,000 annually, would that be something you would turn down? Most would say no. It is for those who welcome such an opportunity that this book is written. Please note that the income continuously earned in a regular stream from this technique does not mean that there is any obligation to take the money earned and spend it. That option exists—but the option to add profits back to the capital being traded can mean enjoying the benefits of compounding. The enhanced return generated by compounding of earnings is not reserved for the long-term investor only.

Our book begins with an introduction and is divided into eight chapters and four appendixes. We start with a brief history of the stock market and the exchanges that have grown up in the United States, providing the foundation for investing and trading stocks in this country. We then cast a critical eye on some of the ways in which the topics of investing and trading are dealt with by many writers working in the investment/trading genre of literature. Chapters 3 through 5 define for the reader the concept of *contrarian ripple trading*. We look at the source of our use of the word *ripples* for the short-term market and stock price fluctuations on which we focus. We describe the key ways in which we adopt a contrarian approach in order to profit from those ripples. We then explain the practical technique that we adopt in our actual short-term trading using these contrarian ripple trading principles. Chapter 6 sets out a number of specific examples in which we have ripple traded our way to profits using our technique. In Chapter 7, we demonstrate "special situations" that constantly occur and bring specific stocks into the orbit of those we trade by "riding the ripples." The need for self-discipline in using our technique and some concluding thoughts close this part of the book. Appendixes A through C provide detail on all of our 1,225 actual roundtrip completed trades from January 1,

2005 to February 28, 2007 and Appendix D sets out those stock purchases that we made in that same period and remained open as the period closed. In other words, Appendixes A through D provide a full and complete documentation of every trade we made in the 26 months covered here.

Aidan McNamara

Martha Brożyna

Wyckoff, NJ, June 2007

Introduction

This book will not make you rich.

It will not tell you how we took $5,000 and turned it into $500,000 in just six months through expert market trading.

It will not now show you how to do the same thing yourself. Sorry.

So why read on? Well, we hope this book offers the reader something rather new and unique in the genre of stock market trading and investing literature. It sets out a method of short-term trading that we call *contrarian ripple trading*. That this book sets forth a technique for trading stocks hardly makes it unique. There are plenty more books that set out to provide pointers to better investing or trading than you can shake a stick at. What makes this book unique is that it backs up its methodology with a genuine and complete trading record. We, the authors, a married couple and nonprofessional traders, have detailed in the appendixes to this book every single stock trade (no exceptions) that we have made for our own account during 2005, 2006, and the first two months of 2007, an end-point dictated by publishing deadlines. Within the body of the book, we have excerpted details from our trading record during this period—1,225 completed, roundtrip trades during the 26 months—to illustrate what we believe to be the fundamental factors that drive the market, how in our view a short-term trader can take advantage of and profit from these factors and to demonstrate the techniques that have allowed us to make such a large number of profitable stock trades during the period. Trading profitably in our case means each and every one of those 1,225 completed, roundtrip trades came with no loss-making trades at all. Yes, that's correct, no loss-making trades at all! And on February 28, 2007, just 48 positions

1

remained open from our 1,246 stock purchases made during the 26-month period—open and awaiting a price recovery so that we can complete what we expect in each and every case to be profitable trades. Of these open positions as of February 28, 2007, 15 were purchases made in the final week of February as the market fell back from its top of 12,796 on February 20, 2007 and eight were bought on February 27 as the market plunged 413 points or over 3 percent that day. This reflects our contrarian approach that is outlined in detail in this book.

We have read many trading/investing books written by experts and investment gurus who are quick to boast about the huge amounts of money that they have made in the stock market. Many seek to define their success in terms such as the following: *I started out with $5 and was able to turn it into $20 gazillion in three months. Clever me. Here's how I did it.* The funny thing is that, as you read on, you find that the authors never actually share their trading record with you. Sure, they detail their favorite methods; but they will often use pretend companies and made-up stocks to demonstrate how they put these into practice. Their explanations are therefore in the abstract. When reading these books, we always have so many questions to ask of the authors. What stocks did they actually buy? How long did they hold on to them before they made those big profits? How many shares did they buy at any one time in any given company? What were their actual profits when they shorted stocks? Which were their profitable trades and which were losers? And how did one side stack up against the other? Sadly, these questions never seem to be answered.

Our book contains no examples of trading tactics using pretend stocks of nonexistent companies. Given that such examples have no basis in reality, they can easily be made to demonstrate whatever writers want in order to provide support for whatever theory they espouse. Our book also does not follow the path taken by many, propounding a trading theory, and then using backtesting to match past results of a stock's or the market's price movement history to prove that if you had done x, then the result would have been y. This kind of backtesting involves a search for proof of an already formulated theory, and thereby typically gravitates towards using as examples those stock price movements that prove the proposed theory correct. However, you can be sure that any stock or market movements that inconveniently work against or disprove the theory will be ignored. In any case, even where it is possible to show that, *with hindsight*, a certain trading technique or investment strategy would have had a successful outcome, it is one thing to look back dispassionately at a chart and note that your theoretical methodology has indeed been borne out by the performance of a stock or group of stocks. It is quite another thing to place hard cash up front, betting in advance on an outcome that, if successful, leads to profits while at the same time knowing that if you are wrong there will be financial losses staring you in the face.

Day traders often start out with a familiarization and practice exercise called *demo* or *paper trading*, where they use pretend money and make pretend trades to gain experience in the day-trading environment without putting real money at risk. Conventional wisdom has it that paper traders consistently obtain better results than they subsequently manage when they switch to using real money and face actual hits to their wallet if their trades do not work out. This is not surprising. Nobody is going to feel that tight knot in the stomach or sweat building up on the brow when all that is at stake is Monopoly money. Just think how taking out a mortgage to buy your first home concentrated your mind, and caused you to fret over all kinds of things that could go wrong given the big commitment you were entering. How easy it is on the other hand to buy hotels on Boardwalk and Park Place, to continue the board game analogy, when the money at risk is just play money. It is our contention that there is more value to a methodology proven in the trial by fire of real market trading with real money on the line than with any that can look great on paper in hindsight, but is not backed up by actual gains and losses in the trader's hard-earned cash.

As you will see later in this book, the white-knuckle nature of our acid test of real trading in the real market is ratcheted up several notches by the fact that our trading method is based on contrarian principles, which we explain in Chapter 4. Pressing the buy button at precisely the moment that most investors and traders would not touch the targeted stock with a 10-foot pole can often take real courage. As a result, we feel that there is a unique qualitative approach in our detailing a trading technique, the value of which is based on 26 months of actual trading experience as against the provision of purely theoretical strategies that tends to dominate the investing/trading literature genre.

As detailed in Appendixes A through D, the period that our trading record covers in this book is the 26 months up until February 28, 2007. This encompasses all of 2005, 2006, and the first two months of 2007. The 26-month period includes 2005, in which the market represented by the Dow Jones Industrial Average essentially moved sideways and was actually slightly down on the year. The following year, 2006, saw a sluggish advance in the first half, followed by a very powerful, gangbusters rally in the second half with the Dow ending up a strong 16.3 percent for the entire year, of which over 12 percent was achieved in that strong second half run. As 2007 began, there was a continuation of that momentum, albeit somewhat choppier, and then a sharp market drop in the closing days of February that brought the Dow to a loss on the year to that point as of February 28 of 194 points or 1.6 percent. Over this 26-month period, the

U.S. stock market represented by the Dow Jones Industrial Average went from 10,784 to 12,269, an increase of 1,485 points. This represents a 13.8 percent gain or 6.4 percent on an annualized basis. A 6.4 percent annualized increase is below the average annual rate of increase of the Dow in the last 10 years (7.9 percent), and it is also lower than the average annual gain by the Dow in the last 100 years, which has been approximately 7.4 percent. (But take care with this number—see Chapter 2.) Please note these percentages relate to gains in the nominal index itself. They do not take account of inflation; neither do they include returns from dividend payouts. The relatively poor showing over the 26-month period covered in this book reflects the market's failure to gain during all of 2005 as well as the pronounced drop on February 27, 2007, which wiped out all gains for the first couple of months of the year and more (see Chapter 4). Indeed, the Dow's entire increase in the 26-month period was essentially achieved from July to December 2006. Otherwise the trend was flat to down.

As can be seen in the appendixes, at the same time that the market was going through this not especially salubrious period, the contrarian ripple method of short-term trading netted us a trading profit of $30,259 in 2005 (and dividends received were an additional $4,093); a trading profit of $45,350 in 2006 (with dividends received in that year of $5,894); and in the first two months of 2007 our trading profit came to $4,734 (plus $369 in dividends). Our before-tax total profit of $90,699 after commissions and dividends represents a return of 28.3 percent or 13.1 percent annualized on our average account balances—cash and stocks in our brokerage accounts. Taking our trading profits and excluding dividends, our annualized return from $80,343 on these same average balances over the period was 11.6 percent. This compares very favorably with the Dow Jones Industrial Average, so we can quite comfortably claim to have "beaten the market."

That does not tell the whole story.

In addition to the simple return percentages that we have compared with the overall market above, there is one additional factor in our trading that must be taken into account in making comparisons between our trading results and "the market." It is our low-risk approach. To describe a short-term trading technique as low-risk appears at first sight to be somewhat counterintuitive. But the low-risk nature of our trading comes from the fact that in our short-term trading methods we are mostly "riding the ripples." This is explained in Chapter 5. For now you should simply need to understand this means we typically buy and sell our individual stock positions at a profit very quickly. Each time a roundtrip trade is completed profitably, we have achieved an increase in our cash balances, and our exposure to the stock market for the amount involved in that specific trading cycle ceases. In other words, we take market risks in short bursts. Not only are we risk-averse, in that we cash out of our profitable trades quickly and continuously, thereby reducing our market risk dramatically, but we display an additional risk-averse trading nature also in that we trade mostly well-established, large-capitalization stocks, many of which are Dow 30 constituents or the equivalent in terms of their size and financial strength. Any comparison of our 26-month record with the market overall, using the Dow as a market proxy, must take into consideration the lower level of market risk that we take in comparison with the equivalent of a fully invested position in stocks that any straight comparison with the Dow presupposes. As you come to grips with our technique, you will see that our contrarian ripple approach has us fully—or close to fully—invested in stocks only when the market is at levels that are low compared to its 52-week highs and lows, such as through the summer of 2005, and mostly in cash at times that the market is posting 52-week highs, such as at the end of 2006 and the beginning of 2007. Following this pattern, our stock positions increased quite significantly again in the final days of February 2007 as the market dropped back, and especially as it took its February 27 tumble and we bought. You can read about this in Chapter 8 and see further detail in Appendix D. What happens if we make a more "apples to apples" or risk-adjusted comparison? By calculating our annualized trading profit without dividends on our available funds that we have on average invested in stocks during the 26-month period, we score an annualized return of 15.5 percent. This compares exceptionally well with Mr. Dow's 6.4 percent return on his fully invested position with concomitant full market risk during the period.

Those statistical purists who point out that comparing our trading profit to the Dow does not take into account paper losses on positions we held at the end of February 2007 might be interested to know that our total gain in value of our brokerage accounts, including cash and stocks calculated as a percentage of the average balances held over two years and two months, was 24.8 percent. That is, 11.4 percent on an annualized basis. This includes brokerage interest received on cash balances, which has not been taken into consideration in trading profit calculations above. If calculated prior to the February 27 market drop, these percentages would have been 28.1 percent and 13.0 percent annualized.

How do we achieve this kind of return on our short-term trading? Check out our record in Appendixes A through C. Of 1,225 profitable, closed, roundtrip trades during the 26 months, 192 were bought and sold on the same day, 350 were bought and then sold between one and three days, and 143 were bought and then closed out at a profit on either the fourth or fifth day following purchase. As a result of such quick-fire trading (56 percent of all completed trades closed within a five-day period) the annualized percentage return on each of these trades was very often in the hundreds of percent as noted against each trade in the appendixes.

Okay, so that probably describes more what we do and not really how we do it. How we do it is the subject of this book, and so we invite you to discover a short-term trading method that is simple, low risk, profitable and, yes, fun. We call that contrarian ripple trading.

This book may not make you rich. But it may nevertheless give you an insight into a stock trading method that can make you money—maybe even enough money so that, like us, you can consider that the earnings you achieve constitute a second or third income for you.

CHAPTER 1

The Buttonwood Tree

The stock market is a source of endless fascination for investors and traders, both professional and amateur alike. Go to any bookstore and you will find an entire section with rows of books dedicated to giving advice on how to make money in the stock market. Often a quick killing or the opportunity to "get rich quick" is what is promised. People from all walks of life are drawn to the romantic allure of instant wealth that seems readily available from "playing the market." Yet apart from this often more superficial interest, the stock market truly is an important factor in the lives of large numbers of people today in the developed economies of the world, and particularly so in the United States.

The American public is actually much more involved in the market than many are aware, going beyond the more obvious direct investments in stocks by individuals or by mutual fund managers who invest on private individuals' behalf. It is true, however, that professional or institutional investors do dominate stock market trading these days rather than private individuals acting on their own. When you examine who these institutional investors are, whether money managers running mutual funds or other investment companies, pension funds, endowment funds, insurance companies, banks, and, increasingly hedge funds, it may seem that they are a world apart from the private individual. Principally these institutional investors are managing the retirement monies, insurance premiums, and savings of private individuals. In a very real sense, they control the financial futures of many millions of Americans. But there is also another way in which the general public is tied in with the stock market. A large proportion of working people in this country are employed at publicly quoted companies, and so the fortunes of those companies and the private individuals who are their employees are also, to a large extent, tied to the ups and downs of the stock market.

What exactly is the stock market? Simply put, it is a market on which equity share ownership in publicly traded companies is bought and sold. The actual venue in which buyers and sellers meet, or more accurately where one is matched with the other, is the stock exchange. It was the joint-stock companies, such as the Dutch East India Company established in 1602, that were the forerunners of today's publicly traded corporations. The Dutch East India Company established a stock exchange to facilitate trading in its own stocks and bonds. That exchange became the Amsterdam Stock Exchange, generally considered the world's oldest. In recent years, the Amsterdam Stock Exchange merged with several European stock exchanges or *bourses* to form a larger, international market called *Euronext*. Euronext is made up of the exchanges of Amsterdam (AEX), Brussels (BSE), Paris (Bourse de Paris), and Portugal BVLP (Bolsa de Valores de Lisboa e Porto) and includes also LIFFE (London International Financial Futures and Options Exchange). Euronext itself has recently merged with the NYSE Group, which includes the New York Stock Exchange.

This brings us to the buttonwood tree. It was on May 17, 1792, under a large sycamore tree—or a buttonwood as it was known in the vernacular of the time—in front of 68 Wall Street in New York, that 24 brokers signed the *Buttonwood Agreement*. This contract stated that the brokers would only trade securities with each other, would abide by a fixed commission rate, and would not participate in auctions. This stock exchange was not the United States' first—the Philadelphia Stock Exchange dates from 1790. However, it was this New York exchange that drafted its constitution as the New York Stock & Exchange Board on March 8, 1817, was renamed as the New York Stock Exchange in 1863, and became the country's and indeed the world's most important and influential stock exchange. Other stock exchanges, both within the United States, such as NASDAQ and a number of regional exchanges, as well as many important international exchanges have grown up over the years and are venues on which stocks can also be bought and sold by the institutional investor, professional trader, or private individual. Professional investors and nonprofessionals alike can choose to use their access to the stock market to allow them to build a portfolio of equity investments to grow their capital, to trade stocks with the aim of making short-term profits—or a mixture of both styles.

After the New York Stock Exchange, traditionally the next most important exchange for many years was the American Stock Exchange (AMEX). It had its origins in the mid-19th century when traders would meet outside the main exchange on the curb on Broad Street near Exchange Place, and thus it became known as "the Curb." Here stocks were traded that were not listed on the NYSE because they were relatively new companies that had not yet established a reputation that would merit a listing on the "Big Board," as the New York Stock Exchange is often called. In 1921, the Curb traders moved indoors into a permanent domicile at 86 Trinity Place. Its name was changed in 1953 to the American Stock Exchange. Today most of the trading done on AMEX is of small-cap companies (those that have market capitalization between roughly $350 million and $1 billion), exchange traded funds (ETFs)—similar to index funds but traded like stocks, and derivatives, which are financial instruments that "derive" their value from some underlying asset.

In 1998, the AMEX was merged with the NASDAQ, which had already eclipsed the AMEX as the principal alternative exchange to the Big Board for younger and less-established companies. NASDAQ, the acronym for the National Association of Securities Dealers Automated Quotation, opened in 1971 as the first electronic stock market in the world, and it initially traded 2,500 over-the-counter securities. Today NASDAQ lists over 3,000 companies, specializing primarily in the technology sector including some very large companies such as Microsoft, Dell, and Intel. Unlike the New York Stock Exchange and the American Stock Exchange, NASDAQ never had an actual physical location where securities were traded because it was always a computerized exchange. Nevertheless in 1999, when the new Four Times Square building was erected in the heart of New York City—on Broadway between 42nd and 43rd Streets—a cylindrical tower located at the northwest corner of the building, the NASDAQ MarketSite, gave the exchange a visible "presence." The NASDAQ MarketSite contains a seven-story screen that is illuminated constantly and is one of the most clearly identifiable sites in Times Square.

At the opening of this chapter, we mentioned that more people are involved with the stock market than probably know. Indeed, over the years there has been an increase in the number of Americans who are owners of stocks whether on an active or a passive basis. Early on in the market's existence, investing and trading were very much the preserve of wealthy, private individuals. Bankers and brokers looked after the investments of the wealthy. If a regular person sought to put his meager savings to work in the stock market, he had to go to the *bucket shops*. Bucket shops were frequently scam operations based on very dubious business practices. Although their customers thought that the bucket shops were placing their orders on the Exchange itself, it was often the case that the bucket shops matched buy and sell orders themselves, with a big spread between the two ensuring a big profit for the bucket shop. In some senses a forerunner of modern-day market makers, but completely unregulated, the bucket shops' business ethics were probably more akin to those of today's so-called boiler-room operations in that they often set out to fleece unsuspecting investors.

Access to the stock market became easier for greater numbers after World War I when many more Americans enjoyed real prosperity for the first time. Concurrently there was a rise in home ownership and a proliferation of household goods, particularly radio sets and telephones. By the late 1920s, millions of people also owned cars as the Ford Model T was mass produced and thereby became more affordable. With the rise of affluence of the average American, stockbrokers, just like other merchants, realized that there was good money to be made in this line of business and they started to advertise their services to the public in much the same manner as companies that were marketing the new consumer goods. More and more people were lured by the prospect of acquiring wealth in this way. Accurate statistics pertaining to the number of stock owners from this period are hard to come by, but one historian believes that between 2 and 14 million Americans in the 1920s were invested in the stock market, including those who had passive ownership in instruments such as corporate stock plans and pension funds.[1] Moreover, there was also a growing number of women who owned shares, and just to give a few examples—50 percent of the shareholders of Pennsylvania Railroad were women (and thus it was mockingly called the "Petticoat Line") and 55 percent of AT&T shareholders were women.[2]

It is not surprising that with the crash of 1929 followed by the Great Depression, the American public tended to avoid Wall Street like the plague. It was only after the Second World War, and particularly during the 1950s, that Americans generally began to show a reviving interest in stocks. Just as with the end of World War I, consumer spending was on the increase, and more and more people were purchasing homes. Suburbs grew and flourished. Most American homes were now equipped with electricity and plumbing and were filled with all kinds of labor-saving devices and gadgets such as dishwashers, toasters, and vacuum cleaners. The middle class, now growing by leaps and bounds, became interested in investing as households now had more disposable income than previous generations, and was attracted by the prospect of making even more. Investing advice became ubiquitous. It could be heard on the radio and read in magazines and newspapers. It was at this time that mutual funds started to gain in popularity.

THE RISE OF THE MUTUAL FUND

A mutual fund pools money from a large number of individual investors and buys a diversified group of stocks, bonds, or other assets. Mutual funds proved advantageous for the small investor who could achieve diversification with a relatively small amount of money. The mutual fund had its origins in the Netherlands in the 1820s, and in subsequent decades it spread to other parts of northern Europe. It made its way to the United States in the early 20th century with the first mutual fund created by Massachusetts Investors Trust in 1924. After the U.S. economy recovered from the crash of 1929 and the Depression, Congress passed the Investment Company Act in 1940 in order to protect investors. The act regulated companies that invested and traded in securities, including mutual funds, by calling on them to disclose information about their operations, finances, and structure. In the decades that followed the mutual fund became more and more a popular investment vehicle.

Aside from setting up safeguards in the form of legislation, the U.S. government made it more tax efficient for Americans to invest in the stock market. In 1981, the Internal Revenue Service (IRS) approved of a system whereby employees could save for retirement through a tax deferred instrument called the *401(k) plan*. This retirement plan was the brainchild of Ted Benna, who worked for a retirement consulting firm. A year earlier, Benna had discovered a small passage in the Revenue Act of 1978 that would allow employees to make contributions from each paycheck before the income is taxed. Taxes would be paid on these monies only when the employee started to withdraw them during retirement. Also, employers could match amounts invested. Over 25 years later, the 401(k) plan has become an important part of retirement planning for many Americans. In 2003, about 50 million people had 401(k) plans totaling $1.8 trillion.[3] Many 401(k) plans offer diverse investment options, including mutual funds, bonds, and money market accounts.

In this way the stock market indeed touched the lives of many Americans. Presently, about 55 percent or $4.94 trillion of all mutual fund assets are in stock funds.[4] Moreover, most 401(k) plans are invested in stock funds. A study conducted jointly by the Employee Benefit Research Institute and the Investment Company Institute shows that at the end of 2005, two-thirds of all 401(k) plans were invested in stocks. This statistic has not changed much over a decade, however. During the period between 1995 and 2005, the percentage of 401(k) accounts invested in stocks fluctuated only between 62 percent and 77 percent.[5]

Investment by the general public in stock mutual funds can be perceived as one factor in the "democratization" of the stock market and thereby the U.S. economy in general. Jay O. Light, a professor at the Harvard Business School, noted this contribution, commenting that mutual funds had made the capital markets easily available to ordinary citizens.[6] However, the level of true democratization has its limits. It is true that in the years leading up to the Stock Market Crash of 1929, the portion of the general public that owned stocks in any shape or form was a wealthy elite. The various developments just detailed led to increasing numbers of private individuals becoming involved in common stock ownership, especially in the post–World War II years and in particular the 1980s onward. This generated a very different picture, with about half of all U.S. households today owning stocks either held directly or indirectly through mutual funds, which form a major part of most people's 401(k) plans. However, given the indirect nature in which the majority of stock holdings are held—using mutual funds—it is still true to say that most private individuals are effectively passive investors and the stock market continues to be dominated by an elite—the elite being today those professional or institutional investors who manage huge amounts of money pooled in funds.

WHY FOCUS ON STOCKS?

They say that history repeats itself. The same can also be said of the economic, business, and financial worlds, which by nature follow cyclical patterns. Over the last decades there have been numerous times when the best investment to be in would be stocks, or bonds, or real estate, or gold—actually this does not happen often for gold, but it does happen as in 2005—or even artwork. While hindsight is always 20/20, it is difficult for anyone to foresee with certainty what area of investment will have its day next. Of course, there are some who consistently do predict these turns correctly. However, once again these are a handful of people with special talents that set them apart from the majority. For example, even those few of us who from time to time give thought to what is happening in the gold market, realized that gold would finally make a come-back in 2005 only after it had actually transpired.

The common stock—equity investment providing partial ownership in corporations—is the one asset class that has consistently outperformed all others over time despite having its own strongly cyclical nature. The post-World War II real rate of return on common stocks investment, net of inflation and including dividends, is approximately 7.1 percent and over any extended period this has bested all other forms of investment.[7] This statistic, however, hides a lot of gut-wrenching ups and downs in the market as well as times when the market has for seemingly interminable periods gone nowhere. In the last 40 or so years, we have seen the listless and lethargic sideways movement of the market in the 1970s, a return to upward movement in the 1980s, the rip-roaring bull market in the unprecedented boom of the 1990s, and the latter's grindingly painful unraveling in the years 2000 to 2003.

While we do not disagree that over time the trend line for stock prices generally is upward, we demonstrate in the next chapter that the way many investment writers present their statistics on the historical "return on stocks" can be deceptive. Nevertheless, it is our feeling and experience that the "wind in your back" provided by the consistent increase in stock values over time, make common stocks the perfect vehicle for the short-term trading strategy that we espouse and that has worked so well for us. The ease and relative low expense of trading these instruments, particularly as far as the large-capitalization stocks are concerned, provide additional underpinnings to the advantages inherent in this approach.

CERTAIN ASSUMPTIONS

We are going to assume that the reader already has a basic understanding of how the stock market works, how a stock transaction is carried out accessing an exchange through one of the online brokerage services, and the basics of corporate America and the market economy or capitalist system in which we live. This book is not designed to go back to the very basics of describing what a stock is, how one goes about trading it, the difference between a stock's bid and ask prices, and how information on stock prices are displayed by the financial press and on brokerage company screens. We also take for granted that the investor has a basic knowledge of such terms as *price/earnings* (P/E) *ratio* and *dividend yield*—although we provide contextual clarification on such things when and where necessary in the text.

Interestingly, many of the investing books that are written by the gurus and pundits of whom we have spoken before assume zero knowledge on the part of the reader, even explaining something as simple as the payment of a dividend in inordinate detail. We even came across one book in which the author wrote out a short dialogue illustrating the way in which an investor should place a call to his broker in order to purchase a stock. This demonstration bordered on the absurd when the author spelled out the exact words with which the reader should greet the receptionist on the phone and ask to speak to a broker! Surely books that seek to help people make decisions that involve stock purchases of many thousands of dollars are the wrong place to provide such hand-holding. Such people with no grasp on the subject matter might be better served if they were discouraged from risking their money in this way.

CHAPTER 2

"In the Long Run, We're All Dead"

Trader or investor? Which one are you? The difference can be very blurred, especially in these days when it is both cheap and easy to trade stocks. "Investing" has something of a more worthy ring to it, and most people are more comfortable thinking in terms of themselves as investors. Perhaps this is because the word "trading" is considered somewhat unseemly, with overtones of gambling or playing games of chance. The financial press tends to toe this line, writing that "investors" are moving into this high-flying stock or deserting that dog in droves, ignoring the fact that precisely the kind of portfolio churn that gives rise to their story would probably more accurately be given the soubriquet "trading." No matter. We like to think in our own rather rigid terms of what constitutes investing and constitutes trading. The difference for us is one of time and risk. The investor takes a medium- to long-term view on his (or her) investment, takes and holds a position, and seeks thereby to grow his invested capital over time, riding out market ups and downs along the way. The upside to such a strategy is that the investor is likely to succeed in his goal should he invest in substantial, established, profitable companies that have viable business models and good growth prospects.

The downside is that the investor ties up his funds for perhaps many years and thus pays an opportunity cost of having the funds unavailable for other purposes during the time they are locked away. He also has to contend with inflation reducing the value of his capital over time. Although it is true that common stocks have proved to be the best hedge against inflation over the years, the investor must still take into account the effects of inflation on any investment strategy especially over longer time periods.

Unforeseen inflation spikes can be damaging to any long-term capital growth plan. Also, as far as market risk is concerned, while the beauty of the medium and especially long-term approach is that investors can ride out market ups and downs, especially as the market trend is generally upward over time, this does not mean that market risks for investors are nonexistent. Ask any investor who bought stocks as the market was in the throes of euphoria in January 2000 (with the Dow Jones Industrials over 11,700) and then watched their investments leak value for almost three years to the lows of October 2002. (The Dow slipped through 7,200 on October 9, 2002). Assuming our investor left his investment intact, and assuming for the sake of this example that his investments tracked the Dow, then the investment would have returned to its original value only by September 2006. Taking inflation into account, the investor would still be sitting on real losses in value to his portfolio.

Trading in stocks, on the other hand, involves taking a short-term position with the goal of exiting with a profit in a relatively short time frame. In order to do this, something must happen to the stock price to send it moving upward. Should the stock languish or go down over an extended period (ouch!), then the trader is left with two choices. Either he turns into an investor and holds the position until it reasserts some basic growth value he has perceived in it, or he sells it in disgust and moves on to the next.

Nowhere is the pressure on the trader to take quick profits or losses greater than in the ultra-short stock holding style known as day trading. The defining characteristic of day trading is that all trading positions, both winners and losers, are closed out at the end of each day. Day traders do this in order to avoid the possible risk of events occurring overnight that may move the market against them the next day. The trick for the day trader is to make sure that the gains from his strategy at the end of the day outnumber the losses, and in such a proportion that it makes his trading worthwhile. Remember that day traders typically try to do this for a living, and they have to watch the market minute by minute, second by second.

There are two principal types of day traders. The first are momentum traders, for whom the watchword is "the trend is your friend." They search out stocks that are moving in a particular direction on high volume and take advantage of this momentum. If a stock is moving up, they buy; if it is moving down, they sell short (more on selling short later). Either way, momentum traders ride the trend in a particular stock.

The second type of day trader are scalpers. They also take advantage of a stock's momentum, but their trading methodology is not as dependent on it as it is for momentum traders. Scalpers can do well when the market is uneven and not trending in any particular direction. They manage to do this by buying or selling short large numbers of shares and quickly selling or buying them back in a matter of minutes or even seconds. They are not looking to make big profits, but focus on smaller profits that are made quickly and repetitively. Scalpers realize that only if they can make dozens of such small profitable trades that will add up over the course of the trading day, can they achieve trading results that are meaningful. As a result, scalping is a high-volume, high-risk game, demanding a substantial outlay of funds for each trade.

Day trading was a much easier endeavor during the bubble years of the late 1990s than it has been in the last few years, and pure day trading has declined accordingly. The practice of trend-following brought more successes in the bubble years because the trend was strong and headed north most days. Stock market activity in recent years, however, has been up, down, and often sideways and not so conducive to the success of typical day trading tactics. That is not to say that day trading has ever really been a great way to make easy money. Even in the golden period for day traders of the bubble years of the late 1990s, most day traders lost money and flamed out in a relatively short space of time. A study done by the North American Securities Administrators Association in 1998 to 1999 found that 77 percent of day traders lost money. The day traders who were successful, however, did not become rich. In fact, they only averaged about $22,000 in an eight month span.[1] The proliferation of day trading facilities during that period was based more on the profits available to those who provided day traders with the tools they needed to trade and whose commissions and fees rolled in whether the day traders' trades were successful or a bust. A historical equivalent of this would be the way that the vendors of pick axes and other supplies to gold miners would be properly characterized as having been the true beneficiaries of the California Gold Rush, rather than the prospectors themselves.

Beyond day trading, but staying with short-term trading, other styles worth a brief mention are swing trading and position trading. Swing traders tend to hold their stocks over the short-term, sometimes even only for a few minutes, just like day traders do. However, unlike day traders, they do not focus on closing all their positions at the end of the day. In fact, swing traders do not mind holding stocks for a few days in order to obtain their desired profits. Position traders identify a price pattern and are willing to allow weeks or even months to allow the pattern to exert itself and permit their profitable exit. As you will see later, our own short-term ripple trading style has elements of both swing and position trading in it.

The short-term trader, whether day, swing, or position trader, eschews the market risk that goes with holding his position for the medium or long-term. His risks are of another kind. The principal one, as mentioned above in reference to day trading, is that the trade will not work out and the trader will have to exit the position at a loss. This risk is so great that most short-term trading strategies take it fully into consideration, assuming that a percentage of all trades entered into will end in losses. The lower that percentage is, the more successful the trading strategy.

One other difference in the approach of investors as compared to traders is that investors feel able more easily to entrust their investment choice to the more stable, large-capitalization stocks. Their stability means that they are less volatile. Short-term traders, on the other hand, are drawn to the smaller, less mature, often technology-sector-based stocks that offer the opportunity for sharp price changes that can be exploited for quick trading profits. In most short-term trading strategies, a stock that moves with a glacial sluggishness is generally perceived as bearing the kiss of death for quick trading profits. However, we turn this concept on its head with our ripple trading method. As will be seen later, thanks to the power of contrarian thinking, we are able to focus on precisely the solid, established and low-volatility stocks that are typically shunned by most short-term traders.

These hard and fast rules of ours on what constitutes investing and trading appear on the surface to be fairly unequivocal or even dogmatic in nature. In reality, investors trade (a lot) and traders invest (especially when they cannot bear to part with that loss-making position that they somehow know will come right in the end). But one thing that nonprofessional traders and investors too often share is a basic lack of knowledge regarding the actual business underlying the company stock they are buying—indeed, they can often be almost clueless on the subject. For the momentum trader or scalper, this is fully understandable and perfectly appropriate. If your purchase is made purely according to chart patterns and trends pointing in the right direction for just a few minutes, then you do not need to have any real knowledge at all of what the underlying stock represents in terms of an actual business enterprise. For anyone who would describe himself as an investor, however, such a blasé approach to the business enterprise in which he is taking a stake would seem to be rather frivolous, to say the least. Yet this is an investing habit that is actually much more pervasive than many would care to admit. An investor will often buy into a position with effectively no real underlying understanding of the economic, financial, or business rationale of his stock purchase other than trusting to the forces of chance or allowing emotions to rule the decision-making process. Such bets can run from the extremely short-term to the very long-term indeed. The buyer may have heard a tip or saw the stock mentioned as "hot" in a newspaper or on a financial TV show and buys clueless about what the company that issued the stock actually does or makes. The buyer does not understand why the prospects of the company whose stock he has bought can really be considered any better than any of the many thousands of other stocks that he could have bought at that moment in time in its stead. Such trading amounts effectively to a throw of the dice. If you practice this form of stock market participation, you could win and you could potentially win big, or you could lose everything invested. In either scenario, should you ever be asked to explain why that particular outcome occurred, you would have great difficulty explaining it in terms other than "the stock went up" (or down)!

Stock market participation in this form provides the instant gratification (or lack of it) of a day at the casino in Las Vegas. Very often shares in young technology companies are bought on this basis by investors who have no understanding of the technology issues that underlie their business model and the true chances of success or failure of the company in which they are investing. There is no amateur investor who feels so smart as the one who buys Applied Nano-Gizmos at $10 only to see it zoom to $60 in a matter of weeks and no amateur investor who feels so foolish when his play on Micro-Doodads Inc. is flushed down the toilet in the same period. Both represent the same decision-making process, and both were equally likely to succeed or fail.

As was noted earlier, there is often a tendency for investing to be considered somehow as morally superior to trading, almost as if it is up there with motherhood and apple pie, while trading is seen as something more fly-by-night, a somewhat more disreputable pursuit more like gambling—even though as pointed out earlier, the same charge can be leveled at much that passes for investing. In our view, investing and trading and all their variants, are completely valid from a moral and ethical standpoint as long as they are legal (not insider trading, for example). Do not think that our musings regarding investing and that we promote a specific method of short-term trading mean that we do not believe in investment strategies that would lock up our money for long periods of time. On the contrary, we believe very strongly that long-term investing is the cornerstone of any long-term savings plan. We have 401(k) accounts for retirement funds and 529 College Savings funds for our children's education tied up in such long-term investments, specifically in large-cap stock mutual funds that we keep fully invested and do not try to time or switch at all. In this way, we take advantage of the returns that the stock market clearly does bring to the diversified investor over the long term.

So why do we not just keep all our money invested in that way, and why are we seeking in this book to bring to the reader the technique of short-term trading for income using common stocks through a method we call *contrarian ripple trading*? The reason is that we perceive a value in generation of an additional income through placement of regular, profitable short-term trades. We have discovered that our contrarian ripple trading method allows us to do this with consistent success—in that we consistently beat the market using this method.

Over the long term, investment in common stock equities is the very best way to obtain a high return in the form of capital appreciation. That is the use to which the long-term investor puts them. Traders in stocks, however, whether day traders or short-term traders, buy and sell continuously with a view to making a profit on each round trip that adds to the cash balance available to the trader for withdrawal or repeated investment—therefore representing a form of income. On top of this, should the short-term trader seek predominantly to use the stocks of well-established, large-capitalization companies for his trading, he will, in similar fashion to the long-term investor, obtain an additional income stream in the form of dividends that will be paid on stocks that the trader has in his position, even if he keeps the holding period as short as possible to maximize trading returns, as we recommend, and does not prolong it in order to capture the dividend.

THE DOW JONES INDUSTRIAL AVERAGE AND THE PETER PAN PRINCIPLE

Many writers on the subject of investing are very eager to demonstrate how the market has continuously gone up over the course of years and decades. This is particularly relevant if their advice is that the investor should buy and hold stocks for a long period of time to maximize future profits. When most investment pundits and academics write about "the market," they are normally referring to a market index that represents the overall market such as the Dow Jones Industrial Average or the much broader S&P 500. If they are talking about technology or younger, growing companies, then the NASDAQ Composite Index is the one they favor. These different market indices track the performances of a certain group of stocks.

The index of choice for most investment writers and others who observe and comment on the market is the Dow Jones Industrial Average, which contains 30 large-capitalization or "blue chip" stocks. These are stocks of large, well-established companies that have over $10 billion in capital. The Dow Jones Industrial Average has quite a long track record since it was first launched in 1896 by journalist and cofounder of the *Wall Street Journal*, Charles H. Dow. Its purpose was to simplify the market by helping investors understand whether stocks in general were going up or down in price on a particular day. Prior to the Dow, investors had to look at the prices of individual stocks and try to work out from these the general state of the market. The Dow Jones Industrial Average therefore has some of the personality of a hoary old index, wizened and weathered by the years and decades. Yet if you look at the constituent companies, you see it is populated by quite a few spiffy, new, and relatively young corporations. How is this possible?

The original list contained only twelve stocks, which were as follows:

- American Cotton Oil Company
- American Sugar Company
- American Tobacco Company
- Chicago Gas Company
- Distilling & Cattle Feeding Company
- General Electric
- Laclede Gas Light Company
- National Lead Company
- North American Company
- Tennessee Coal, Iron and Railroad Company
- U.S. Leather Company
- United States Rubber Company

Other than General Electric, it is quite likely that many of our readers have never heard of any of these companies. Yet they represented some of the most important industries of their day, and were at that time the leading corporations within those industries. The first average, calculated simply by adding up the stock prices of the 12 companies and dividing the sum by 12, was 40.94. The index increased its number of component companies over time. The companies included in the index were also subject to regular changes until the first Dow Jones Industrial Average with 30 companies was published on October 1, 1928. At that time, the index of the finest U.S. industrial companies comprised the following:

- Allied Chemical
- Allied Can
- American Smelting
- American Sugar
- American Tobacco
- Atlantic Refining
- Bethlehem Steel
- Chrysler
- General Electric
- General Motors
- General Railway Signal
- Goodrich
- International Harvester
- International Nickel

- Mack Trucks
- Nash Motors
- North American
- Paramount Publix
- Postum, Inc.
- Radio Corporation
- Sears, Roebuck & Company
- Standard Oil (New Jersey)
- Texas Corporation
- Texas Gulf Sulphur
- Union Carbide
- U.S. Steel
- Victor Talking Machine
- Westinghouse Electric
- Woolworth
- Wright Aeronautical

By the time the Dow Jones Industrial Average closed above 1,000 points for the first time on November 14, 1972, it consisted of the following companies:

- Allied Chemical
- Aluminum Company of America
- American Can
- American Telephone & Telegraph
- American Tobacco
- Anaconda
- Bethlehem Steel
- Chrysler
- DuPont
- Eastman Kodak
- Exxon
- General Electric
- General Foods
- General Motors
- Goodyear
- International Harvester
- International Nickel
- International Paper
- Johns-Manville
- Owens-Illinois Glass
- Procter & Gamble
- Sears, Roebuck & Co.

- Standard Oil of California
- Swift & Co.
- Texas Corporation
- Union Carbide
- United Aircraft
- U.S. Steel
- Westinghouse Electric
- Woolworth

The current makeup of the Dow Jones Industrial Average, effective from April 8, 2004, is as follows:

- 3M Company
- ALCOA
- Altria Group
- American International Group
- American Express
- AT&T
- Boeing
- Caterpillar
- Citigroup
- Coca-Cola
- DuPont
- Exxon Mobil
- General Electric
- General Motors
- Hewlett-Packard
- Home Depot
- Honeywell International
- Intel
- IBM
- Johnson & Johnson
- JP Morgan Chase
- McDonald's
- Merck
- Microsoft
- Pfizer
- Procter & Gamble
- United Technologies
- Verizon
- Wal-Mart Stores
- Walt Disney Co.

These different renderings of the Dow Jones Industrial Average demonstrate that the use of this index as if it is unchanging and somehow carved in stone can be misleading. The use of the index as a statistical proof of the history of "the market" is in truth compromised by the constant changes in its component parts. The same holds true for any of the other market indices. Yet it is convenient for those preaching long-term investing strategies to use graphs and quote statistics indicating the progress of the market over many years, using the Dow Jones Industrial Average in particular, and thereby seeking to prove not only the ever onward and upward nature of market movements, which do correspond to reality, but much more tenuously that of individual stocks comprising "the market." Using charts based on the Dow Jones Industrial Average, investing books are very eager to assert and "prove" that if an individual had invested $x in "the market" in 1957, meaning in certain stocks of that time, his investment would be worth a huge multiple of $x today. However, this would depend on which stocks he selected, as many of the companies that made up the Dow 50 years ago are no longer around or have hit a bad patch and either still exist in a different guise, or as part of another company, or which along the way may have lost investors all or some of their investment.

Please do not misunderstand our position on this. As the rest of this book shows, we are great proponents of the idea that the stock market contains the very best way to make real inflation-beating returns on invested capital. However, the self-serving use of the Dow Jones Industrial Average as "the market" to make long-term comparisons by many investment writers on the historical return of individual stocks falls for us under the overall rubric of what Mark Twain so aptly described as "lies, damn lies, and statistics." As we have shown, the Dow Jones Industrial Average throughout its history has been replenished constantly by stocks that represent companies that are the most successful within the industries that are most important in their particular period. The editors of the *Wall Street Journal* (owned by Dow Jones & Company) do a kind of housecleaning of the Dow Jones Industrial Average every few years, bringing in companies that are dominant in the economy of their day, and throwing out those that are no longer considered dominant enough, either generally or in their own sector. Therefore, they ease out the old-economy, smokestack, buggy-whip making has-beens of yesteryear, and replace them with zippy bright new-economy stars in growth mode. The regular replacement of an index with dominant companies in growth sectors and the removal of those stocks that are either from declining industries, or are just declining companies, means that the value of comparisons between the indices in different time periods is severely diminished, and does not reflect accurately and should not be quoted as an accurate reflection of likely returns on positions in individual stocks over long periods.

You can see from more recent examples how these changes work and what was behind the decisions. On November 1, 1999 low-growth Chevron, Goodyear, Sears Roebuck, and Union Carbide were replaced in the index by higher growth and certainly at the time more fashionable, Intel, Microsoft, The Home Depot, and SBC Communications (now renamed AT&T). On April 8, 2004, low-growth International Paper, Eastman Kodak, and AT&T—the original company of that name, subsequently acquired by SBC Communications which itself took on the venerable name—were replaced by Pfizer, Verizon, and American International Group (AIG). Apples compared with apples?

It is disingenuous for proponents of long-term investing to point to an index that contained Texas Gulf Sulphur, Victor Talking Machine, American Smelting, and International Harvester in 1928 and compare it with an index that today contains Citigroup, Coca-Cola, Intel, Microsoft, and Procter & Gamble and conclude that you can draw a direct line of growth from one to the other. Nor can these writers demonstrate retroactively the wisdom of an investor having bought into any individual stock in the 1928 market, or indeed to use the progress of the market in the intervening 79 years to extrapolate forward into the future the prospects for an investment over the long haul in any one individual stock today.

The same is true of the other indices. The S&P 500, which is the second most important index, containing 500 companies that are important industry leaders in all sectors of the U.S. economy, is also constantly refreshed by additions of fast-growing companies and demotions of slower-growing ones. Moreover, companies that are acquired by larger, more successful companies are deleted and are always replaced in the index with promising up-and-comers.

What is the lesson to be drawn from all of this? There is no doubt that "the market," meaning a grouping of company stocks as an investment class, makes impressive upward progress over long periods of time. However, if "the market" is defined, as it typically is, by one of the popular indices and especially the Dow, then historical "proof" of the increase in market prices over long periods of time, using comparisons of these indices calculated years apart is far too simplistic and can be misleading. On the contrary, one has to recognize that such comparisons seriously mask the significant rotations of sectors within the overall market that are always taking place. Developments in technology, lifestyle choices, and general business and consumer trends are subject to changes that can be cyclical in nature, as certain industries or companies and their products come in or out of fashion or prominence. These developments can even be transformational in nature. Just think of how our lives have been transformed by the invention and development of the microchip or integrated circuit. Not just computers, but automobiles, telephones, and every conceivable household appliance are crammed with these devices. As a result, there is an overall increase in the quality of life for all, except possibly for those whose fortunes were tied to the vacuum tube industry. U.S. companies continue to be innovators and highly successful in this field and investors in companies like Microsoft and Intel have benefited handsomely.

The only way that comparisons of indices over many years can truly be considered accurate is for the investor who puts his money into a market index fund, which is managed to replicate the movements of the index on which it is based. In this scenario, any new stocks added are reflected in the fund, and the old stocks are removed so the link to the index as it is redefined continues. (See Chapter 5 for some comments on index funds and ETFs.) Otherwise, you cannot directly extrapolate from the historical trend lines of any index the likely success of any individual stock in which you may choose to invest over the very long-term. Put bluntly, individual stocks potentially have a shelf life and are perishable, even though the overall market over time may go marching on.

BUY AND HOLD?

The strategy of holding a stock over a long period of time has many advantages. The most obvious one is that it keeps costs down. An investor's profits are taxed at a lower rate when he holds his stocks over a longer period of time. Moreover, commission costs are also lower because the investor is not trading frequently. The best returns come over a long period of time because the holding period covers both the lows and the highs, but over the long term, the market in general tends to go up.

Traditional investment writing has particularly supported the buy and hold strategy, emphasizing especially the "hold" part of this equation. In so much investing literature, however, as has been noted above, the Dow's rise over the years is used, in our view erroneously, to illustrate the wisdom of buying or holding any one particular stock. So it would be stated that if Mr. Investor had the foresight to invest $100 in "stocks" in 1972, when you will recall the Dow was first at 1,000, then the stock he invested in would be worth over 10 times that amount today. There are two problems with this. Assuming Mr. Investor put his money into a specific company's stock, and let's call it *XYZ Inc.*, there is a fault in logic that we explained above, whereby it is simply incorrect to extrapolate from the performance of the Dow how any 1972 component (Bethlehem Steel anyone?) or noncomponent stock would have performed. Second, such comparisons also leave unanswered the question of what investor really wants to leave a stock position in place untouched for that amount of time—35 years in this example. In this scenario, Mr. Investor may have started to set aside money for his retirement quite early on, adopted a buy and hold strategy, and 35 years later he still holds the same position and is now ready to retire. But how common is this investing practice really?

Some investment writers like to go back many more years to make similar comparisons, sometimes comparing the market 80 or 100 years ago or more with today's market to indicate the wisdom of long-term buying and holding of stocks. This brings to mind the story, most likely a fable, of the Native Americans who sold Manhattan to the Dutch for $24 in glass beads in 1626. The moral is one of an incredible investment opportunity lost by these Native Americans not having held on to Manhattan, given the real estate value of the island today. This ignores one small fact. Both alleged buyers and sellers are long dead today! When the experts compare the investments made many decades or even centuries ago to today's investments, as if these truly demonstrate realistic returns, it is useful to remember the quote from John Maynard Keynes, "In the long run, we're all dead."

In recent years, however, it has been less fashionable for investment gurus to suggest that the only way forward in investing is to buy a stock and then simply forget about it for many years. For example, Peter Lynch has revised this strategy and urges investors to do "six-month checkups" on their stocks, which includes checking on the price/earnings ratio and seeing what the company is doing in order to ensure that earnings go up.[2] In a similar vein, Jim Cramer has called on shareholders to avoid "buy and hold" but to embrace the practice of "buy and homework," in which the investor researches thoroughly and often the companies that he owns.[3] Other writers today are eager to espouse short-term trading strategies, a reflection of the shift in trading mentality that has taken hold in recent years, and has fueled also the heady recent growth of hedge fund trading in stocks as well as other financial instruments. Professionals and amateurs alike feel more and more comfortable with the short-term approach and the search for quick profits.

INVESTING MYTHS DEBUNKED

In the last section, we discussed some of the disingenuousness that surrounds discussions on the ever-upward trend of the market, and therefore of individual stocks within it. Now we touch on a few other gripes that we have with much of the advice often proffered by investment experts' writings. There is certainly plenty of advice out there for the Average Joe who is looking for the best way to use his savings in order to make money from investing. With all of the many and varied "how-to" books, each containing its own sometimes bewildering, often contradictory advice on investing and trading styles and systems; it is no wonder that most readers either throw their hands up in horror or end up more confused after reading them than before they opened up the cover. Despite the intention of each writer to contribute something new to the genre, interestingly, there are a number of common themes within investment literature that are written about ad nauseam. On closer inspection, these themes seem to provide unnecessary complication or even misinformation and propagation of myth to the investing advice mix.

Many investment writers stress timing. For some reason, many of them suffer from a strange obsession with market tops and bottoms, particularly the beginnings and ends of bull and bear markets. As will be seen from Chapter 3, this is an obsession that appears to have its foundation in Dow Theory, an investing strategy with a long pedigree that has influenced the thought and actions of investors and traders alike for over a century, and is the forerunner of technical analysis. It has to be understood, however, that bull and bear markets represent shifts in sentiment that happen only every few years or so. The length of time that the entire bull/bear cycle runs may take many years, possibly up to a decade or more. Yet such writers whose focus is on spotting these tops and bottoms will happily expend an acre or so of the Amazon rainforest explaining how to recognize the signs that a market bottom or top has been reached. There were dozens of books published just in the past two decades alone, and a handful published as far back as the 1960s, on market timing. Many of them simply review different theories about how markets are timed and invite the reader to choose his or her favored approach as, for example, the introductory work, *Complete Idiot's Guide to Market Timing*. Others, however, believe they discovered the market timing philosopher's stone and try to instruct their readers in how to time the market's up and down cycles. The scenario is usually as follows. When the point has finally been reached where the market has reached a bottom, they instruct the investor to make an insightful purchase at precisely the "right" price level. Then, these writers advise that the intrepid investor must scrutinize closely for similarly clear signs that a market top has been reached. Again, the investor must time everything just right, thus achieving the goal of cashing out at precisely the moment when investment earnings are maximized.

It is a feat of almost impossible brilliance for anyone to succeed in spotting *exactly* when the market has hit the bottom or top. Unfortunately, neither the professional nor the lay investor has a crystal ball to tell when the market is at its high or low. Neither does a bell ring at that point. Moreover, what is an investor to do if he missed the opportunity provided by a market low? Does he now wait several years or decades until the market again reaches a secular low and presents him with another appropriate buy signal?

Even when market pundits are not trying to accomplish something as ambitious as identifying a market top or bottom, many do claim that they are able to spot an individual stock's top or bottom. This is where the technical analysts enter into the picture with their various charts and symbols like dogi stars, shaven heads, hammers, and hanging men. They attempt to interpret all kinds of bizarrely named patterns that can be read from charts illustrating past stock movements in an attempt to predict what their next directional move will be. Here is an excerpt from Toni Turner's *A Beginner's Guide to Day Trading Online*: "If the next candlestick after the Evening Dogi Star is a white real body, the Dogi warning is negated."[4]

Hmmm.

There most certainly is no shortage out there of those who claim that they have all the answers. Even when they are not promising to teach others how to interpret the signs, there are those who promise that they can provide the tools necessary to achieve success. (California Gold Rush syndrome again perhaps?) There are dozens of Web sites that lure the investor/trader with promises that their fortunetelling market experts can signal the precise moment when the investor should buy or sell stocks, mutual funds, or bonds if the investor is unable to do it himself. Some promise that they can pinpoint and help the investor avoid any approaching market crashes. It must be noted that all these sites charge subscription fees of varying fatness. We have also noted a revival in investing seminars, advertised through infomercials on late night TV, that promise to provide insights and tools for successful stock trading and indicating that those who sign up can be on the road to "financial independence." The latter is typically illustrated in the infomercials by a big house and pool in a sunbelt setting, a big car and lots of time to play golf or for other leisure time activities. The implication is clear. "Financial independence" means getting rich without having to work.

HOMEWORK, THEN BUY?

Back in the world of more mainstream investment advice, many investment writers such as Jim Cramer concentrate much of their content on the topic of research and hammer home that the investor needs to do extensive research into any stock he or she proposes to buy. Most of these books advise the reader to scrutinize the annual report, quarterly reports, and 10k reports filed by the company. They go into exhaustive detail explaining how the balance sheet and income statement of a company work. They then apply the information gained from the balance sheet and income statement to obtain ratios that will give a picture of how the stock price level relates to elements taken from those financial statements, such as price/cash flow ratios, or price/book value ratios. Some investing advice books suggest that the prospective investor should talk to the senior management of the company or listen into conference calls given by the company's management to discuss quarterly earnings. Such a privilege used to be reserved for the financial analyst community, but in more recent times, it has been theoretically opened up to all-comers.

In his former life as a commercial banker, including stints working in credit analysis departments, coauthor Aidan McNamara was trained to work with balance sheets and income statements. This enabled him to figure out whether the company to which the bank intended to lend money had the financial strength and cash flow to repay those loans. One half of the couple writing this book is therefore literate in financial statements. Nevertheless, we do not agree that the financial information that the annual or quarterly reports or 10k filings impart have any *real* urgent relevance to either the individual long-term investor or to the short-term trader who is using our approach to trading. Why?

The Average Joe is simply not going to learn anything new from these statements. There are hundreds, and sometimes thousands of equity analysts on both the sell-side (those working for the investment banks and brokerage houses who distribute securities to investors), and on the buy-side (those who do proprietary research for institutional investors—pension funds, mutual funds and the like), all engaged in crunching every last number released by the company. They parse endlessly comments made by management and seek to make buy, sell, or hold decisions based on every strand of available information all day, every day. It is ludicrous to suggest that a private individual, picking up and reading the annual report when he has a spare moment, will possibly glean some additional insight from an obscure footnote somewhere in the text that everyone else has missed. It is naïve to expect the average person can home in on some nugget of price-moving information from the balance sheet or income statement that the research professionals have not already noticed. Yet this is precisely what many investing books recommend that their readers do, claiming that the investor will gain an edge by making the effort to carry out precisely this kind of research.

It may be counterintuitive, and sound to some like heresy, but it is our belief that there is not a lot of point in either the long-term investor or the short-term trader immersing himself in the minutiae of the company's business and financial reporting because all that information is already reflected in the stock price. This is especially true as far as the larger well-established companies are concerned. Please note, however, that this view by no means puts us in the camp of the *Efficient Market Hypothesis* (EMH) brigade.

The EMH was first theorized in the 1960s by Eugene Fama, an economics professor at the University of Chicago nominated for the Nobel Prize. The hypothesis posits that all important financial information about a particular company is already factored into the current stock price. The EMH is often combined with the *Random Walk Theory*. This theory states that stocks follow a "random walk" meaning that the movement of stock prices does not follow any kind of pattern; prices are simply "random." Thus, even by looking at past movements, it is impossible to predict how a stock will perform in the future. Combining the EMH and Random Walk Theory one can conclude that it is impossible to beat the market.

Yet this is clearly not the case. The EMH and Random Walk Theory are wrong because time and again some very bright people have managed to beat the market well and consistently. With all due modesty, we claim this for ourselves. As we have made clear above, we share the view with EMH theorists and with Dow Theorists (see Chapter 3) that all financial, economic and political factors that could affect a stock price are factored in, including all that research on the company done by professional analysts. On the other hand, however, where the EMH and Random Walk theorists have it wrong is in their discounting the effects of fear and greed on both the overall market and the prices of the individual stocks within it. We believe that the principal drivers of market and individual stock movements are the raw human emotions of fear and greed. However much a stock price may reflect all relevant financial information, and be pushed higher and lower based on new information that comes into the public domain, it is the conflicting emotions of fear and greed of millions of investors (both professional and lay), that in the end are the predominant factors moving prices of individual stocks and of the overall market. It is by understanding the nature of these human emotions, and taking advantage of the irrational actions they often cause investors to take, that the short-term trader can make money using a contrarian approach, while essentially disregarding most of the torrent of financial information that is generated on each company and its stock every day.

This is not to say that we believe the investor/trader should have no interest in learning about the company in which he is taking an investment or trading position. On the contrary, as we set out in Chapter 4, a very important element in our trading strategy, and one we believe to be of fundamental importance to long-term investors too, is the principle of "know your stock." Being knowledgeable about the company you are investing in or trading; its business, what it does, makes and sells, and to whom—all this is grist to the mill of a successful investing or short-term trading strategy such as ours. This information is available from daily use of companies' products, reading the business and financial press, watching financially oriented programming on TV, keeping up-to-date generally on trends in the economy, industry and the specific corner of the market in which the company operates. It involves essentially keeping your eyes open. However, what it does not mean is trying to divulge from the company's financial statements nuggets of financial information that will give you "an edge" over other investors/traders. You will not find anything there that is not already in the stock price. Remember too that a company's reported financial statements are based on historical cost accounting. Also, they represent a best efforts attempt to provide a snapshot of where the company is today financially, not where it is going. Both investors and (to a lesser extent) traders are looking to the future when they put their money into a company and the idea that the financial statements provide the backing for the investment/trading decision seems to us like trying to drive while firmly focused on what is going on in the rearview mirror. Remember that our comments here apply specifically to the lay investor attempting to take the raw financial data and working out investment decisions based on it, something that is a standard piece of advice in investment advice literature. Insights provided by professional analysts can be helpful in getting an up-to-date all-round feel for what is going on at a company, often without the selectivity of more "newsy" aspects that is the tendency of financial journalism. If your online broker offers research, and all invariably do, then find one or two research companies that you can access that way and use these to round out your knowledge of companies that you are monitoring or considering for purchase. Our own favorite is the Argus Research Company, whose research is available free online to clients of Charles Schwab & Co. Again we emphasize that the purpose of using this research is to round out knowledge on your target companies, while not getting bogged down in the nitty-gritty of financial ratios and other arcane information that the research also sets out for you. One exception to this is an insight into the company's cash position and net debt position. Research houses such as Argus will always point out those companies that have a particularly strong cash position, and as we point out in Chapter 5 this can be a useful piece of information to assist in a buying decision.

A theoretical exception to our argument that detailed knowledge of the financial information of a company provides no particular edge to the individual investor or trader is exhibited in the advantage that company insiders may have, at least in theory, when it comes to trading stocks in the market. Corporate insiders are defined as a company's officers and directors, and any beneficial owners of more than 10 percent of a class of the company's stock. Such stockholders are obliged to file with the Securities and Exchange Commission (SEC) a statement of ownership and to report their insider transactions within two days of the date the transactions occurred. It is illegal for such insiders to trade when they are in possession of material information that is still not public. Insider information gives those who possess it such a tremendous advantage to profit from big moves in a company's stock price that acting on such information is deemed so unfair as to be illegal. Once information is in the public domain, however, and the company's stock price has moved in accordance with the news' positive or negative implications, the information has no additional value—it is already reflected in the stock price.

THE COST OF TRADING: IT'S NOT AS BAD AS THEY MAKE IT SOUND

A favorite hobbyhorse of many writers in the investment genre, especially of those who espouse buy and hold strategies and dismiss short-term trading techniques, is that frequent trading is to be avoided because of the various costs it generates. We have already noted above that additional costs are generated by this strategy. One of the biggest ones that is the subject of grumbles is taxes. Should a trader buy a stock and then sell it a short time later, he has generated a capital gain on which capital gains taxes will be payable unless the transaction is done through a tax-sheltered account such as a Roth IRA.

It was Benjamin Franklin who famously said that "in this world nothing is certain but death and taxes." Should anyone be successful at trading or investing and generate profits rather than losses in this activity, sooner or later he or she should expect Uncle Sam to come calling to claim his cut. This is true even of income generated in a traditional tax-deferred IRA, as opposed to the Roth version mentioned above. Of course, nobody likes to pay taxes. Equally, however, when we go out to work to a paying job, as most of us do, we accept the inevitability that a significant portion of our earnings will be siphoned off by the tax man. Strangely, while we accept that the income earned from our jobs will be taxed, many of us are fixated on tax-avoidance in our investing habits. We are also encouraged in this by financial advisors. This tax phobia has such a hold on some people that it reaches the point where they will even accept lower returns on their investments as being more desirable so long as they come tax-free.

Do not misunderstand us on this point—there can be very good reasons to choose an investment path that enables you to reduce or even eliminate a tax burden. For example, the tax deduction on mortgage interest is one of the economic underpinnings of making home ownership such an attractive investment in the United States. But should you decide to go down the road of generating an extra income from stock market trading, then paying taxes on that income, whether as part of your annual tax filing or on a tax-deferred basis once an IRA is cashed out, has to be understood as being part of the territory. In order to demonstrate the absurdity of people's tax phobia on investments, ask yourself this—how many people decide that they will no longer go out to a paying job any more because they have to pay tax on the income they earn there?

Coauthor Martha Brożyna's father has an expression he often uses in this context, "I want to pay a million dollars in taxes." When the person he says this to looks at him as if he has just sprouted a second head, he explains, "if I pay a million dollars in taxes, then just imagine how much income I've made." The kind of person who can take advantage of the ability to trade for an extra income is the kind of person who will not be upset that his taxes have gone up from one year to the next. He will understand that this rise in taxes is simply a reflection of the increase in his overall income for the year generated by profits on his trading. This is even true taking into consideration the higher capital gains tax payable on short-term gains as opposed to those made on positions held over 18 months. Again, just as you would not turn down a promotion at work because the higher salary would mean paying more in tax, the differing levels of taxation applied to long-term and short-term trading gains should not dissuade you from trading if this seems the more lucrative path overall for you.

Along with vilifying the payment of taxes, many investment writers point out, quite rightly, that the more trading a person does, the more he will have to pay in commissions to his broker. Until relatively recently, commission costs generated by trading would have been a huge impediment to a trading strategy involving the making of a significant number of roundtrip trades in stocks. However, for traders who are seeking online execution only, the cost of trading these days is relatively small. At the time of writing this book, we pay just $5 per trade with our principal online brokerage E*TRADE (with rates set this low as we are legacy Brown & Co. clients, with $5 commission rates grandfathered from our former brokerage house which was acquired by E*Trade in 2006); $7 per trade with Scottrade, and $9.95 per trade with Charles Schwab. Nevertheless, many authors of books that rail against trading argue that commissions eat away at all or most of the trader's profit. This is because active traders can do dozens of trades a day, so commission costs can really add up. It is certainly true this could be particularly onerous to a trader if some of his trades are loss-making. After all, the trader has to pay commissions regardless of whether he makes a profit or loss from his trade. This circumstance does not affect our method, however. We always factor in the costs of commission for doing a roundtrip trade when calculating the price at which we intend to sell our stock. More importantly, we do not sell at a loss, preferring instead to wait, maybe even for months until the stock goes back up. (See more on selling with our method in Chapter 4 and check out Appendixes A through C for the full record of our profitable closing sales.)

A third transaction cost that investment writers, correctly, point to is the spread between the bid and ask price—the trader buys at the ask price and sells at the slightly lower bid price and this difference constitutes a real cost. The cost of the bid/ask price spread is really only an issue, however, if the stock being bought and sold is small and thinly traded. This is especially true of a NASDAQ quoted stock, although even there spreads have been forced to come down in the last years. The bid/ask spread that is usually found with the well-established large-capitalization stocks that are traded mostly on the New York Stock Exchange is typically just one or two pennies a share, and as such represents a very small "cost of doing business."

Moreover, the spread between the bid and ask price has been reduced in recent years because of changes made in the way stock prices are quoted. For most of the stock market's history, pricing was done through whole dollar amounts and fractions (half, quarter, one-eighth). This system was based on the Spanish real which was divided into eighths. Between 2000 and 2001, U.S. stock markets converted all their stock prices from fractions to decimals. As a result, whereas the lowest typical spread in the old system using fractions had been 1/16th or 6.25 cents, now the use of decimals allowed for narrower spreads, a development, which was further encouraged both by competition between market makers (and Internet-based market places known as *electronic communication networks* or ECNs) as well as regulatory pressures.

The three types of costs just examined are used by investment writers in their warnings against "churning" or what they perceive as excessive trading. While we agree wholeheartedly that nobody likes to pay taxes, commissions, or bear the additional small expense of the spread between bid and ask prices, we feel that the approach of certain investment writers to these costs is still one that is somewhat biased owing to a general preference for buy and hold strategies. We like to think of the gaining of an extra income through short-term trading in the same way as taking on an additional paying job. Just as taxation, expenses, cost of commuting, and, perhaps, purchase of professional clothes such as business suits would not turn most away from a job that provides real returns in the form of a good income—so the costs that go along with active short-term stock trading can be seen in the same light.

In this chapter, we have sought to share with the reader some of our thoughts on both investing and short-term trading and how both topics typically tend to be covered by investing advice literature. It is now time for us to turn our attention to the short-term trading technique that it is this book's mission to espouse. Let us now introduce some of the foundations on which we have built our contrarian ripple trading method. We start with an explanation of the term we have chosen for our short-term trading strategy, "ripple trading," and for this we turn briefly to an examination of Dow Theory in Chapter 3.

CHAPTER 3

Tides, Waves ... and Ripples

T he name we have chosen for our style of contrarian short-term trading, "ripple trading," comes from the ocean metaphor term "ripples" used initially by Dow Theorist Robert Rhea (pronounced *ray*) in his 1934 book *The Story of the Averages*.[1] Rhea used this word to describe the short-term fluctuations that Dow theorists identify as one of the three recurring trends that characterize the movements in prices of the stock market. Dow Theory is based on observation and study of these recurring trends and is thereby said to lend predictive powers to the observer who has the skills to interpret them. Rhea gave the name *tides* to the primary trends, otherwise known as *bull* or *bear markets*. The intermediate or reaction trends, rallies, or corrections, he called *waves*. *Ripples* are how Rhea described the short-term fluctuations that occur from day-to-day or over periods of up to a few weeks.

We have adopted Rhea's ripples to illustrate the short-term market trends and fluctuations that we focus on for our short-term trading activity. However, it would only be fair to Rhea to mention that he would in no way have endorsed or used our contrarian ripple trading concept as you will see in this chapter. Indeed, our own short-term trading theories and practice have a complicated relationship with Dow Theory. To illustrate this further, we are presenting a brief summary of Dow Theory—where it came from, how it influenced heavily today's technical analysis, and the component parts of it that have also had an influence on our own short-term contrarian speculative trading.

THE DOW THEORY

The theory had its beginnings in editorials written from 1900 to 1902 by Charles H. Dow in the *Wall Street Journal*. Dow's good friend S. A. Nelson tried to persuade him to put these ideas into a book. Dow resisted, and so Nelson wrote it himself. He published *The ABC of Stock Speculation* in 1903 following Dow's death the previous year. The book included 15 of Dow's seminal *Wall Street Journal* editorials on the subject of speculation in the market. It was in this book too that Nelson first coined the term "Dow Theory." The theory was subsequently expanded upon and refined by William Peter Hamilton, Dow's understudy and the editor of the *Wall Street Journal*, in editorials titled "The Price Movement," as well as in his book, *The Stock Market Barometer*, published in 1922. However, it was left to Robert Rhea to organize and summarize the theory more fully. Rhea was confined to bed for many years with tuberculosis and a damaged lung. He used this time of enforced physical inactivity for study of business and the markets and to hone his understanding of the trends that, according to Dow and Hamilton, characterize the market. In his 1932 book, *The Dow Theory*, Rhea wove together the various strands of the theory, including 252 editorials by both Dow and Hamilton, setting them out in a structured way designed to be of practical use to the individual investor. As mentioned above, it was in Rhea's 1934 work *The Story of the Averages*, that he used ocean metaphors to describe the three basic trends of Dow Theory. "I like to think of Dow's three movements as being the tide, the wave, and the ripple, all acting, reacting, and interacting at the same time. Consider a rising tide: as part of the tide we may have an oncoming or a receding wave, but on the wave may be an incoming ripple, or perhaps a ripple acting against the tide."[2]

According to both Hamilton and Rhea, there are certain key assumptions that need to be accepted in order to understand and use Dow Theory. The theory asserts that the primary trend of the overall market cannot be altered through market manipulation, even though individual stocks are subject to short-term and even medium-term manipulation. A focus on market manipulation today seems a little antiquated and a reflection of the times in which the Dow Theory was formulated, the late 19th century, when market manipulation indeed was rife. Today the market is much broader and deeper compared to what it was over 100 years ago or during the Depression pre-World War II time of Rhea's writing, so manipulation of the entire stock market today would appear to be a much more ambitious and probably impossible endeavor. It is true that individual stocks can be manipulated, particularly smaller stocks, through accounting fraud, the deliberate spreading of rumors, and big investors deciding to act in concert while taking short positions. Also individual market manipulations such as the Hunt brothers' attempt to corner the silver market in 1980 or the manipulation of California's Energy market in 2000 and 2001 by Enron and other energy trading companies are perfectly possible to envisage in modern times. Manipulation of the overall U.S. stock market today, however, appears to be a concept lacking any real feasibility.

Another major assumption that followers of the theory are advised to accept is that every known fact is already discounted in the market. In other words, stock prices reflect all available information, including all hopes, disappointments, fears, and other emotions of market participants, as well as all extant knowledge of economic factors. These include interest rate trends and earnings expectations for all companies quoted on the market. Political events such as presidential elections and domestic and external strife are also included. Only the unknown and unknowable, such as catastrophic "Acts of God" are not reflected in current prices. (See our take on this in Chapter 2.)

A third assumption that adherents to Dow Theory accept is that the Theory itself is not infallible. It can guide the investor in his understanding of what the trends mean, but is not immutable science.

The Dow Theory concentrates on identifying the primary trend because followers of the theory believe that the correct recognition of that trend is the best means to making money in the market. As Rhea put it, "The correct determination of the direction of this movement (primary trend) is the most important factor in successful speculation."[3] These primary trends can last many years, and correspond to what is usually termed either a bull or bear market. In Dow's day, these terms had not yet come into use and the primary trends were still generally called "booms" and "panics." In Rhea's parlance, the primary trend is like a "tide," and the point at which the primary trend changes from bull to bear or vice versa is described aptly as a turning of the tide.[4]

Secondary "reactions" move against the prevailing primary trend for a time, with a life span of perhaps a few weeks to several months. These are called *market corrections* when they are on the downside and go against a prevailing bull market—or *market rallies* when on the upside against a prevailing bear market. Robert Rhea dubbed these moves *waves*. For Dow Theorists, secondary reaction moves are considered to be the means by which the market ensures that excessive speculation and possible overheating or cooling of markets is kept in check. Of course, there is always the possibility that corrections and rallies are mistakenly identified as a change in the primary trend; but it is one of the aims of Dow Theory to identify these trends correctly in order to ensure that speculative market activity takes advantage of them and is not stymied by them. This is not very easy to do, however, as even the staunchest followers of the Dow

Theory would admit. Rhea considers the secondary reaction as the "most deceptive" of trends.[5]

Finally, there are daily fluctuations that can move with or against the primary or secondary trend. Their defining characteristic is that they are short-lived, lasting from a few hours to a few days, and then reverse themselves. In Rhea's lexicon, these fluctuations are the ripples. According to Dow Theory, while short-term market movements can be useful when grouped together to aid analysis of the bigger picture of secondary or even primary moves, these ripples are insignificant when identified or analyzed on their own. Followers of Dow Theory believe that these short-term fluctuations have no real importance or value in pointing to primary or even secondary trends and are no more than background noise. Rhea was certainly very dismissive of any attempt to make money by exploiting these short-term fluctuations:

> *It will be seen that these minor movements rally and decline, back and fill, and generally perform in a manner most perplexing to the man who is trying to watch each day's fluctuations in hopes of scalping a few dimes out of a few shares of stock while paying commissions, taxes and brokerage.*[6]

In retrospect, Rhea can be viewed as the first observer of markets to have provided a strong critique of day trading as a money-making practice.

Bulls and Bears

Dow Theory sets out three distinct stages to a primary trend bull market as follows.

Stage 1: Accumulation. This is the first budding stage of a bull market or "boom" in the vernacular of Dow's day, when there is still great pessimism regarding the future. As expectations rise that things will improve, stock prices begin to rise also. There is increasing recognition that a bull market is underway. Nevertheless, this growing optimism is tempered by lingering fears and doubts that what is happening is simply a rally within a continuing bear market. This is the stage when the smartest and most perceptive of value investors see their opportunity to come into the market at cheap levels.

Stage 2: General advance. This stage takes hold as improving business conditions and a boost in business confidence increase valuations in stocks. Here trend followers buy in as the market consistently makes new highs and the investing public is filled with increasing confidence.

Stage 3: Excess. Speculation is rampant and pushes the market ever higher. Valuations are excessive and the general public is fully involved in the market. Everyone believes that a new era is at hand and all are overly optimistic regarding the future. This sounds like Alan Greenspan's "irrational exuberance" and will be familiar to all who were watching the market in the late 1990s into the year 2000.

For Dow Theorists, the primary trend bear market, or "panic" as was still the accepted terminology in Charles Dow's day, also has three stages that mirror the three stages of the primary bull market.

Stage 1: Distribution. This is the point where the "smart money" starts to move out of stocks; but the majority of investors are still willing buyers because they feel that the market still has a long way to go on the upside. The market, however, starts to look tired.

Stage 2: General decline. This downward trend is characterized by deteriorating business conditions, falling revenues, and shrinking profits.

Stage 3: Despair. At this point, there is no good news around. The economic outlook is bleak and nobody wants to be involved with the stock market, which appears to be a loser's game. There is a generally pervasive lack of confidence in the future. The despair stage continues until all of the bad news is fully priced into stocks, then the cycle can begin again. It is at this stage that financial reporting may adopt a very negative tone on the prospects for the market. The most often quoted example of this is the *Business Week* cover story of August 13, 1979, "The Death of Equities," which foretold the forthcoming demise of stocks as the Dow languished at around 840, a prognosis that clearly now seems somewhat premature with the Dow above 12,000, as of February 28, 2007.

Peaks and Troughs

Dow Theorists seek to identify the primary trend using what is known as *peak and trough analysis.* An uptrend is detected by prices forming a series of higher highs and higher lows. A downtrend is characterized by prices setting a series of lower highs and lower lows. Additionally, it is also an important part of the theory that the Dow Jones Industrial Average and the Dow Jones Transportation Average both confirm the trend. Until 1897, there had been just one stock average maintained by Dow Jones & Co., but at the beginning of that year separate averages were established for railroad and industrial stocks. Today's equivalent of the early Rail Average is the Dow Jones Transportation Average. It is normally to be expected that the Transportations lead the confirmation of any trend, as stocks in that index are especially cyclical and, by definition, highly susceptible to economic changes. However, Dow Theory holds that the certainty of a new trend can only be considered to have been firmly established when both averages confirm each other's evidence of it.

Trading volume is also said to provide additional evidence of which trends are in place. "A market which has been overbought," according to Rhea, "becomes dull on rallies and develops actively on declines; conversely, when a market is oversold, the tendency is to become dull on declines and active on rallies. Both markets terminate in a period of excessive activity and begin with comparatively light transactions."[7]

As previously mentioned, the Dow Theorists in no sense shy away from looking at what they are trying to achieve as "speculation." However, they look rather askance at short-term speculation/trading. Rhea voices the rather low level of importance he places on the ripples in his *Story of the Averages*, asserting that the study of the ripple fluctuation, or the minor trend as it is also termed, warrants only 10 percent of serious study time.[8] As Dow Theorists see it, the study of ripple fluctuations provides little predictive information from the price data to point to the trends that truly interest them, the primary bull and bear trends.

For Dow Theorists, the principal reason that there should be any examination of short-term fluctuations is to ascertain whether these start to form patterns over time, which may be valuable in helping to identify the more important primary and/or secondary trend. One of the patterns that may be formed by ripple fluctuation movements is a so-called "line." Hamilton many times referred to "lines," which were really trading ranges where the market moves sideways for two to three weeks or longer. According to Dow Theory, such trading ranges indicate either accumulation or distribution, but which one it actually is will only become apparent once the market breaks out to the upside or downside.

THE AUTHORS AND THE DOW THEORY

Our affinity for Dow Theory comes from the insights that it gives us into trends that underlie market price movements over any period of time, whether it be long-term, medium-term, or short-term. Dow Theory provides a foundation for technical analysis, or *chartism*, which focuses on attempts to divine future market moves from patterns in historical market data using charts of historical price movements. We do not count ourselves squarely among the mainstream chartists, as we believe the kind of technical analysis that has developed from the study of charts suffers from a tendency to seek too much certainty in the predictive value of patterns. However, our use of a contrarian trading strategy based on price history rather than reliance on company fundamentals, as will be outlined in subsequent chapters, clearly places us in the technical analysis camp to some degree. Our ripple trading method, and especially our practice of "riding the ripples" do, however, fly in the face of the philosophy of Dow Theory with the latter's focus on the longer trends and its assumption that the short-term fluctuations cannot be used in profitable speculation, which is contradicted by our own trading record. When we seek to capture a new stock position at a less expensive level by timing the purchase to a point where that stock is close to a fifty-two-week low, we acknowledge and put our faith in the existence of longer-term technical trends within the market. Dow Theory was the first line of conceptual thinking to posit that such trends do exist.

We consider Dow Theory as having some particular value to the long-term investor because it offers some useful techniques for attempting to call the tops and bottoms of bull and bear markets. However, as we have previously indicated, the limitations to the usefulness of such techniques are not insignificant. From the point of view of the short-term trader, the observations regarding trends do lend a sound and useful background to an assessment of the current trading environment, but do not directly provide assistance in buying and selling over a short-term time period. For the short-term trader and, to some extent, the long-term investor, the theory also concentrates too much on the overall market rather than the price performance of individual stocks. As we observe in Chapter 4, the perception that stocks move up and down as a group is central to our own short-term trading strategy because the effect is even more true over the short-term, even day by day, as it is over the medium and long-term. However, Dow Theory's single-minded focus on "the market" with what might be considered something of a dogmatic approach may possibly reflect the much smaller universe of stocks of Dow's and Hamilton's day. Whatever the truth of the underlying principle, that stocks all tend to move as a group following the same trends, at the end of the day what we buy are individual stocks rather than the overall market. As a result, although we are very happy to take advantage of the short- and medium-term fluctuations, we also take full note that individual stocks do go against the prevailing trend with sufficient regularity to allow essentially at all times certain stocks to present themselves as good targets for purchase, whatever the direction of the primary trend, bull or bear.

Overall Dow Theory still holds value for us as a descriptive tool that succeeds extremely well in defining market movement patterns and providing a framework of reference as to how they work. We acknowledge a debt to Robert Rhea for his succinct use of the ocean metaphors to describe these patterns and we have employed one of his metaphors to describe our own method of short-term trading—the trading of the ripples. Ironically, while it is the short-term fluctuation ripples that hold a special attraction to us and on which we focus, this is something completely contrary to the underlying principles of successful speculation espoused by Charles Dow and his followers.

THE ELLIOTT WAVE PRINCIPLE

The *Elliott wave principle* was first advanced by Ralph Nelson Elliott in the 1930s in a series of articles and books. Elliott's theory was rediscovered and popularized by Robert Prechter who, together with stock market analyst A. J. Frost, published *Elliott Wave Principle: Key to Stock Market Profits* in 1978. Elliott's wave principle has intriguing similarities to Dow Theory, not least of which is its proposition that stock market prices move in waves. In contrast to Dow Theory, Elliott considered his wave patterns to be as valid a predictive device over any time period in the market that is observed, from the entire history of the market down to a chart setting out market price movements over just a 5- or 10-minute period.

Elliott's theory bases itself on the same principle as Newton's Third Law of Motion in Physics—that every action is followed by a reaction. In the financial markets this can probably be reduced to its most basic level in the assertion that what goes up must come down. The Elliott wave principle also claims an underlying correlation with the Golden Ratio (1.618) associated with the Fibonacci Sequence of numbers, publicized by the 13th century Italian mathematician Leonardo da Pisa, known as Fibonacci, and derived from earlier mathematical theories developed in India. The supposed scientific and arithmetic underpinnings of Elliott's theory lead to a very rigid principle that holds that market moves follow a constant pattern of five waves in the direction of the main trend, bull or bear, followed by three corrective waves. The cycle in a bull market runs up, down, up, down, up, followed by down, up, down. In a bear market the five/three pattern is neatly reversed. The wave pattern that is exhibited here is said to reflect the constant swings of investor psychology from optimism to pessimism and back again. We are certainly believers in this type of pendulum swing from optimism to pessimism, as well as its effect on markets even if we prefer to classify these primary emotional drives as "greed and fear" (see Chapter 4). In common with many critics of the Elliott wave principle, while we feel comfortable with the desire to replace outright chaos or even a "random walk" with patterns that can help predict future price movement, it is the rigidity of the five/three pattern that we find unrealistic and a little too suggestive of an almost religious predetermination—as so much that is Fibonacci-related tends to be. We like to mix our acceptance of the existence of patterns in the markets with a judicious recognition of the equally important existence of the more chaotic nature of the effects of human emotional drives.

KONDRATIEFF WAVE

For those who like their waves or cycles in both the economy and markets to be even more long-term, there is the Kondratieff Wave that originated with the ideas of Russian economist Nikolai Kondratieff (1892–1938). This school of thought posits a very long cycle, between 50 and 60 years, affecting modern capitalist economies. Ironically, Kondratieff himself helped develop the first Soviet Five Year Plan. But his writings were considered critical of certain aspects of the Soviet planned economy and he was sentenced to death by Stalinist officials and executed in 1938 after a period of imprisonment in the Gulag. In our view, the waves of such long duration that Kondratieff identified are probably of little more than academic interest. (see Chapter 2, In the Long Run, We're All Dead," in which we point out that over very long periods of time trends lose their relevance even to long-term investors.) Clearly the relevance of so-called supercycles to anyone pursuing a short-term trading strategy would be minimal to nonexistent.

WATER, WATER, EVERYWHERE, BUT NOT A DROP TO DRINK

As our comments here show, we do not hitch our wagon to any particular theory based on market waves. We are, however, completely supportive of the concept that market movements contain patterns that recur over and over again and thus can be indicative of future trends in the market. Where these patterns run over the longer term, such as bull or bear markets, they can be considered cycles. Where they are short-term, lasting days, hours, minutes, or perhaps even just a few seconds, they are better thought of as fluctuations. In any case, the important thing to keep in mind is that they are always there, constantly recurring and providing runes for the market observer, whether trader or investor to ponder. One of the problems that we see with these patterns, aptly given oceanic, or perhaps more properly littoral metaphorical names, is that they may provide some useful guidance to the market observer in his quest to understand where the market is coming from and maybe in which direction it is going. As a result, those writers who stand behind one or other of the wave theories generally set out to advise their readers the best times to buy and the best times to sell stocks as an asset class, based on the patterns that they have discerned. However, they generally leave this important question unanswered: If this is a good time to buy stocks, which particular individual stock or stocks should I buy?

With the acknowledgment that there are patterns, trends, cycles, and fluctuations in every market, in the next two chapters we look at some of the reasons that they work in this way. We also examine how we take that extra leap to use recurring market fluctuations to select individual stocks to buy and how we choose the specific times at which we make our purchases.

CHAPTER 4

Ripple Trading à la Contrarian Style

U nder our short-term trading strategy, we buy stocks according to contrarian investing principles. In following a contrarian approach, we owe a debt of gratitude to the high priest of contrarian investing, David Dreman. However, because our contrarian strategy is part of a very short-term trading technique, it does not really directly follow the tenets outlined by Dreman in his books.[1] While we recognize Mr. Dreman as the dean of contrarian investing, he is an investor and not a trader. His investing strategy involves the discovery of truly misunderstood, beaten down stocks with great but not immediately obvious growth potential that allows him to get in at the ground floor and then—if right in his analysis—make a superb return as the company and stock right themselves. This is a wonderful form of investing—and Mr. Dreman is a very smart man with a tremendously disciplined approach. However, he is also extraordinarily well-heeled and so can easily afford an investing style in which large sums of money can be invested according to these kinds of contrarian precepts. He holds large positions until the investments turn around and generate the sizable returns he is looking for and that affirm his investment style. He also runs quite a large business enterprise these days, the investment advisory firm Dreman Value Management LLC where he has employees and professional research tools available to him to help him analyze the contrarian quarry that he stalks. Unfortunately, because most of us are playing with very limited sums of money with no staff to back up our research efforts, we can ill afford to match Mr. Dreman's plays. Yet, as this book demonstrates, a lack of such significant resources does not hinder successful application of our contrarian ripple trading method.

What is it then that we mean by "contrarian principles"? Contrarian investing is usually defined in the simplest way as "going against the crowd." Yet we consider such a characterization to be potentially misleading. Should someone practice the contrarian approach merely by slavishly doing whatever the crowd is not doing at any given time, he would surely have mixed success. There would be as often an adverse outcome as a positive one, as it is clear that the crowd is not always wrong. When someone yells "Fire!" in a crowded movie theater and everyone rushes for the exits, the contrarian who refuses to join the crowd will gain the advantage of having his choice of seating in the now empty room . . . or he or she may just suffer a fiery fate.

A good description of contrarianism comes from Anthony Gallea and William Patalon III's book, *Contrarian Investing.* The authors start with the premise that contrarians are essentially misunderstood by most. Because contrarians are a small minority who question the wisdom of what "everyone" is doing, they are often stigmatized as grouchy pessimists who are only out to rain on everyone's parade. Most people perceive the contrarian as someone who desires to contradict the majority's action merely for contradiction's sake. Gallea and Patalon argue that this is far from the truth. In fact, it is their claim that contrarian investors are very much acting as part of the crowd in their own way—the big difference being that they just do things a few steps ahead of the rest of the crowd. True contrarians buy good stocks that no one is showing much interest in at that particular moment. When the majority of investors eventually come around to the realization that the stock in question is indeed a good investment, they all come piling back in and push up its price. At this point, the contrarian is comfortably holding on to his position that he bought at a much lower level and is sitting on a profit.[2]

A cornerstone of our own version of trading in a contrarian style lies in a recognition that by definition stocks trade at more expensive levels when they are in favor with the investing community, including both professional institutional investors and private individuals. Conversely, those stocks that are not generating great buying interest from the investing community trade at less expensive levels. Our contrarian approach in our trading is to make our best efforts to buy the stocks we trade at times that they are at relatively cheaper price levels rather than at more expensive price levels. On the face of it, this sounds like a very obvious thing to do; but it is a contrarian approach precisely because it goes against what the majority of investors/traders perceive the value of the particular stock to be at the specific time it is purchased. Our contrarian strategy also acknowledges that the market overall is sometimes relatively more expensive and sometimes relatively cheap. Indeed, most individual stocks exhibit the same relative expense or cheapness as the overall market at the same time for reasons that we cover shortly. As a matter of principle we concentrate on buying at times when bargains are to be had and mostly avoid buying at those times when the market overall and individual stocks within it are pricey. (Chapter 5 covers this in detail.)

SUPPLY AND DEMAND/GREED AND FEAR

We often talk of buyers and sellers of stocks in metaphorical terms. For example, "buyers stayed away in droves" rationalizes a down market. Such expressions are used, including by us in this book, as if there can be an uneven number of buyers and sellers and it is this factor that drives stock prices up or down. In reality, the number of buyers and sellers of a stock is always exactly equal, as there can be no sale or purchase without both a buyer and a seller. What is actually at work is a balancing of supply and demand through the mechanism of price. In a smoothly functioning market economy the prices of everything bought and sold are governed by supply and demand. So it is too with the stock market. Companies issue a limited number of shares, so when this finite number is then subsequently traded on a stock exchange, the level of supply in that particular stock on any particular day is constant and unchanging. It is the level of demand for the stock that fluctuates, however, and the dynamic by which the fixed supply and the shifting demand are kept constantly in a state of equilibrium is through the mechanism of price.

This raises the question of what it is exactly that causes the price of any given stock to fluctuate fairly strongly, as most do each and every day. The theoretical cause of the changes in demand for a stock during the trading day is that demand is raised by increased expectations regarding the prospects for the stock and decreased by dampened expectations. However, if this were all that were going on, one would expect to see very little change in most stocks' prices from day to day or during the course of any trading day, except for those for which quarterly numbers are reported or other specific company news is released. But most stock prices actually do move around quite vigorously, moving up and down and bouncing around each and every trading day. Clearly something else is going on here. The demand for individual stocks as well as the demand for stocks as a group forming the overall market are both driven by a constant struggle among all investors, both professional and amateur, involving the two major emotions that affect people's investing and trading habits—greed and fear. The combined effects of the interplay between greed and fear in investors' and traders' emotions drive the demand for and thereby the pricing of each individual stock up and down, constantly throughout the day. Interestingly, as stock prices are affected by the prevailing currents of optimism and gloom that wash constantly over the market, as a result the vast majority of stocks exhibit price movements that are remarkably similar to each other's. The overall market too, as measured by market indices, exhibits exactly the same movements up and down that characterize the majority of individual stocks, and this is as would be expected as the overall market is nothing more than a grouping of those stocks. However, we feel that it is too simplistic to conclude that the direct connection of individual stock prices to overall market movements is a one-way street. The truth is more nuanced. In fact, as traders and investors watch the overall market as much if not more than they do the prices of any individual stocks, it is their perception of what is happening to the Dow that affects dramatically their view as to whether they should be buying or selling individual stock positions. It can be the subject of some debate here which is the chicken, which the egg in this subtle cause and effect conundrum. Regardless, we believe that it is the constant change of sentiment in the investment community, lurching from positive to negative and back again regarding the outlook for stocks, reinforced with data read from the Dow Jones Industrial Average Index that actually spurs the majority of individual stock buys and sells. It is this that drives the market even more than individual stock price fluctuations caused by stock-specific news. Related to this point, it is interesting how the market often has difficulty passing through important psychological milestones such as the round number 1,000 markers—Dow 10,000, 11,000, 12,000, and so on. It is clear that investors become more excited and nervous around these levels and trading is affected accordingly. Clearly this has nothing to do with company fundamentals, news, interest rate trends, economic and political developments, and the like. It is an indication that the market index value—and essentially that of the Dow Jones Industrial Average—is one of the prime influencing factors on whether investors/traders are in the mood to jump in and buy or seek to sell individual stocks.

Although the laws of supply and demand cause an ebb and flow in stock market prices in the same way as they affect pricing in any other kind of human economic activity, it is interesting to note that the stock market is the only place where people are actually happier buying when prices go up and are reluctant to buy when prices go down. It is really a strange phenomenon. Can you imagine hordes of people arriving at a shopping mall the day after Thanksgiving when many retailers lure shoppers by marking down their prices, and being disappointed at the bargains? Would it not surprise you to see all these would-be customers returning to the parking lot upset and empty-handed and with the intention of coming back when prices have risen again? Sounds crazy, doesn't it? In the stock market, down days represent those days on which stocks go on sale. By definition, they are also days on which there is a greater reluctance to buy stocks. Up days in the market, on the other hand, are naturally days in which most individual stock prices are also up, and ironically, they are the days that buyers start to salivate and open their wallets. Investors and traders are buying up a storm, and the pricing power is back in the hands of the seller. It is a classic case of crowd mentality at work—people are buying because others are buying. But this is clearly illogical because it means that investors/traders are as a rule happier paying higher prices. As Warren Buffett once cannily put it, "You pay a very high price in the stock market for a cheery consensus."

As has been mentioned earlier in this book, it is interesting that many writers on investment topics happily use the general upward rise over the years of the Dow Jones Industrial Average to prove to their readers the wisdom of buying and holding individual stocks over time. Yet, when these same experts turn to individual stocks, they tend to proffer advice on the buying and selling of these as if all that moves stocks are their own internal dynamics as a stock and as a company. As noted, we strongly believe that it is the direction of market movements on any given day or even longer term, that actually provides *the* most fundamental driver of individual stock price movements, whether their direction is up or down. It is no coincidence that the short-term fluctuations we perceive and take advantage of in individual stock prices mirror so closely those in the overall market—they are to all intents and purposes the same fluctuations.

Just to emphasize the important point that we make here, the main driver of any individual stock's price movement is the movement of the overall market. As the overall market fluctuates constantly, with a day or two of a rising market followed by a day or two of a falling market being the norm, so too do the prices of individual stocks fluctuate in very similar patterns. It follows from this that a buyer of a stock has a choice. He can either buy at a relatively cheaper level on a day and at a time that both the overall market, as well as the stock he is purchasing, are down in price, or he can do the opposite, buying at a relatively more expensive level on a day and at a time that both the market and the stock are relatively more expensive than they were just hours or days before. We prefer to aim for the former course of action.

STOCKS ON SALE

If you look at the 52-week chart of almost any stock's price, you will be hard-pressed to find one that has maintained a continuous unchanging flat-line type level. The stock of each and every company will see times during a 52-week period where its price is toward the top of its range and other times when its price is near the bottom of that same range. This is true even of a stock that has done nothing but advance during the 52 weeks. Such a stock will have been close to the lowest point of the year at the start of the period and close to the highest point at the end of the period. In the case of most stocks, however, there is some element of price fluctuation in evidence.

One of the key elements of our version of contrarian buying is to buy into new stock positions exclusively on those days when they are on sale, that is, on days when the market is down, and at times during the day when the market is down as the market often fluctuates between positive and negative territory during one day. It is also a cardinal principle of our trading method that an individual stock should only be bought as an initial purchase when general market movements coupled with factors driven by the stock's own internal dynamics have driven the price of that individual stock to the relatively lower levels of its 52-week range. The internal dynamics of the stock would include sector or company-specific news, financial results, or other factors that may have pushed the stock lower in recent times, whether this is with the general trend in the market or against the prevailing trend. (For stocks we buy as part of our "riding the ripples," technique a different strategy applies—see Chapter 6.)

It is not the case that the best contrarian plays will necessarily be those stocks that are truly "out of favor" or have been "beaten down." In many cases such stocks may certainly be good buys because they are being offered at pricing levels that are appreciably lower than where they once stood. But a truly out of favor stock can also have obtained that status for a number of different reasons. The stock may be within an industry sector that is now in decline. The company may have experienced some kind of accounting shenanigans by its management which have just now been made public. Perhaps a new competitor has come along and eaten the company's lunch. Therefore, just because a stock is out of favor does not mean that it is a screaming buy. The trader needs to have a greater understanding of the exact reasons why the stock has fallen so far out of favor in order to assess whether the price drop presents a great buying opportunity or a signal to stay clear. Often great buying opportunities are opened up for the discerning trader, however, by irrational panicked selloffs in stocks that have no critical underlying weakness, but are overreactions to some unexpected bad news of one kind or another.

Fortunately for the short-term ripple trader, our contrarian buying strategy as detailed thus far does not depend on the trader seeking out those stocks that have hit hard times because of structural flaws in their business model or critical management missteps. Neither does our contrarian ripple trading strategy have to rely on the assumption that whatever factors drove such stocks down will eventually be corrected and thus allow them to rise again, phoenix-like from the ashes. There certainly is room in our trading strategy, however to profit from purchases of stocks that have been knocked back temporarily, usually by one piece of news or an earnings report. We look at some examples of these in our recent trading record in Chapter 7. However, even in those cases where we swoop in to buy a stock that has been temporarily knocked down by company-specific events or news, what we are doing is essentially still following the basic principle of buying good stocks because they are, or have now become, relatively cheaper, rather than targeting stocks that are, or have become, cheap for a reason in that they are unattractive stocks of intrinsically low-value companies, possibly with deep-seated problems.

Sometimes there is a sudden reevaluation of an individual stock by the market, particularly following some very positive or negative news, normally unexpected, usually based on a quarterly earnings report. Positive news of this kind can cause a stock to jump, whatever is going on in the overall market and the same is true for negative news, which can cause a sudden big drop in the company's stock price. Interestingly, as we note in Chapter 7, even positive quarterly results can sometimes lead to a sharp drop in a stock's price and thereby sometimes a great buy signal for us. Our contrarian approach means that we look closely at the stock that has been revalued downward swiftly owing to this kind of news. We look on a sharp price drop caused by circumstances such as these as being the catalyst that can place the stock into buying territory again. The stock is now a lot cheaper than it was, so we can buy it inexpensively compared to its recent trading range. We also know from experience that stocks that are knocked back suddenly in this way often overshoot dramatically to the downside. They then have a tendency to recover quickly.

The principal factor that drives individual company stocks to behave in this way, and open up good buying opportunities for the contrarian buyer, is the action taken or not taken by the professional institutional investors who now exercise almost total domination over the market. It has almost always been considered a truism in the past that the small, private investor is the one who does all the wrong things. He or she buys only when the bull market is approaching its frothy apogee and sells fearfully when the market is fast approaching a bottom from which a recovery is imminent. In this popular view, professional investors take a much more considered and rational approach to their investment decisions. After all, this is what they do for a living five days a week and they must therefore be experts. However, as it is the professional investors who dominate today's market, it is to the professional investors' actions that we must look when we seek to identify the behavior of market participants that allows a contrarian short-term ripple trader to profit from his contrarian trading strategy.

It is true that both professional and lay investors do appear to be prone to selling their holdings as panic sets in at market bottom. Both also lose all sense of reality and think buy, buy, buy in the heady atmosphere of a market top. In every sense, however, it is the professional investors' actions that drive market direction; and in more normal market conditions, where neither a market top nor bottom is close by, it is the sometimes apparently irrational behavior of professional investors that is the most striking. There are good, logical reasons for this phenomenon.

The market today is truly the stamping ground of the professional investment community. One statistic shows that 70 percent of shares in major companies are controlled by institutions.[3] Portfolio managers at pension funds, insurance companies, and mutual funds control huge amounts of money earmarked for investment in stocks. Their investing decisions represent often huge bets that can make them look like geniuses if they pay off, but equally can result in humiliating failure if they do not. What puts further pressure on portfolio managers is that their successes and failures are usually judged in a short-term time frame by their bosses, who are senior executives at the pension fund, insurance company, or mutual fund where they are employed, their investor clients themselves, and even for some of the more high-profile ones—the press and general public. For example, asset management company Legg Mason's star value investor and contrarian fund manager Bill Miller was often the subject of stories in the financial press in 2006 when he failed that year to beat the market for the first time in 15 years. There has for years been a sharp media focus on the investment successes and failures of whichever manager is running Fidelity's Magellan Fund, partly owing to the size of the fund, but also to some extent owing to a public curiosity regarding a fund run by Peter Lynch for 13 years.

Fund managers are fully aware that their investment decisions and the outcomes generated are placed under a microscope and their performance is judged often on the basis of fairly short-term results. In such a closely monitored environment, loss-making bets are really not an option. So playing it safe is generally the order of the day. As a result, professional investors as a class do tend to play it safe to such a degree that even if they identify a contrarian play as being one they feel will be ultimately profitable, they still avoid it. In fact, as Peter Lynch explains it, fund managers in their day-to-day investment decision making take pains to find reasons *not* to buy a particular stock and come up with all kinds of explanations such as "it was in a nongrowth industry," "it was too small to buy," or "the employees are unionized," when the real reason to avoid buying is a fear to make that commitment in case the company fails.[4] They simply do not feel comfortable making unpopular buys as this leaves them exposed to a risk of being caught in a position that could cause them embarrassment with their bosses, peers, or clients. After all, while a professional investor risks being pilloried for making a purchase, investment, or trade that does not work out, he will conversely never have to face criticism for *not* having bought into a stock position that subsequently would have made money.

Therefore, when news breaks on a stock that exerts strong downward pressure, often the stock is pushed further down to an unrealistic degree, as professional money managers decide that they do not want to touch it with the proverbial 10-foot pole. If they already hold it, they may try to get out of their position as they fear, not what the stock may ultimately do once it recovers, but the embarrassment of being caught with what is right now almost unanimously considered as a big "loser" in their portfolio. Another characteristic of institutional investors' buying and selling in the face of major news is that there is nothing subtle or graceful about it. As these big investors move in and out of their positions wielding huge blocks of shares, their grace and poise is that of a hippopotamus dancing the ballet on roller skates. When several big institutional investors move at the same time to unload a stock that has been the subject of a negative announcement, the effect on the stock price can be a sharp dramatic fall. Once the stock has been pushed down to levels where the only way for it to go realistically is up, the professional investors come piling back in. This can sometimes be a few hours after a selling frenzy occurs. But it more normally takes place only when they have seen a day or two of recovery and can feel emboldened in their purchase. Note that such pressures on professional investors are huge when the stock has fallen with a thud. This same dynamic is at work each and every day to a greater or lesser degree, even with stocks that have fallen back for relatively small percentages. It also reflects the fact that institutional investors simply do not have any need to dribble stocks in and out of the market. Their buys and sells on each and every occasion involve fairly significant blocks of stock. This will itself each time cause a certain amount of reverberation and then fluctuation in the stock's price that will take a little time to settle down.

Individual private investors do not have this pressure of bosses monitoring their every investment decision. They do not have to explain their motives for buying a particular stock to anybody but themselves (and occasionally their spouse). Moreover, because lay investors tend to have day jobs, they do not have the time to spend eight hours a day thinking about their investments. By not spending all day, every day thinking about and watching the market, they also have a lethargy factor built in that prevents them from joining the herd that temporarily stampedes out of an irrationally falling stock, where the fall is driven by institutional investors' sudden unwillingness to own it. Also, whether the private individual buys or sells and whatever the circumstances under which he does so, this never has any real effect on the market as the volume of the stock traded is just too small to have a significant impact. Oddly enough, as a result of all these factors, nonprofessional investors actually tend to have something of a calming influence on the market, while it is the professional investors, (more logically considered traders?) who tend to drive volatility. In any case, and whatever the principal cause, exaggerated downward price swings or any clear ripple fluctuations generated by institutional investors' market action offer a great opportunity for the short-term ripple trader to get into a position at a cheaper price before the fluctuation ceases and the stock price returns to some kind of equilibrium.

THANK GOD IT'S MARLBORO FRIDAY!

On the subject of overreaction to negative news, coauthor Aidan's favorite story regarding the tendency for the professional investing community to overshoot on the downside when hit with bad news relates to an event that took place 14 years ago. This may be prehistory for some market participants, but it remains superbly illustrative as to what can happen when news hits the market that is almost universally considered to be negative and is unexpected. On April 2, 1993, on what became known as "Marlboro Friday," the cigarette manufacturing giant Philip Morris, (stock symbol MO and since renamed Altria Group), announced that it would cut the price of its flagship Marlboro cigarette brand by 20 percent to fight its corner against lower-priced generic cigarette brands that were increasingly taking market share from the iconic brand leader, with its Marlboro Man lone cowboy symbol. The reaction in the market was immediate and sweeping. Equity analysts, who virtually all had buy ratings on the stock the day before, switched almost to a man to sell ratings, something rather amazing at a time when analysts tended to avoid using the sell rating and stuck to either buy or hold to avoid upsetting their relationships with the companies they covered. The analysts and professional investing community interpreted the slashing of prices as an admission by Philip Morris that the Marlboro brand faced defeat from the generic cigarette brands. They were certain that Philip Morris's action indicated they were throwing in the towel on the idea that they could continue to charge a premium price for a premium brand. Philip Morris's stock plunged 23 percent that day, which raised an interesting conundrum, at least in Aidan's mind. How could it be that a stock that was 23 percent more expensive yesterday was rated a buy and now is rated a sell at much cheaper levels today? Aidan bought 300 MO at $16.71 on April 6, 1993 (adjusted for MO's three-for-one stock split in April 1997), and it was the stock he traded most during 1993 and 1994. Fourteen years later MO stock trades close to $90. Despite the fact that Philip Morris and later Altria Group have been engaged in almost constant legal battles that have targeted them as one of the major manufacturers of a product that kills hundreds of thousands each year, they as a company and their shareholders have essentially flourished through the intervening period. In fact, against seemingly all odds, MO has proved itself to be a very good long-term investment. Actually, it could be argued that it is because of Altria's constant battles with litigation, bad press, and government action against it that it has remained such a superbly successful company. This may sound counterintuitive, but the fact is that the barriers of entry into what at the end of the day is a classic example of a low-tech, easily manufactured, and distributed product have been kept artificially high owing to the perceived highly negative aspects of the tobacco business. Ironically then, the constant attacks to which the company has been subjected from a large number of different constituencies have allowed the Philip Morris unit of Altria and the few other smaller established cigarette manufacturers and distributors such as R. J. Reynolds (a unit of Reynolds American Inc.) and Lorillard (owned by Loews Corporation through tracking stock Carolina Group), to operate in a rather cozy semimonopolistic business environment. Investing in Philip Morris/Altria has appeared at any and all times over the years to be an especially contrarian bet—and has worked out superbly.

It should be added that the reason that the market got Marlboro Friday's effects so spectacularly wrong at the time is that the fear, generated by Philip Morris's move on that day, that premium pricing for premium brands was to all intents and purposes dead, "the death of brands" as it was then termed, was 100 percent incorrect. Subsequently we have seen that the economy has continued to be dominated by companies who sell highly recognizable premium brands supported by heavy marketing and advertising campaigns.

CATCHING A FALLING KNIFE?

Problems, some of which were genuine, others of a Marlboro Friday nature, caused by false or exaggerated perceptions, affected a number of stocks during the 26-month period covered by our trading record at the end of this book. Examples of such hard-hit stocks are Biogen Idec (BIIB), Morgan Stanley (MWD, since changed to MS), UnitedHealth Group (UNH), BP Plc (BP), Wm. Wrigley Jr. Co. (WWY), Legg Mason (LM), and Black & Decker (BDK). Their prices were driven down significantly on at least one occasion as institutional investors in particular fled faced with bad news or negative perceptions. In each case, professional investors were unwilling to buy, yet willing to sell the stock for prices several dollars below the price they had considered quite reasonable just a few days or weeks earlier. As their avoidance of the stock in question drove the price down, these fearful professional investors did not feel comfortable diving in for what ought to have been considered a bargain by any rational investor. They feared that if the stock continued in the same downward trend, even for a short while, then they would look like losers to their bosses and their peers for buying the stock.

There is an old saying on Wall Street that justifies the stand-away attitude in such circumstances—"Don't catch a falling knife." This warns investors or traders from being tempted to buy a stock that is falling sharply. The thinking is that the stock can go knifing through the buyer's hands and continue its plunge. The contrarian trader, however, often gleefully catches that knife and profits as the stock rebounds once the professional investors feel comfortable enough to go back in once again and buy the stock. As well as being true for individual stocks, this kind of approach is also the rule in the overall market on days when stocks take a serious tumble. An excellent example of this is what happened on February 27, 2007. Following negative comments by former chairman of the Federal Reserve Alan Greenspan regarding the possibility of a recession in 2007, a 9 percent drop in the Chinese stock market, and with investors already jittery over the possibility that U.S. and Asian markets had overheated, the Dow plunged 413 points or a little over 3 percent. For a part of the afternoon, the Dow was showing a loss of 543 points. It later transpired that the extent of the collapse in the index was more apparent than real, the result of a computer glitch that had affected the calculation of the Dow and its communication to the markets—heavy trading volumes appeared to have temporarily overloaded the system. Nevertheless, the drop in the market made it clear that overall institutional investors were not willing buyers, seeing the market as a falling knife that they did not want to get beneath. For a contrarian, however, a market environment such as that of February 27, 2007 looks like a great buying opportunity. In our case, we took full advantage with a series of ripple trade purchases as the market fell and buy signals started to flash for stocks that we had previously bought and sold: Motorola, Dell, Corning, Weatherford International (bought twice, sold once during the day), SLM Corp., Eli Lilly, and Statoil. One new stock position was also purchased—Texas Instruments. What constitutes the buy signals for our ripple trading is covered in Chapter 5.

The majority of trading opportunities that arise day in and day out in the market for the contrarian ripple trader are not those that involve such sudden dramatic meltdowns of the market falling off a cliff as on February 27, 2007 or in temporarily pariah stocks of the kind that Chapter 7 examines. Our contrarian strategy in no sense involves waiting until such special situations arise and otherwise sitting on our hands waiting for the next strongly contrarian buy opportunity to come along. Our contrarian purchase technique strategy is primarily based on a recognition that essentially all stocks, including those of highly successful, well-established and growing companies, are subject to fluctuations in their price level during the course of a year. As a result, these stocks present themselves at various times in the year as relatively expensive or relatively cheap compared to the historical range in their prices during the preceding 52-week period. We believe that under all circumstances an established, large-capitalization stock is a better buy when it is closer to its lows for the year than when it is flirting with its highs. This follows from the simple observation of the typical fluctuations of almost any stock over a one-year period. If Nike Inc. has fluctuated during a 52-week time period between $75 and $92 as was the case during 2005, then it is our contention that the time to buy Nike stock was when it was closer to $75 than when close to $92. Please note that the operative word here is *closer*. We are not suggesting that the trader should take out his crystal ball and call the absolute bottom of any stock's trading pattern. The trick is for the investor to give himself a higher chance of a move to the upside in the relatively near term when the stock is towards the lower end of its trading range *and* when the market overall, including the stock he is looking to buy, is having a down day.

THE THEORY OF FLUCTUATION

What gives the trader the ability to presume that a stock bought under these circumstances will go up in the relatively near future? A guiding principle of contrarian investment thinking is that what goes down will usually come back up. The concept is called "reversion to the mean," and it usually appears to work. However, while we are certainly contrarian in our buying strategy, we do not hold the conviction that what is at play in most cases is a reversion to any mean. Such a concept assumes that there is some kind of "fair price" of the stock and while the actual market price may deviate upwards and downwards, the stock always finds itself drawn back to that fair value pricing point as if pulled by some kind of irresistible gravitational force. Our difference of opinion with this view concerns the existence of such a mean price or fair anchor price. We see the dynamic of what appears to be a reversion to the mean at work in most if not in all stocks, but we feel that what is really going on is a simple, natural fluctuation in price. Any fluctuation, of course, has its mathematical mean or midpoint, but we do not feel that there is any force pushing the stock price toward that price point other than a statistical coincidence. This difference of opinion with the "reversion to the mean" crowd may just amount to a splitting of hairs. After all, the resulting contrarian buy signal is the same—buy low. However, in the interest of understanding better the mechanics that drive prices in the market, the concept of "reversion to the mean" is better replaced by a "theory of fluctuation." This posits that individual stocks as well as the overall market itself move in waves or cycles, which are evident in the very short-term, medium-term, and over the long-term, too. As short-term traders, it is the short-term fluctuations that we take advantage of, and exactly how we do this is covered in the next chapter.

CHAPTER 5

What to Buy, When to Sell?

I n Chapter 4, we clarified why we take a contrarian approach in our
short-term trading method, looking at a stock for initial purchase when
it is trading at levels toward the lower ranges of its 52-week trading
history and not considering it as a buy target when it is toward its highs
for the year. In this chapter, we further detail how we decide to make an
initial buy of a stock for the first time—and how we then seek to "ride the
ripples" in that stock as we trade in and out of it and profit from its regular
day-to-day or other short-term price fluctuations.

THE DOW JONES INDUSTRIAL AVERAGE FORMS A BACKDROP

As a backdrop to our initial buy decision, we consider the price levels of
the overall market in relation to its 52-week high and low. Because most
individual stocks move as a group, the market will be around its lows for
the year and therefore relatively cheap when most individual stocks are as
well. The overall market will be moving toward its highs for the year, and
therefore relatively expensive, when most stocks are trading at higher levels. So we try to test the temperature of the overall market by assessing
the point that it is at in relation to its 52-week high and low. The best index
to use in order to assess the market in this way is the Dow Jones Industrial Average. Information on the highs and lows for the Dow, as well as
individual stocks, are within anyone's reach. They can be found in charts

that are readily available for access on the Web site of your online broker. Such charts can also be found on publicly accessible websites such as MSN Money and Yahoo! Finance. Finally, this information is also obtainable in the stock price listings in the financial press, especially the *Wall Street Journal* (although we are sad to see that recent changes in the *Wall Street Journal's* page size format have left their stock tables with less information than they used to provide).

Why should you look to the Dow Jones Industrial Average? After all, this index has certain built-in disadvantages over other indexes. We already pointed out in Chapter 2 that there is a danger in using the Dow as a guide as to how investments in any of its component stocks have done over long periods of time, as the index is regularly "housecleaned." Indeed, almost all of the original companies listed in the early Dow either no longer exist or have been merged into other companies. Over a more short-term or medium-term time frame admittedly, this problem with comparisons is not a major one. But there are other, theoretically more cogent disadvantages to using the Dow Jones Industrials as a representative or proxy for the overall market. As an index of just 30 stocks, the Dow is by definition very narrowly based, and this narrow base should surely invalidate its ability to serve as a reflection of an overall market comprising many thousands of stocks. Also, the Dow is price-weighted, meaning that movements of the more high-priced stocks in the Dow have more influence on the overall average than lower-priced stocks. In other words, a 1 percent move in IBM, which traded approximately between $73 and $97 in 2006, affects the average disproportionately more than a 1 percent move in AT&T, which traded between $25 and $36 during the same period. Clearly, this is something of an illogical anomaly as the actual dollar price of any individual stock should be basically irrelevant in comparison to others in the index. So with these disadvantages in mind, why would we suggest that the Dow is the index to use when seeking an overall market backdrop to provide a comfort level for our decisions regarding buying into new trading positions? The answer is simple. Whatever its failings as a true market indicator, the Dow is the index that the financial press and the general public use as a market proxy. When someone asks how is the market doing today, the answer will not come back that the S&P 500 is up 12 points, unless the person asked is a professional investor in which case he may have a broader-market based index preference, and it will not come back that the NASDAQ is down 20, unless the person being asked is especially technology stock obsessed. Instead, the answer that "the market" is up 10 points will indicate that the Dow Jones Industrial Average is up 10 points that day. Whatever the logic of everyone using this index to measure market movements, its value lies purely and simply in the fact that it has that level of acceptance. When you are trying to assess how the public and investors, large and small, perceive the market on any given day in order to help make an informed trading buy on a contrarian basis, to all intents and purposes the Dow *is* the market.

Assessing whether the market is closer to its 52-week highs or lows then allows the trader to make a general judgment as to whether it is likely to be a good or bad time to be a buyer. Therefore, as our approach is a contrarian one, the most auspicious time to be a buyer is when the levels are toward the low side. Please note, however, that we are not recommending that stocks be purchased only when the Dow itself is running along its lows for the year. When the Dow is running at lower levels, the trader should be more willing to buy rather than to sit on cash and wait. When the Dow is running at higher levels, the investor should exercise caution about committing too much money. However, he is unlikely to sit on his hands completely at any time, whatever the state of the overall market, as one stock or other in his monitored "portfolio" may give buy signals even at high market levels. Just to recap this point, the position of the Dow in relation to its 52-week high and low levels is therefore essentially a backdrop evaluation for the contrarian ripple trader. Low levels should increase the feeling of comfort that buy signals are well worth acting on. The traffic light is green. High levels indicate caution, while not ruling out that a good buy signal can still be generated by a particular stock. The traffic light is amber, not red.

A "PORTFOLIO" OF STOCKS TO MONITOR

Before we move on to the question of what constitutes a buy signal and when it should be acted on, one other important question worth answering is how we are we able to screen all the stocks in the market to identify those that are generating the buy signals we are looking for. The answer is that we cannot and do not try. Certainly there are many computerized stock screening programs out there that will do this kind of work. But for a trader to screen on this basis goes against our "know your stock" rule, as outlined in the rest of this section. Just like everyone else, we have reasonable familiarity with a number of stocks; but there is a much larger number, counting in the thousands, with which we do not. Familiarity means knowing what the companies in question do as a business, what they manufacture and sell, their basic business models, and why in general terms the prospects for at least moderate growth for the companies are good. Monitoring of these stocks also leads to familiarity with their recent price history, historic price ranges, and the like. We call the list of stocks that we monitor in this way our "portfolio" of trading stocks. It is not a portfolio in the usual way that the word is used—a list of actual investments made and currently held by an investor. But in the framework of our short-term trading strategy, we feel that the word "portfolio" fits the bill squarely for the list of stocks we monitor.

At first blush, the need to identify individual companies' stocks to purchase on this basis may seem to contradict our contention that our strategy is simple and easy for Everyman to understand. However, we believe that everyone with at least some education and some basic knowledge of what is going on around them in the commercial and business world will have a reasonable level of understanding of some of the major U.S. companies which will allow them to put together a ripple trader's "portfolio" as described above. The necessary comfort level may for some only be there with a relatively small number of companies, perhaps limited to those that cater directly to consumers/the general public and therefore companies that most people interact with as customers on a daily basis—for example, Procter & Gamble, Nike, Microsoft, McDonalds, Johnson & Johnson, Wal-Mart, and AT&T. But many traders will have some reasonable familiarity of maybe several dozen publicly traded companies and not just a handful.

If the trader is a regular reader of the financial press (*Wall Street Journal, Barron's, Fortune, Forbes, Business Week*, etc.) or a viewer of financial TV programming (CNBC in particular) or has a job that brings him into closer proximity to the business world, the number of companies that he is able to monitor for the purposes of our trading strategy will grow accordingly. Actually, for all intents and purposes, most people also have a superb opportunity to benefit from what is a kind of insider trading, but one that is perfectly legal! Let us explain. Most people hold jobs at some kind of company, each of which operates in its own specific industry sector or area of the economy. By the very nature of employees' day-to-day contact with what is going on in their industry or area of the economy, they are very well placed to have a wonderful insight into the various merits and demerits of the companies operating in their close business environment, including the company where they are employed. Please note this is nothing to do with possession and use of material financial insider information, which is illegal. It is simply a reflection of the fact that if you work at a financial services company such as a bank or insurance company, or at a supermarket chain, a pharmaceuticals company, or a manufacturer of household cleaning materials, you will have a better idea than the vast majority of the investing public as to the business trends in your industry and in your corner of the economy. You will be better placed than most to assess the general performance of your company as well as that of all its major competitors. It makes perfect sense to use this kind of legal insider knowledge to employ in your ripple trading strategy, should you be using our method, by including several or all of these especially familiar companies in the "portfolio" of stocks that you will monitor for trading purposes.

BUYING WHAT YOU KNOW

As we noted above regarding our own practice, we would suggest that any trader using our method makes it an iron-clad rule that he include in his "portfolio" of monitored stocks only those on which he can, even in the form of a three-minute soliloquy, provide a reasonably informed description of the company underlying the stock and of its business. Please note that we are not suggesting here that the trader should be able to talk about the company in the style or with the base of detailed knowledge and levels of research of a financial analyst. But it does mean that the trader should have the discipline of this self-imposed knowledge requirement to help him focus only on those stocks for which he personally perceives there to be a basic rationale for purchase of the stock. This ensures that the trader does not chase hot tips or stocks that have caught his imagination for fleeting or superficial reasons.

Apart from the power of legal "insider trading" already mentioned, from the viewpoint of exploiting familiarity with companies and their products, there are stocks of companies whose products you are familiar with because you purchase and use them. Peter Lynch, in his investing books, popularized the notion of using your experience of things you buy to help you make stock-buying decisions.[1] This can be very helpful. We certainly agree that if you regularly shop at Wal-Mart and see that the checkout aisles are clogged with people pushing overstuffed shopping carts, this may quite validly spur you to add Wal-Mart Stores to your "portfolio" of monitored companies. The same would be true if your doctor were to prescribe Lipitor for you and you were to ruminate on and calculate how much you, or your medical insurance, will be contributing to Pfizer's coffers during your course of treatment. Reliance on our technique, however, would still mean that your decision to buy Wal-Mart Stores or Pfizer would be triggered by their being closer to their 52-week low than 52-week high. However clogged with shoppers those aisles may be, and however prescription-happy those doctors may be getting to lower your cholesterol, if the stock price of these companies is up close to its 52-week high then you can be sure that those booming sales are already factored in.

In connection with using personal experience as your guide when it comes to which stocks to purchase, you have to understand that this method also has its limits. We noted with some distaste that one online brokerage company tried during its 2005 television advertising campaign to appeal to active traders by using commercials based on buying decisions relating to the investor/trader having become aware of the heavy use by consumers of a product. In one such commercial, their client discovers and buys a jeans-manufacturing stock because his daughter pleads for money to buy a pair of jeans *everybody* is wearing. In another commercial, the client buys a shoe manufacturer's stock after discovering that everyone in the road-race he is participating in is wearing that manufacturer's running shoe. Clearly it is ludicrous for anyone to buy a stock they did not know even existed moments before, purely and simply because they discover somebody, or even lots of people, are using a product, and likely just one of many products, that company manufactures.

The number of companies that can be comfortably monitored and traded according to this strategy depends on the level of the trader's familiarity with U.S. companies and his (or her) level of general business knowledge. Our "portfolio" of stocks is relatively broad for two reasons. Firstly, Aidan has been following this trading strategy for a number of years and each year has added companies to his "portfolio" as they have arrived on his radar screen for one reason or another. Secondly, through his professional life and interests, Aidan has developed a fairly extensive knowledge of corporate America, as well as of major international companies (see Chapter 6). As a result, the number of companies that he monitors (latterly together with Martha) has increased to around 200. As you can see in the appendixes, we traded in and out of around 130 stocks in the entire period covered and, therefore, at one time or another we traded the majority of the stocks we monitor in our "portfolio."

Another big difference in the choice of a contrarian ripple trader's "portfolio" compared to the stocks generally targeted by investors becomes apparent as we look deeper into the premise behind and mechanics of our contrarian ripple trading method. Given the nature of the short-term trading dynamic, the contrarian ripple trader does not need to seek out and identify those stocks that are set to grow dramatically, or that he believes have the propensity to grow very fast in the future, like those 10 baggers that Peter Lynch sought out. Finding a 10 bagger involves finding a stock to invest in that will return 10 times your investment. This is a very worthy goal. But it is one that is really hard for anyone to achieve on anything like a consistent basis. You would need to have Peter Lynch's talent for picking stocks or be willing to bet on relatively young companies, thereby assuming the market risk that involves, or willing to hold positions in larger stocks for the years it will take for them to make these kinds of gains. It is certainly true that those investors who are able to spot the kinds of companies that are set to break out to the upside consistently end up being the most successful. After all, Warren Buffett and Peter Lynch gained their sterling reputations for a reason. But most stock-picking advice does tend to revolve around the idea that any investor will naturally be looking for the undiscovered gems that are about to start a great growth spurt, and thereby provide that kind of phenomenal return on investment, whether in the short-, medium-, or long-term. For those who hold this out as the gold standard of investing, those stocks that may seem to hold out only the promise of potentially staying bound within a price range over an extended period of time are normally not considered potential members of the winners' circle and therefore tend to be shunned. With our method, on the other hand, even slow-growing, stodgy, unfashionable stocks will do fine for us, as long as they are currently selling cheaply on a relative basis and hold out the promise of being good candidates for repeated, short-term, ripple fluctuation–based trading.

BUY SIGNALS

So what are the buy signals that we are looking for? Just as the Dow's running high or low will provide a good indicator of whether it is generally a good time to be buying into trading positions, the buy signals for any new trading position in a stock we have not owned before, or have not traded in recent months, is delivered up by the individual stock's own current price in relation to its 52-week high and low.

Through our regular monitoring of what we have described as a "portfolio" of stocks, we can manage with ease our search for stocks that are coming into buy territory and that are not as yet being traded by us on a repeat ripple trade basis. (This is clarified later in this chapter.) If we are buying a stock for the first time or one we have not traded in some considerable time so that comparisons with the previous trading range make little sense, we make our buy decision based largely on the one important factor of where the stock is trading in relation to its 52-week trading range. On any given day, we may find that some of the stocks we monitor have wandered into a territory that is emphatically in the lower reaches of their 52-week trading range. A stock trading at $42 where its high for the year was $55 and its low for the year was $40 would be the kind of correlation we would be looking for. Note there is no hard and fast rule—this part of the method is more art than science. Should a stock be trading roughly in this low ball park area, however, then it is useful to take a few additional factors into consideration when making the decision to buy into a new position for the first time. The most important of these, and a fundamental discipline that helps us decide whether and when we should buy an individual stock, is the market trend of the day. We make the buy decision on a new stock position only when both the market overall, in the form of the Dow Jones Industrial Average, *and* our chosen stock are showing a reasonable loss for the day. This again reflects our contrarian viewpoint, which maintains that you buy when sale time comes around. It makes no sense to pay good money today for something that by nature fluctuates in price and is more expensive today than it was yesterday. However, the reader should note that both the overall market and the individual stocks within it can at different points in a volatile day's trading be sometimes above and sometimes below the previous day's close. Therefore, we can find ourselves buying on a generally up day if the market and the stock we have pegged as a possible buy are *at the point of purchase* both below their closes of the previous day.

There are other factors that we may take into consideration for the purchase of a stock for the first time or after a long hiatus that we would like to mention. One is the stock's price/earnings ratio, or P/E ratio for short. The P/E ratio is the company's stock price divided by its earnings per share and is essentially a yardstick for the trader/investor to judge how much each dollar of the company's earnings per share costs to buy right now. A comparison with that same company's P/E numbers over time can help establish whether the market is valuing those earnings at a higher or lower end of the historical scale. As contrarian buyers we would prefer to buy the company's earnings for less rather than more, so therefore where the P/E ratio is lower, meaning that a lower valuation has been applied by the market. Looking at this ratio can help confirm a buying decision initially predicated on the much more important statistic of the relation of price to 52-week high and low. But beware, as contrary to the views of many investment writers, comparisons of P/E ratios of two or more companies, even in those operating in the same industry sector, tell you little if anything at all worth knowing about the relative attractions of the stocks being compared owing to the vagaries of accounting between different companies. This is the case even though all U.S. companies do their financial reporting using *GAAP* or Generally Accepted Accounting Principles. For us, therefore, the value in using the P/E ratio is in its ability to help us evaluate historical price comparisons on one company's stock that we may be considering for purchase.

Also, a very useful and helpful factor that often assists the buying decision is the dividend yield of the stock in question. Many years ago the collection of dividends was considered almost the sole reason for investing. The idea that it could be worthwhile investing in a stock that paid a low dividend or even, heaven forbid, no dividend at all would have been anathema for any serious investor. In recent years, however, and especially during the go-go years of the late 1990s, the perceived value of dividends was turned on its head. Dividend payments were seen as the preserve of old-line economy companies and utilities, useful for income-oriented investors such as the proverbial widows and orphans but really for no one else. Serious investors were more interested in stocks that paid a low dividend or no dividend at all, something that came part and parcel with the fast-growing companies of the new economy. Clearly money reinvested by a company in its own fast-growing business at a high internal rate of return was worth more to the investor than a dividend that would be subject to tax and then would need to be reinvested in some way. It was believed that investors would not be able to find alternative uses of their dividend income that could match the heady returns that investments in many companies were at that time perceived to be making—at least on paper.

After the boom of the 1990s turned to bust, dividends made a comeback. This was due partly to a perception that the ability to pay dividends in cold, hard cash certifies a company as a serious business enterprise with a mission to reward its shareholders in something that goes beyond pipe dreams. Moreover, dividends are back in fashion also in part because of legislation making the taxation of dividends less onerous to stockholders. The Jobs and Growth Tax Relief Reconciliation Act of 2003 changed the dividend taxation rate. In the past, dividends were taxed just as regular income would be, and the rate could be as high as 38.6 percent. Now the top rate dividends could be taxed at is 15 percent (and 5 percent for lower incomes). There are some exceptions to this rule, such as the length of time the stock is held or the kind of corporation that is paying out the dividend. For example there are foreign corporations that pay dividends that do not fall under the Act. Nevertheless, the tax break certainly helps attract investors to dividend paying companies. Today even companies like Microsoft and Intel are dividend payers.

For traders following our strategy, the payment of dividends is a strong plus. This seems counterintuitive—surely as short-term traders we are not in positions long enough to see the benefits of dividend payouts. Not so. It is true that many, and actually most, of our trades will go through the "roundtrip" cycle in one, two, or just a few more days. (Check out Appendixes A through C to see just how often we managed this.) This means that on those trades we are very unlikely to catch a dividend record date and thus entitlement to the dividend with that trade. Later in this chapter, you will see that one of our governing disciplines in this trading strategy is that we hold our position in a stock until it reaches our targeted profit figure. Some stocks we may hold for several months or more as they drift down further from our buy point or languish just shy of where we bought them. Dividends received from these companies help keep us happy during this holding period.

The other signal that a higher yield sends us is a reaffirmation that the stock is trading at relatively lower levels to its regular trading range. The yield is the amount of the dividend payout expressed as a percentage of the stock price. As a stock rises in price and becomes more expensive, its yield falls and vice versa. When a company increases its dividend payout, however, the yield rises. So the yield combines a picture of how generous a cash payout is available with the stock, as well as a rough gauge of whether the stock is expensive or cheap in relation to the level of that dividend payout. A dividend yield that has trended higher over the recent past for the company whose stock we consider for purchase is a good sign of either a lower price level or a more generous payout—or hopefully both. An attractive dividend yield, therefore, while in no sense the main reason for buying, nevertheless provides a useful reaffirmation of our initial buy choice.

These previously mentioned factors are important considerations for evaluation of potential candidates in which to make an initial stock purchase. Another additional factor to add to the mix, which can be helpful but is in no sense a vital must-have in the buying decision, is a consideration of whether the stock is of a company that is known to be cash-rich and to carry low levels of debt. For many investors looking to invest in companies with powerful growth prospects, such stocks have a huge disadvantage and are probably better avoided. Their return on capital is diluted by their cash hoard, as the return they earn on those cash balances is always inferior to what a growing business will aim at as a satisfactory return on its capital. In other words, high levels of cash balances and cash equivalents act as a drag on performance.

Theoretically, such cash-rich companies should return their excess capital to stockholders in the form of dividends or through share buybacks, in order to maximize their return on the capital they employ in the business, leaving stockholders to decide for themselves how to use the extra cash. So why is it that we would look with positive eyes on companies that have a larger part of their net assets in cash than they would appear to need for their business operations? From our point of view as short-term ripple traders, the stock of a cash-rich, preferably low-debt or debt-free company is attractive precisely because the company's high cash position can tend to exert downward pressure on a stock as it detracts from its attractiveness to investors looking for growth. Buying a stock more cheaply is a positive for us, and if the real value of the company's core business is its market price minus its cash balances, then that means such companies are selling even more cheaply than they may at first appear. Remember, too, that these cash balances mean that such companies are in a position to pay out or increase dividend payments or engage in stock buybacks if they choose, moves that are positive to the stock price and our trading position if we happen to own it at the time such an announcement is made. A company that is already engaged in returning excess cash to shareholders already has that positive action reflected in its stock price and so we cannot profit from it through a purchase of the stock now. Companies such as Goodyear Tire and Gateway are low-growth companies that are well stocked with cash. But there are other companies that are large, highly successful and well-known to be flush with cash. Exxon Mobil, Microsoft, Johnson & Johnson, Pfizer, Cisco Systems, and Motorola are good examples. Note that pharmaceutical companies need to hoard cash to fund their hefty R&D expenditures and some oil companies have built huge cash piles in recent periods as revenues have gushed as a result of high oil prices.

Gimlet-eyed readers may note that on the face of it our predilection for cash-rich companies contradicts our view that the nonprofessional investor or trader gains little or nothing by immersing himself in a company's financial statements (as we stated in Chapter 2). It is true that such information can be obtained by delving into a company's balance sheet; but we ourselves prefer to be guided on this point by research from our favorite stock research companies—honorable mention was given to Argus Research in Chapter 2—or, alternatively, by just checking general information on cash-rich companies that can be easily elicited through simple research carried out online.

In recent times, there has been one additional reason to feel comfortable with a company that sits on a cushion of cash. Private equity firms are increasingly circling such companies as possible acquisition targets. Private equity firms run investment pools that buy controlling stakes in private companies or take public companies private—in both cases with a view to managing the companies for a future profitable exit through an *IPO* (initial public offering of shares) or through the sale of its investment to another company in the same or a similar industry, (strategic buyer), or another private equity firm (financial buyer)—in either case aiming for a profit on the transaction overall. Cash-rich companies hold out the opportunity for the private equity firms to extract for their own benefit some of the excess liquidity by paying themselves substantial special dividends after they have taken control and then having the company take on debt to fuel growth, while tightly reining in costs and shedding non-core assets. All of this allows the private equity firm to win twice over, with its planned profitable exit somewhere down the line, preceded by an early cash drawdown through dividends that provide them with an upfront additional return on their investment.

For stockholders in public companies, even the hint of private equity interest in their company can put the stock price into overdrive. This occurred with the stock of marketing services and information provider Catalina Marketing (POS), which spurted 20 percent on December 8, 2006, when it announced that it had received an unsolicited approach from an unidentified private equity firm and had hired investment bank Goldman Sachs to evaluate this and other possible offers. On this news Catalina Marketing stock jumped $4.88 to close at $29.11. We sold our 100 shares in Catalina Marketing on that day for $28.06. They had been bought November 27 for $24.65, and we netted a profit on them of $331. We traded in and out of Catalina Marketing a couple more times over the next few weeks as they backed down from that initial jump in price. Interestingly, Catalina Marketing subsequently decided not to proceed with negotiations with any bidders. According to press reports there were several bids on the table, all at around $30 a share. Then on February 21, 2007, ValueAct Capital Master Fund LP made an unsolicited $1.5 billion offer for the shares in Catalina that it did not already own, representing an offer of $32 per share. On the date the bid was announced, Catalina's shares jumped 10 percent to close at $32.02. Did we kick ourselves, having last bought and sold 200 shares in Catalina Marketing just one week before on February 14, with our sale being made at $27.64? No, we did not, and see our comments regarding the futility of obsessing on the "what ifs" following a stock position sale later in this chapter. Ultimately private equity firm Hellman & Friedman offered $32.50 per share in cash for Catalina, and this sweetened bid won out.

Increasingly, even major public corporations with household names are coming into the sights of private equity firms who also find themselves awash with liquidity. These can additionally jointly pool resources with other private equity companies through so-called club deals to aim at even the largest targets. Also, never rule out the corporate raiders such as Carl Icahn who are skilled in spotting opportunities with companies they consider inefficiently managed. Icahn announced January 30, 2007, that he had acquired 33.5 million shares or 1.4 percent of Motorola's stock and was seeking a seat on the board with a view to tapping into the company's net cash, generally reported as amounting to almost $11 billion. Mr. Icahn's proposal was that this cash hoard should be given back to shareholders in the form of a special dividend and through stock buybacks. Icahn bluntly pronounced Motorola's use of its capital to be inefficient and said of the company's management, "If they want to be money managers they should get a job on Wall Street."[2] Motorola stock jumped almost 7 percent on news of Icahn's actions, thereby demonstrating the value that can accrue to existing stockholders of a company when an attempt is made to unlock this kind of cash balance value.

Finally, one last piece of information that can give an enhanced comfort level looking at a stock that may be bought, but that is not currently in any sense fully captured in any company's financial reporting, is in the area of patents and intellectual property. Intellectual capital is generally poorly reflected in companies' balance sheets, reflecting the fact that financial statements are still constructed according to historic cost principles, and therefore fail to value fully the often huge future earnings potential and therefore real value of these assets. Companies such as IBM, Intel, Microsoft, Micron Technology, Applied Materials, Broadcom and Motorola are consistently prolific innovators in their research & development (R&D) activities and have all in recent years been major recipients of large numbers of patents.

HOW MUCH TO BUY?

We have now made the decision to buy a stock based on the factors outlined in the previous section. How many shares do we buy? We typically buy 100 shares, unless the stock in question is trading at a price of less than $30 or so when we consider buying 200. The appendixes set out what we actually did in this regard in the 26-month period we cover there. What happens next? As our practice is to buy when both the market and the price of our chosen stock are moving down in relation to their previous close, the most likely thing that happens next is that our stock drops at least a little further. Although it would be nice to see each stock we buy immediately turn around and head north just because we bought it, this is unrealistic. So, for a short time at least, we are used to seeing our stock purchases continue on a downward track. However, given our discipline of buying when both market and individual stock price are down on the day, the power of a contrarian buying strategy, and the nature of ripple fluctuations that form cornerstones of our trading strategy, mean that at some point later that day, if not in the next few days, we normally see the turnaround in the stock's price movement that we are looking for. Should this not happen, we continue to hold the stock on the understanding that we bought it at a relatively low point in its trading range for the year and so the chances are good that it will come back up over the next weeks or maybe months to the point where it will meet our target point for sale. Should it take months for this to happen, then we are consoled by the dividends we will be earning if the stock is a dividend-payer.

Should the price continue to drop in the stock that we bought, we may purchase more of the same stock a few days or perhaps weeks later when it has dropped a dollar or two from our original purchase price. We do this sometimes once or twice, but rarely as many as three times. It would be a mistake to build up too large a position in any one stock, just in case there actually is some huge underlying problem with that specific company that could see it crippled or go bankrupt—like Enron or WorldCom. The watchword here is *diversification.* So in the interest of not keeping all our eggs in one basket, we limit ourselves in the number of times that we will go back to purchase a position again at a lower level following an initial purchase to two or occasionally three times.

WHEN TO SELL

The above describes the ways in which we screen for buy signals on stocks within our monitored "portfolio" where we are either buying a stock position for the very first time, or coming back to a stock that has not been bought and sold in a considerable amount of time. Actually, most of our purchases do not involve even the simple process described above, as in the majority of our trades we "ride the ripples." Before we look at what that technique involves, however, this is an opportune time to look at the other side of the buy signal coin and examine the issue of when to sell.

In many "how-to" investing books, the authors give as much space to the sell decision as they do to the buy decision. The guru guide offers an insight into the signals that indicate that the upward trend of the chosen stock has run its course and now a red light is flashing telling us to sell, sell, sell! Another common approach states that you should ride your profits and quickly take your losses—often through the disciplined placing of stop-loss orders—one that has indeed become something of a classical approach to the issue of selling in short-term trading strategies. Clearly this is an approach that has merit, as it quickly separates the winners from the losers and by backing the former and cutting the latter seeks to give predominance to the winning trades. Should the strategy work, it will cover the costs of the losers as well as make an overall trading profit. While this is a perfectly valid approach to short-term trading, its rigorous application would be counterproductive when tied to our practice of buying shares that are trending down with our implicit acceptance that the downward trend may continue for a little time before reversing. To our mind, given our contrarian approach, quickly cutting losses would necessarily result in too many positions being sold as losers, to the extent that it would be impossible to make enough profit from those that immediately bounce back and score gains. Equally, given that it is our practice to buy stocks when they are relatively close to the lows of their 52-week range, we feel that patience and expectation of their recovery over time makes the best sense for us for those that continue to decline afterward. Our results in Appendixes A through C bear this out. In conclusion then, the buy signals that we use for targeting our purchases make our trading method essentially incompatible with the popularly advocated strategy of riding winners and cutting losers.

Moreover, as our trading technique seeks to allow us to take advantage of the short-term fluctuations that we see in stocks over a period mostly of just a few days, we do wish to ensure that we take our profits quickly on those positions that go up, in order hopefully to be able to take advantage of a downdraft coming as part of the normal ripple fluctuation of markets and the individual stocks within it. So we ride the ripples, not our profits, which we discuss in the next section of this chapter.

The sell strategy we follow has the advantage of being the simplest part of our short-term trading method and is encapsulated in the following simple rule: You sell when you make a predetermined profit. During most of 2005, we stood ready to sell once the profit on any stock that we had bought reached $40 net of brokerage commissions. Late in 2005, for all of 2006 and into 2007, we switched this number to $50 except for stocks that we were selling on the same day that we had bought them, in which case we sold them at the $40 minimum. There is no hard or fast rule on the actual amount that a trader following our strategy may use. However, if you choose to utilize our short-term trading strategy, you do need to have the ability to follow your preset selling discipline with determination, as it is the only way in which you can earn profits from repeat ripple fluctuation trading described later in this chapter. With our quick-fire approach to selling, a stock often continues to rise in price after we have sold, as we are by definition selling during a climbing trend, at least as far as that stock is concerned. We do not lament over any additional price rise forgone. It may be difficult for many not to obsess about how much money could have been made if one had just waited a little longer. A good example of this is demonstrated by what happened with Catalina Marketing mentioned earlier in this chapter. But remember that the stock could easily have turned down again without any profit having been made. Indeed our trading strategy is predicated on the observation that over the very short term stocks do tend to fluctuate in price, rather than making a strong unwavering move either upward or downward. In any case, it helps to recall the old trading adage, "Nobody ever went broke taking a profit."

The astute reader, after looking at Appendixes A through C, might ask why, if we target a $40 or $50 profit figure, we made profits on some trades in the hundreds of dollars and very often far in excess of our minimum profit requirement—as much as $993 on a 14-day position in MBNA Corp. and $879 on a four-day position in Genentech, both in 2005; and $651 on a 25-day position in Adobe Systems in 2006. The answer is that as amateur traders who have day jobs, we only get the opportunity to look at our positions from time to time during the day (and some days we have more time to devote to monitoring our "portfolio" than others). While we have a threshold profit figure and allow ourselves to be guided by it, in many cases when we look at where our positions are, we have already scored a much higher profit. This is certainly an added bonus for us. Notice that we do not place limit orders to have stocks sell as soon as they reach our required margin of profit. While we do like the discipline of following a profit margin strategy which will cause us to sell if we check our open positions and find that one or more have reached the target, we find that the leaving of a certain element of flexibility in selling often results in our making some additional money because the stock price can often blow through our target price. This is especially true if, as in the case of MBNA mentioned above, the stock has benefited from a takeover bid from another company—Bank of America, in this particular case. This notwithstanding, it is an important element of our strategy that the necessary discipline is always there to sell unquestioningly and without hesitation when we do check the price and see that we have broken through the sell signal level. More words on self-discipline are expressed in Chapter 8.

As mentioned earlier, in those cases where we have purchased a position in a stock, a continuing decline in the price of the stock often motivates us to buy a second position at lower levels. Note, however, that where we come to sell the second position bought at lower levels, the criteria used are based on the same profit margin target over purchase price as applies to any of our trades—so we are not engaging in "dollar-cost averaging." Dollar-cost averaging involves increasing positions in a stock already held, but made at a lower cost level so that the average cost of the entire position in that stock is lowered. Typically with a dollar-cost averaging strategy the entire position would be sold at a profit calculated on the average cost of the position overall. With our method, however, every distinct purchase is sold at our predetermined profit margin, or held until that level is attained.

It should be noted that our method of selling the last stock purchases rather than the first is known as a *last in, first out* (LIFO) approach. When tax time comes around, this is the way trades need to be reported for this method to work without a great deal of additional complication. Although the most common way for multiple trades in the same stock to be reported to the IRS is on a *first in, first out* (FIFO) basis, the IRS allows LIFO accounting of trades as long as the approach is consistent throughout the filing.

RIDING THE RIPPLES

Apart from the advantage of locking in a certain profit, there is another good reason that the discipline of cashing out a stock at a predetermined price applies in our method. The principal value in our short-term trading strategy derives from the ability it gives us to buy and sell the same stocks over and over again to take advantage of their natural price fluctuation or ripple. As can be seen from our trading record in the appendixes, almost all of our trading actually involves this practice of trading the same stocks over and over again—always at a profit. We call this "riding the ripples" and its successful practice is the key to successful short-term contrarian ripple trading. By adopting this method of trading, we take advantage of the typical very-short-term fluctuations of all stocks. The decision-making process to target a purchase point when riding the ripples could not be more simple. Once we have bought a stock and then sold it, then should the stock in the next few days or weeks drop back to that same level at which we bought it before, as so often is the case owing to the natural short-term fluctuation in stock prices (the ripple), then we buy again and hopefully the cycle will quickly go full circle once again over the next hours or days. As the initial decision to enter a stock position has been made based on the contrarian indicators detailed earlier in this chapter, as a result subsequent buys, however often they may be made as part of a continuous riding of the ripples, are by definition also imbued with that same contrarian rationale. This holds true, even if the thought process that goes into the future purchases is a very simple one, representing essentially no more than an automatic reaction to the stock price hitting or going below the price level of the previous purchase.

Whenever we ride the ripples of a particular stock, we do not necessarily apply the rule of buying only when the overall market is well down for the day. The fact that the ripple fluctuation of our stock has brought it back to the point where we bought it in a previous roundtrip provides a buy signal even where the market is up on the day. The exception to this would be when the market is very strongly up on the day—over 45–50 points on the Dow—in which case we prefer to wait for a downdraft in the overall market. Also, where the market overall trades at very high levels compared to its 52-week trading range, as at the end of 2006 and beginning of 2007, we often wait for a definite fallback in the market, even by a small margin, before buying a stock at its previous purchase price. We believe this represents good contrarian caution on our part.

There are other scenarios that allow us under our method to buy a stock at a time that the market is trading higher on the day. One of these is a special situation purchase when a stock has fallen heavily owing to circumstances specific to that stock. Also, oil and gas or gold stocks often are bought against a higher trending market as these typically run counter-cyclical to the overall market trend. (See Chapter 7 for more about both scenarios.)

In Chapter 6, we provide several detailed illustrations of how the ripple trading method can be made to work profitably over and over again. A good sense can also be gained from the following summary that sets out the stocks that were most traded by us in the 26-month period covered by our trading record. Stocks in this trading record are ranked by number of completed roundtrip trades. As everywhere in this book, profit numbers are net of brokerage commissions.

- Nike Inc.—40 completed trades with a profit of $2,723
- Corning Inc.—34 completed trades with a profit of $2,260
- Morgan Stanley—31 completed trades with a profit of $1,669
- Intel—28 completed trades with a profit of $1,589
- Johnson & Johnson—27 completed trades with a profit of $1,507
- Genentech—26 completed trades with a profit of $3,302
- Suncor Energy—26 completed trades with a profit of $1,735
- Commerce Bancorp—26 completed trades with a profit of $1,480
- Procter & Gamble—24 completed trades with a profit of $1,533

- General Motors—23 completed trades with a profit of $2,301
- Eli Lilly—23 completed trades with a profit of $1,297
- Bristol-Myers Squibb—21 completed trades with a profit of $1,622
- Time Warner—21 completed trades with a profit of $1,205
- Peabody Energy—20 completed trades with a profit of $1,683
- FedEx—18 completed trades with a profit of $1,257
- CIT—17 completed trades with a profit of $995
- Wal-Mart Stores—17 completed trades with a profit of $993
- Anheuser-Busch—17 completed trades with a profit of $992
- Goodyear Tire & Rubber—17 completed trades with a profit of $932
- Central Fund of Canada—17 completed trades with a profit of $876
- Tyco International—17 completed trades with a profit of $846
- Adobe Systems Inc.—16 completed trades with a profit of $1,569
- Catalina Marketing—16 completed trades with a profit of $1,239
- Reuters—16 completed trades with a profit of $873
- United Technologies Corporation—16 completed trades with a profit of $865
- Bausch & Lomb—15 completed trades with a profit of $1,163
- Vodafone—15 completed trades with a profit of $974
- Qualcomm—15 completed trades with a profit of $966
- Anadarko Petroleum Corporation—15 completed trades with a profit of $925
- Lloyds TSB Group—15 completed trades with a profit of $820
- General Electric Co.—15 completed trades with a profit of $777
- Microsoft—15 completed trades with a profit of $755
- ConocoPhillips—14 completed trades with a profit of $780
- Pfizer—13 completed trades with a profit of $737
- Weyerhaeuser—12 completed trades with a profit of $746
- Barrick Gold—12 completed trades with a profit of $715
- BP—12 completed trades with a profit of $707
- Coca-Cola—12 completed trades with a profit of $698
- Carnival Corporation—12 completed trades with a profit of $660
- Repsol YPF—10 completed trades with a profit of $785
- Advanced Micro Devices—10 completed trades with a profit of $745
- 3M—10 completed trades with a profit of $662
- Abbott Laboratories—10 completed trades with a profit of $572
- Caterpillar—10 completed trades with a profit of $561
- DuPont—10 completed trades with a profit of $558
- Juniper Networks—10 completed trades with a profit of $531
- Clear Channel Communications—10 completed trades with a profit of $485
- Electronic Arts—9 completed trades with a profit of $895
- UBS—9 completed trades with a profit of $739

- GlaxoSmithKline—9 completed trades with a profit of $702
- Gateway—9 completed trades with a profit of $680
- Fortune Brands—9 completed trades with a profit of $532
- News Corporation—9 completed trades with a profit of $422
- St. Jude Medical—8 completed trades with a profit of $663
- Goldman Sachs—8 completed trades with a profit of $534
- Cadbury-Schweppes—8 completed trades with a profit of $485
- Colgate-Palmolive—8 completed trades with a trading profit of $458
- Unilever—8 completed trades with a profit of $411
- iStar Financial—8 completed trades with a profit of $382

One of the first things that you should note from this list is that the vast majority of repeat ripple-traded companies in it are large, well-known, established corporations. We have included in this list only those stocks that were repeatedly bought and sold through a minimum of eight roundtrip trades during the 26-month period in our record. Just beneath this arbitrarily chosen threshold are a number of other companies that were regularly traded in the period, but did not quite reach eight trading roundtrips. The following are companies that we traded in and out of six or seven times each in the period: Exxon Mobil, Ford Motor, Walt Disney Co., Kellogg Co., Alcoa, Wm. Wrigley Jr., Co., Cisco Systems, Yahoo!, Dell, UnitedHealth Group, CVS, Dow Jones & Co., State Street Corp., Micron Technology, Molson Coors Brewing, Bank of Montreal, Teva Pharmaceutical, Ahold NV, El Paso Corp., International Game Technology Inc., Washington Mutual and Statoil ASA.

As you examine the list of stocks we traded, which are detailed in full in Appendixes A through C, notice that among the many familiar household name companies are some that are probably not so familiar, such as Avaya (AV), a communications systems company; Biogen Idec (BIIB), a biotechnology company; Juniper Networks (JNPR), a designer and seller of Internet networking products; The Cheesecake Factory (CAKE), a chain of casual restaurants; Catalina Marketing (POS), an operator of behavior-based marketing programs for retailers; and CKX Inc. (CKXE), a company that owns the rights to the names, images, and likenesses of Elvis Presley, Muhammad Ali, and others, as well as the American Idol TV show. Does inclusion of such clearly smaller and less well-established companies go against our rule of focusing on the well-established large-capitalization, dividend-paying stocks? Yes, it does. We believe that there is always room for inclusion of a little bit of what Jim Cramer would call "mad money," meaning those slightly more off-the-wall bets that involve a little more risk. Such purchases should be fine as long as you can discipline yourself in a few ways. You should keep the amount of trading in stocks of smaller, less familiar companies to a relatively small proportion. You should also follow even more faithfully the rule of buying when these stocks are close to their 52-week lows and on down days for both the individual stock and the market overall.

Lastly, despite the fact that these stocks are less familiar to the man or woman in the street, *you personally* need to be familiar enough with the company whose stock you buy to be able to describe what it does, how it makes its money, and what its general business prospects appear to be. It is even more vital to have familiarity with your stocks of smaller companies than with the stocks of larger, better-known companies that will make up the bulk of your monitored "portfolio." You should also note that "mad money" stock trades are quite appropriately very *underrepresented* in the list of the most ripple fluctuation traded stocks earlier in this section. The low-risk nature of our ripple trading technique is largely achieved through our concentration on companies that have large market capitalization and are well-established and well-known, not just to professional investors, but to the general public.

ALL STOCKS ARE EQUAL?

If you look at how our trading strategy is applied to the 200 or so companies that we monitor regularly to assess their ripeness for purchase on the basis outlined earlier in this chapter, you might think that we treat all of them exactly alike. That is not strictly true. There are certain stocks that we are fans of. Indeed, if we were in the business of "buying and holding," these would be among the principal components of our investment portfolio. As a result of their position in the markets they compete in, the quality of their management, their history of regular and consistent growth, and what we perceive as their overall good prospects, we consider these stocks very promising growth vehicles. If we bought and held these stocks, however, we would probably find that several of them would indeed perform extremely well over the long run, but one or two would perhaps disappoint. Indeed, we believe this to be the most common investment outcome for those following a buy-and-hold strategy.

Because our strategy is a short-term trading one, we trade these stocks in much the same way as any others in our monitored portfolio. The one difference is that we allow them a little more on the upside from their 52-week lows when we buy into them after a hiatus. In other words, with these favored stocks, we do not typically have a problem with buying them when they are around the midpoint of their 52-week high-low range; and we do not necessarily wait for them to retreat further before buying them, as we would with most of the stocks we monitor. Please note, however, that no such favoritism enters into the decision on when we sell them—the same profit target applies to these stocks as to any others in which we take a trading position.

Which are our favored stocks? They are United Technologies Corporation (UTX), Nike Inc., (NKE), Procter & Gamble, (PG), Goldman Sachs, (GS), Johnson & Johnson, (JNJ), Colgate-Palmolive (CL), Diageo Plc (DEO), Lloyds TSB Group (LYG), Microsoft (MSFT), and Intel (INTC). This list of preferred companies is by definition a very personal one, and each person trading on our technique would have their own list of such companies. Note that it is a short list—just 10 companies—and is made up exclusively of large corporations, all of which would by general public consensus be considered well-established and highly successful. Moreover, all of them pay reasonable dividends, always an added bonus if we are forced to sit on positions in them for some time. It should also be noted that a couple among them, Goldman Sachs and Colgate-Palmolive, were traded by us relatively lightly in the period, eight times each, and Diageo even fewer times than that. This was simply because during 2005, 2006, and early 2007 their prices were consistently hitting new highs and thus did not provide many opportunities for us to ripple trade with the comfort of our contrarian approach.

A WORD ON ETFS

Exchange traded funds (ETFs) are a fast-growing group of instruments that enable investors to invest in or traders to trade in what are essentially index funds, but which can be bought and sold like stocks throughout the trading day. Index mutual funds were themselves pioneered by John Bogle and his company The Vanguard Group, and the first index mutual fund launched in the mid-1970s was Vanguard's 500 Index Fund that tracked the S&P 500 Index. (Index funds aimed at institutional investors were already in existence). Tracking the index means that funds contain stocks that are component parts of the particular index that is being tracked, so that their returns are close to matching those of the underlying index. This has the added advantage of keeping administrative costs down as the buying and selling of securities to keep it tracking the index does not require stock-picking talent or research—it is essentially a formulaic process. Index funds were often the subject of scorn in their early days given that they were purposefully set up in such a way that their returns would match the index they tracked, minus some relatively small expenses, and therefore they achieved for their investors a real return that was just marginally below the average. Over time, however, index funds have earned greater respect and attracted large sums of investors' money as it has become increasingly clear that the goal of matching, let alone beating the market averages has been a goal that is tough to reach for the majority of actively managed funds. As a result, the promise of a return that would be guaranteed to track closely one of the major index averages has increasingly been perceived as an attractive prospect for many investors.

On the surface the principal difference between an exchange traded fund and a regular index fund is the one already mentioned, that the ETF can be traded on an exchange throughout the trading day just like a stock. The first ETF to be launched in 1992 was the Standard & Poor's Depository Receipts index—SPDRs or "Spiders" for short. Like Bogle's first index fund, it tracked the S&P 500. Over the last few years, however, the number of ETFs has ballooned, as have the trading volumes associated with them. The general development of ETFs in the recent past, however, has moved away more and more from the tracking of broad market indices such as the S&P 500 and Wilshire 5000 Total Market index, or the Dow Jones Industrial Average—where the ETF is known as "Diamonds"—to much more narrowly based sector (and especially hot sector) ETFs. Despite their having descended from their index mutual fund ancestors, the characteristics of ETFs and the ways in which they are most typically utilized are very different. Whereas the index mutual fund based on a broad market index provides a diversification tool for the long-term investor, who can thereby invest in an entire index without individually buying the component parts, the ETFs are a tool beloved of and used frequently by short-term traders, hedge fund managers etc. Their value to the trader is that it is possible to make a bet on a sector, even a very narrow one such as cardio devices, for which there is a Healthcare ETF (HHE), without picking one particular stock within that sector. They also allow the trader to go long or to short that sector depending on the bet he wishes to place. So as short-term traders why do we not use ETFs? Our problem with ETFs is really more practical than conceptual. There is in theory no reason why the broad-based index ETFs such as "Spiders" or "Diamonds" could not be ripple traded. We would however be concerned, even without empirical knowledge to back this up, that baskets of stocks by design dampen volatility. Volatility plays its part in generating the fluctuation that enables us to trade the ripples. As far as the more narrowly based ETFs are concerned, the main reason that we shy away from them is that we lean very heavily on the comfort level provided by our "know your stock" rule. These sector-focused ETFs are also baskets of stocks, even if the sector focus is narrow, and this blurs for us the principle of "know your stock." These narrowly focused ETFs also often have a short history so a comparison of their current price with historical price movements is difficult. In a major market correction the likely weak track records of many over their short lives could make them suddenly very unattractive to investors and traders and might well cause large numbers of these ETFs to be discontinued owing to a lack of trading volume. However, for a short-term contrarian ripple trader who would feel comfortable taking the time to familiarize himself with some ETFs, there is no reason why one or two of these could not be included in his monitored "portfolio" of stocks. There would need to be an awareness, however, that by the nature of the ETF marketplace today, new ETFs tend to be designed to track "hot sectors" and therefore have a tendency to attract hot money that rushes, emotion-driven, into the latest fad or sector of the month. The contrarian trader looking to ride the ripples may find that many of these fad or hot sector-based ETFs contain precisely the kinds of stocks he needs to avoid if he is to stay true to the contrarian underpinning of our technique.

'TIS THE SEASON . . .

Views and opinions abound on when are the best times during the year to load up on, or sell out of, stocks. Statistically, September is the month that shows the biggest tendency for stock market declines. October scares some people because some major market crashes have taken place in that month including 1929 and 1987. We hear about "summer rallies," but find that concept is contradicted by the old adage, "Sell in May and go away." There is a "Santa Claus rally," closely followed by a "January effect." All of these have grains of truth or even more rational reasons underlying them. (The influx of new cash into mutual funds and then into stocks that originally caused the January effect spawned a Santa Claus rally that anticipates that inflow, for instance). In our view, the techniques we use for short-term trading are valid throughout the year, whatever month we are in and whether the market in that month is following the path prescribed to it by market lore or not.

Mark Twain summed up the best way to view the timing of buying stocks by month of the year when he wrote:

October. This is one of the particularly dangerous months to invest in stocks. Other dangerous months are July, January, September, April, November, May, March, June, December, August and February.

CHAPTER 6

Contrarian Ripple Trading in Practice

I n Chapter 5, we discussed the factors that traders should consider when assessing the suitability of specific stocks to purchase, ideally seeking to establish a trading pattern of "riding the ripples," whereby the same stock can be bought and sold repeatedly for profit each time. We now illustrate how this works in practice by providing real examples of how we bought and sold in and out of certain stocks regularly in 2005, 2006, and early 2007. We have selected as examples two stocks that we traded during the period numerous times, Eli Lilly and Wal-Mart Stores, as well as one additional stock with a twist, Corning Inc. We then follow up with four examples of stocks that experienced similar up and down trading ranges, but where the stock price was quite dramatically affected by specific company news and developments. These stocks are Nike Inc., Morgan Stanley, Johnson & Johnson, and Commerce Bancorp.

RIPPLE TRADING: SOME PRACTICAL EXAMPLES

Eli Lilly

Eli Lilly (LLY) is a major pharmaceutical company based in Indianapolis, Indiana. It manufactures and sells a number of well-known brands of medication such as Zyprexa, Prozac, and Cialis. In common with other healthcare stocks, Lilly has recently been subjected to a number of pressures within its sector caused by worries about drug development pipelines, the effects of generic drug competition, and regulatory risks. It has not, however, had to face any major traumas such as Merck experienced when it withdrew its top-selling pain-killer Vioxx from the market for heart safety reasons and then had to endure a subsequent bombardment of lawsuits. Neither has Eli Lilly suffered the executive management turmoil that affected both Bristol-Myers Squibb and Pfizer. Indeed, Eli Lilly has experienced general corporate stability over the last couple of years. Also, in common with other pharmaceutical manufacturers and healthcare sector companies, Eli Lilly has world demographic changes on its side, in particular aging populations.

We bought and sold Eli Lilly 23 times in the 26 months from January 1, 2005, and netted $1,297. One position remained open as of February 28, 2007, as we had bought it while ripple trading back into stocks during the market plunge of February 27. Each roundtrip was made up of 100-share lots bought and sold as follows:

Bought 2/9/05 at $55.12	Sold 2/14/05 at $55.78	Profit = $46
Bought 2/15/05 at $55.05	Sold 2/15/05 at $55.71	Profit = $45
Bought 2/17/05 at $55.09	Sold 2/25/05 at $55.83	Profit = $54
Bought 3/14/05 at $54.74	Sold 4/13/05 at $55.87	Profit = $92
Bought 7/25/05 at $54.77	Sold 7/28/05 at $55.28	Profit = $41
Bought 8/3/05 at $54.79	Sold 9/6/05 at $55.40	Profit = $47
Bought 8/3/05 at $54.75	Sold 9/6/05 at $55.42	Profit = $57
Bought 9/19/05 at $54.68	Sold 12/13/05 at $55.43	Profit = $65
Bought 4/4/06 at $54.81	Sold 4/5/06 at $55.42	Profit = $51
Bought 4/6/06 at $54.81	Sold 6/30/06 at $55.43	Profit = $52
Bought 7/18/06 at $54.70	Sold 7/19/06 at $55.75	Profit = $95
Bought 7/21/06 at $54.58	Sold 7/21/06 at $55.14	Profit = $46
Bought 7/21/06 at $54.70	Sold 7/24/06 at $55.42	Profit = $62
Bought 8/11/06 at $53.93	Sold 8/14/06 at $54.48	Profit = $41
Bought 8/11/06 at $54.07	Sold 8/15/06 at $55.19	Profit = $92
Bought 8/18/06 at $54.39	Sold 8/18/06 at $54.87	Profit = $38
Bought 11/13/06 at $53.94	Sold 11/15/06 at $54.55	Profit = $51
Bought 11/16/06 at $53.82	Sold 11/16/06 at $54.34	Profit = $42
Bought 11/21/06 at $53.73	Sold 12/5/06 at $54.43	Profit = $60
Bought 11/21/06 at $53.71	Sold 12/5/06 at $54.35	Profit = $50
Bought 12/7/06 at $53.88	Sold 2/1/07 at $54.62	Profit = $54
Bought 12/7/06 at $53.88	Sold 2/5/07 at $54.53	Profit = $51
Bought 2/23/07 at $53.83	Sold 2/26/07 at $54.58	Profit = $65
Bought 2/27/07 at $53.81	Position still held at 2/28/07	

Wal-Mart Stores

Wal-Mart Stores (WMT) is the Bentonville, Arkansas-based retail giant that grew from a single store opened by Sam Walton in Rogers, Arkansas in 1962 to become the world's largest retailer. Its huge size has brought with it its own problems, including the challenge of continuing the heady growth for which it became known, as well as its growing status as everybody's favorite corporate punching bag, whether this is for alleged exploitation of its nonunionized workforce or the perceived negative effects of its big-box stores on local businesses. The stock has trended steadily lower over the last couple of years, but has provided excellent trading opportunities for those who wished to take advantage of lower stock prices—bargain hunting that to a certain extent mirrors Wal-Mart's own "everyday low prices" sales philosophy. Its stock has provided traders with the opportunity to profit from the contrarian bet that Wal-Mart can still be a growth story owing to expanding international operations and newer product lines such as liquor, electronics, prescription medicines, and gas retailing in the United States.

During 2005 and 2006, we made 17 roundtrip trades in Wal-Mart Stores and netted $993. Each purchase and sale involved 100 shares. Two positions of 100 shares each in Wal-Mart Stores remained open as of February 28, 2007. These were bought in separate accounts and are not a duplication in our records.

Bought 1/28/05 at $52.33	Sold 2/2/05 at $53.04	Profit = $51
Bought 2/10/05 at $52.26	Sold 2/15/05 at $52.87	Profit = $41
Bought 2/22/05 at $52.13	Sold 3/3/05 at $53.05	Profit = $72
Bought 2/25/05 at $51.21	Sold 2/28/08 at $51.99	Profit = $64
Bought 3/10/05 at $52.29	Position still held at 2/28/07	
Bought 3/10/05 at $52.29	Position still held at 2/28/07	
Bought 4/1/05 at $49.45	Sold 6/15/05 at $50.11	Profit = $56
Bought 6/16/05 at $49.45	Sold 7/8/05 at $49.97	Profit = $42
Bought 8/19/05 at $46.76	Sold 10/31/05 at $47.26	Profit = $40
Bought 1/5/06 at $45.55	Sold 1/11/06 at $46.41	Profit = $76
Bought 1/13/06 at $45.48	Sold 1/25/06 at $46.09	Profit = $51
Bought 2/6/06 at $45.16	Sold 2/9/06 at $45.76	Profit = $50
Bought 3/2/06 at $45.06	Sold 3/16/06 at $46.08	Profit = $92
Bought 4/28/06 at $45.07	Sold 5/1/06 at $46.06	Profit = $89
Bought 7/14/06 at $43.91	Sold 7/24/06 at $44.53	Profit = $52
Bought 7/26/06 at $43.80	Sold 7/28/06 at $44.48	Profit = $58
Bought 8/1/06 at $43.83	Sold 8/3/06 at $44.49	Profit = $56
Bought 8/23/06 at $43.84	Sold 8/28/06 at $44.47	Profit = $53
Bought 12/19/06 at $46.00	Sold 12/29/06 at $46.60	Profit = $50

Corning Inc.

Another stock that we traded regularly throughout the 2005, 2006, and early 2007 period was Corning Inc (GLW). Corning is a manufacturer of glassware, fiber optic cable, specialty ceramic materials, and glass substrates based in—no surprises here—Corning, New York. The company was founded in 1851, and its historic achievements include the development of the glass for Thomas Edison's light bulb. Until 1989, the company was known as Corning Glassworks, hence the stock symbol.

Corning's technological advances in the production of optical fiber made the company and its stock a darling of the dot-com boom years of the late 1990s as the breakneck expansion of the Internet made fiber optical cable production appear to be a business with almost infinite growth prospects. When the bust came, it hit Corning hard as the high-flying stock plummeted from a high of around $113 a share to as little as $1 in just under two years. Hapless stockholders faced the fact that Corning's management had bet the company on a market, telecommunications equipment, that had then suffered near-collapse.

Corning's diversity of businesses, including its traditional basic glass and ceramics businesses in which it is a world leader, has helped set it on the road to recovery. Corning is also well positioned to lead the surge in demand for LCD (liquid crystal display) screens for flat-panel TV. Increasing demand for fiber optic cable in the last year or so has also helped, especially now that Corning is no longer so dependent on the vagaries of that one sector.

During 2005 and the early part of 2006, Corning's stock price evidenced a strong recovery as a general appreciation of the bright prospects for Corning's LCD glass business took hold. A correction took the stock price back down somewhat in the early summer of 2006 followed by another recovery. The regular fluctuation in Corning's stock price encouraged contrarian ripple trading in this stock. Corning has been different from most of the stocks that we have traded in the time frame covered by our record in this book in that it traded generally at a significantly higher level in 2006 and early 2007 than in 2005, reflecting its status as a stock on the road to recovery following its near-death experience. We bought and sold Corning Inc. 34 times during the period covered and netted $2,260 in trading profits. We held a position of 200 Corning Inc. as of February 28, 2007, another position we ripple traded back into as the market fell heavily February 27.

Each trade in 2005, with the one exception we note in the following table, was of 300 shares as follows:

Bought 12/28/04 at $11.74	Sold 1/3/05 at $11.98	Profit = $51
Bought 12/28/04 at $11.75	Sold 1/7/05 at $11.90	Profit = $31
Bought 1/3/05 at $11.74	Sold 1/18/05 at $11.94	Profit = $40
Bought 1/20/05 at $11.70	Sold 2/8/05 at $12.01	Profit = $74
Bought 1/21/05 at $11.68	Sold 2/8/05 at $11.88	Profit = $46
Bought 2/9/05 at $11.72	Sold 2/14/05 at $11.92	Profit = $40

Bought 2/16/05 at $11.71	Sold 2/16/05 at $11.92	Profit = $42
Bought 2/16/05 at $11.68	Sold 2/16/05 at $11.91	Profit = $55
Bought 2/18/05 at $11.71	Sold 4/8/05 at $12.13	Profit = $107
Bought 2/22/05 (250 shares) at $11.52	Sold 3/3/05 at $11.76	Profit = $46
Bought 3/8/05 at $11.38	Sold 3/15/05 at $11.58	Profit = $46
Bought 3/15/05 at $11.36	Sold 4/6/05 at $11.68	Profit = $77
Bought 4/12/05 at $11.70	Sold 4/12/05 at $11.87	Profit = $41
Bought 4/13/05 at $11.71	Sold 4/20/05 at $12.33	Profit = $167

At the end of April, Corning's stock price rose sharply and we ceased to trade it. The stock price reached $29.61 on April 21, 2006, and then, in line with the rest of the market, went through a correction dropping to a 2006 low of $17.50. We started to trade it again on June 7 when the pull-back from near $30 had reached $22. At this point, we were trading 200 shares each time, as they were somewhat more expensive than the price at which we had been trading them the previous year. We returned to a 300-share trading strategy once the stock dipped below $20 in December 2006 as follows:

Bought 6/7/06 at $22.01	Sold 6/9/06 at $22.61	Profit = $109
Bought 6/12/06 at $20.95	Sold 6/14/06 at $21.39	Profit = $78
Bought 6/19/06 at $21.93	Sold 6/26/06 at $22.25	Profit = $54
Bought 6/27/06 at $21.85	Sold 6/28/06 at $22.36	Profit = $92
Bought 7/10/06 at $21.70	Sold 7/17/06 at $22.01	Profit = $52
Bought 7/17/06 at $21.69	Sold 7/17/06 at $22.01	Profit = $45
Bought 7/18/06 at $21.70	Sold 7/19/06 at $22.11	Profit = $61
Bought 7/25/06 at $21.67	Sold 8/29/06 at $21.96	Profit = $48
Bought 9/5/06 at $21.68	Sold 9/5/06 at $22.01	Profit = $56
Bought 9/7/06 at $21.53	Sold 9/8/06 at $21.83	Profit = $50
Bought 9/8/06 at $21.43	Sold 9/8/06 at $21.75	Profit = $54
Bought 9/11/06 at $21.52	Sold 9/11/06 at $21.85	Profit = $56
Bought 10/26/06 at $21.30	Sold 11/16/06 at $21.62	Profit = $54
Bought 11/20/06 at $21.03	Sold 11/22/06 at $21.42	Profit = $68
Bought 11/27/06 at $20.97	Sold 11/29/06 at $21.29	Profit = $54
Bought 12/1/06 at $21.01	Sold 12/5/06 at $21.32	Profit = $52
Bought 12/7/06 at $21.00	Sold 1/25/07 at $21.69	Profit = $128
Bought 12/12/06 (300 shares) at $19.80	Sold 1/12/07 at $20.01	Profit = $53
Bought 1/17/07 (300 shares) at $19.66	Sold 1/24/07 at $20.29	Profit = $179
Bought 1/25/07 (200 shares) at $21.05	Sold 2/5/07 at $21.37	Profit = $54
Bought 2/27/07 (200 shares) at $20.85	Position still held at 2/28/07	

BOARDROOM WOES OPEN UP OPPORTUNITIES

Nike Inc.

Nike (NKE), the sports footwear, apparel, and equipment marketer, got its start as a result of the brainwave of entrepreneur Philip Knight in the early 1960s that low-priced, high-tech athletic shoes imported from Japan could compete with and challenge the dominance of German running shoes such as Adidas and Puma. The idea was sound. Over 40 years later, Nike Inc. is the largest sports apparel company in the world. Nike traded between $75 and $109 during the period covered by our record in this book. At the beginning of 2005 and then at the end of 2006 into early 2007, however, it was trading at levels that made it too expensive for our strategy, based on the contrarian guidelines we follow. Nevertheless, for much of the period we were comfortable buying and selling Nike as follows, with 100 shares bought and sold each roundtrip, except where noted, as follows:

Bought 4/15/05 at $76.26	Sold 4/19/05 at $77.62	Profit = $116
Bought 4/20/05 at $76.25	Sold 4/21/05 at $78.12	Profit = $166
Bought 4/29/05 at $76.11	Sold 4/29/05 at $76.87	Profit = $56
Bought 8/30/05 at $78.25	Sold 8/31/05 at $78.96	Profit = $51
Bought 9/2/05 at $77.98	Sold 9/9/06 at $79.05	Profit = $87
Bought 9/20/05 at $80.41	Sold 9/22/05 at $81.22	Profit = $71
Bought 9/23/05 at $79.92	Sold 9/23/05 at $80.61	Profit = $60
Bought 12/9/05 at $85.52	Sold 12/12/05 at $87.56	Profit = $194
Bought 12/19/05 at $87.40	Sold 12/20/05 at $88.07	Profit = $57
Bought 12/21/05 at $84.00	Sold 12/21/05 at $84.56	Profit = $46
Bought 12/21/05 at $84.31	Sold 12/21/05 at $84.98	Profit = $57
Bought 12/30/05 at $86.75	Sold 1/9/06 at $87.48	Profit = $52
Bought 1/6/06 at $85.71	Sold 1/9/06 at $86.56	Profit = $75
Bought 1/12/06 at $86.56	Sold 2/23/06 at $87.19	Profit = $53
Bought 1/13/06 at $85.54	Sold 1/13/06 at $86.12	Profit = $48
Bought 1/17/06 at $85.67	Sold 2/22/06 at $86.29	Profit = $52
Bought 3/2/06 at $85.89	Sold 3/3/06 at $86.54	Profit = $55
Bought 3/2/06 at $85.89	Sold 3/3/06 at $86.44	Profit = $41
Bought 3/7/06 at $84.66	Sold 3/7/06 at $85.20	Profit = $44
Bought 3/7/06 at $84.52	Sold 3/9/06 at $85.15	Profit = $53
Bought 3/27/06 at $85.24	Sold 3/30/06 at $85.82	Profit = $48
Bought 3/30/06 at $85.20	Sold 4/3/06 at $85.80	Profit = $50
Bought 3/30/06 (92 shares) at $85.16	Sold 4/3/06 at $85.82	Profit = $46
Bought 4/3/06 at $84.83	Sold 9/22/06 at $85.56	Profit = $65
Bought 4/7/06 at $83.95	Sold 6/23/06 at $84.57	Profit = $52

Bought 4/17/06 at $81.49	Sold 4/18/06 at $82.12	Profit = $53
Bought 4/26/06 at $81.49	Sold 4/28/06 at $82.14	Profit = $55
Bought 4/28/06 at 81.48	Sold 5/1/06 at $82.18	Profit = $60
Bought 5/3/06 at $81.40	Sold 5/8/06 at $82.10	Profit = $50
Bought 5/3/06 (98 shares) at $81.11	Sold 5/8/06 at $81.70	Profit = $43
Bought 5/15/06 at $81.36	Sold 5/16/06 at $82.00	Profit = $54
Bought 5/16/06 at $81.25	Sold 6/2/06 at $82.07	Profit = $72
Bought 6/5/06 at $81.13	Sold 6/12/06 at $81.78	Profit = $55
Bought 6/13/06 at $81.01	Sold 6/13/06 at $81.66	Profit = $45
Bought 6/27/06 at $83.67	Sold 9/22/06 at $85.56	Profit = $181
Bought 6/28/06 at $80.52	Sold 6/30/06 at $81.37	Profit = $65
Bought 7/5/06 at $79.78	Sold 7/5/06 at $80.45	Profit = $57
Bought 7/6/06 at $79.80	Sold 7/24/06 at $80.51	Profit = $51
Bought 7/25/06 at $79.76	Sold 7/27/06 at $81.08	Profit = $122
Bought 7/27/06 at $79.65	Sold 8/31/06 at $80.50	Profit = $65

We bought and sold Nike no fewer than 40 times during 2005 and 2006, netting a trading profit in the two-year period of $2,723. It is worth pointing out that for much of the time that Nike traded at lower levels, sentiment was adversely affected by managerial conflict at the top of the company. Nike cofounder Philip Knight handed over the reins to outsider William Perez, who had previously been president and CEO of SC Johnson & Co. in December 2004. Perez served as chief executive officer at Nike for just 13 months, only to be ousted abruptly in January 2006 and replaced by Nike insider Mark Parker. Internal tensions between Knight, chairman during the tenure of Perez, and his new CEO appear to have had a negative impact on the share price for much of the period. This negativity was excellent news for contrarian buyers such as ourselves because it gave us ample opportunity to trade in and out of Nike at the lower end of the stock's price range. This situation provides a very good example of how a contrarian approach can often make for a winning bet on a stock. Nike's stock was constantly pressured as investors mulled over the growing rift between the company's top managers, perceiving that this strife made the company less attractive as an investment.

However, the contrarian trader keeps the situation in perspective. Nike sells athletic footwear and other apparel based on an amazingly powerful brand identity with its famous "swoosh" logo. This brand identity is one of the most successful ever marketed, and provides that same product quality and brand cachet no matter who is CEO. The bottom line is that the shopper goes into Foot Locker and buys Nike merchandise because he wants the shoes with the swoosh, and he does not really know or care who is running the company.

Morgan Stanley

Another active ripple trading stock for us in 2005 and 2006 was New York investment banking company Morgan Stanley (MWD until it changed its stock ticker symbol to MS on January 17, 2006). This so-called "bulge bracket" investment banking powerhouse, one of the premier U.S. investment banking houses with its huge retail brokerage arm and almost $700 billion under management, owes its present size and structure to the 1997 merger of Morgan Stanley and Dean Witter, Discover & Co. Morgan Stanley traded between $47.50 and $80 in the two years 2005 and 2006 and climbed to a high of just shy of $85 in early 2007.

In March 2005, Morgan Stanley's stock suffered a severe downdraft for two reasons. First, there was a very public executive management power struggle at the top of the company, involving a feud between CEO Philip Purcell and a group of dissident shareholders and former directors that became increasingly public as well as vitriolic. Second, the company had a high-profile legal setback when financier Ron Perelman won a $1.45 billion lawsuit against Morgan Stanley in a case relating to Perelman's sale of his interest in Coleman Company to Morgan Stanley-advised Sunbeam in 1998. At least partly as a result of both of these factors, Morgan Stanley's stock was depressed for much of the year, falling from a high of $60 in February 2005 to a low of a little over $47 in May 2005.

Unlike the situation with Nike described above, both of these factors had a depressing effect on Morgan Stanley's stock price for very good reasons. The huge amount of money that was awarded against the firm clearly had major negative implications for the value of the company. Also. in contrast to a manufacturing/consumer goods company such as Nike, publicly feuding senior executives will have a very real effect on an investment bank's corporate advisory business. Companies may shy away from seeking advice from an investment bank where that bank's own senior management ranks are in turmoil. However a contrarian bet on the stock at precisely this time states that the trader considers the damage to the company and its stock to be temporary, not permanent.

Apart from another mini-swoon in May and the early part of June 2006, the stock recovered quite strongly to the low $80 levels in the overall strong market of December 2006 and hit new highs in early 2007, before dropping back to the mid-70s in the market sell-off of late February.

During the 26-month period covered by this book we bought at times of relative weakness, 100-share lots each time as follows:

Bought 4/12/05 at $53.99	Sold 4/12/05 at $54.62	Profit = $42
Bought 4/13/05 at $53.79	Sold 7/25/05 at $54.34	Profit = $45
Bought 5/2/05 at $49.93	Sold 5/5/05 at $50.60	Profit = $46

Bought 5/10/05 at $49.61	Sold 5/12/05 at $50.14	Profit = $43
Bought 5/10/05 at $49.69	Sold 5/23/05 at $50.34	Profit = $51
Bought 5/13/05 at $49.22	Sold 5/19/05 at $49.94	Profit = $51
Bought 5/24/05 at $49.17	Sold 5/25/05 at $49.75	Profit = $48
Bought 5/31/05 at $49.03	Sold 6/1/05 at $49.57	Profit = $44
Bought 5/31/05 at $48.98	Sold 6/1/05 at $49.75	Profit = $63
Bought 6/3/05 at $48.89	Sold 6/7/05 at $49.41	Profit = $42
Bought 8/5/05 at $52.61	Sold 8/10/05 at $53.14	Profit = $43
Bought 8/12/05 at $52.77	Sold 8/15/05 at $53.52	Profit = $65
Bought 8/16/05 at $52.96	Sold 9/29/05 at $53.48	Profit = $42
Bought 9/13/05 at $52.55	Sold 9/14/05 at $53.05	Profit = $40
Bought 9/14/05 at $52.52	Sold 9/29/05 at $53.14	Profit = $42
Bought 10/12/05 at $51.96	Sold 10/17/05 at $52.60	Profit = $44
Bought 10/19/05 at $51.35	Sold 10/19/05 at $51.87	Profit = $42
Bought 11/3/05 at $52.61	Sold 11/10/05 at $53.36	Profit = $65

After November 2005 and several months following Philip Purcell's ouster and replacement by John Mack (whom Purcell had forced out of Morgan Stanley in 2001), Morgan Stanley stock began a recovery. It climbed to a high of $66 in early May 2006 before falling back as general market sentiment weakened. With the stock down almost 10 percent, we came back in and traded at weaker levels until Morgan Stanley's price again recovered strongly along with the yearend surge of the general market.

Bought 5/17/06 at $59.89	Sold 5/18/06 at $60.54	Profit = $55
Bought 5/18/06 at $59.91	Sold 5/18/06 at $60.48	Profit = $47
Bought 5/18/06 at $59.93	Sold 5/19/06 at $60.55	Profit = $52
Bought 5/22/06 at $59.60	Sold 5/26/06 at $60.60	Profit = $90
Bought 5/22/06 at $58.35	Sold 5/22/06 at 58.98	Profit = $43
Bought 5/24/06 at $58.23	Sold 5/25/06 at $59.59	Profit = $126
Bought 5/30/06 at $59.07	Sold 5/31/06 at $59.78	Profit = $61
Bought 5/31/06 at $59.03	Sold 5/31/06 at $59.55	Profit = $42
Bought 6/5/06 at $58.72	Sold 6/7/06 at $59.36	Profit = $54
Bought 6/12/06 at $58.27	Sold 6/12/06 at $58.93	Profit = $46
Bought 6/12/06 at $58.25	Sold 6/21/06 at $59.29	Profit = $84
Bought 6/16/06 at $56.64	Sold 6/19/06 at $57.28	Profit = $54
Bought 6/19/06 at $56.59	Sold 6/20/06 at $57.26	Profit = $57

During these relatively short interludes of weakness we bought and sold Morgan Stanley 31 times and netted a trading profit of $1,669.

Johnson & Johnson

While the fluctuations in stock price of both Nike and Morgan Stanley were due in part to the effects of boardroom battles and management changes, the pharmaceutical, healthcare products, and medical device giant Johnson & Johnson (JNJ) was not affected by such issues. Nevertheless, there was significant pressure on the stock during the year between July 2005 and July 2006 largely relating to Johnson & Johnson's on, then off, then on again, then off again merger plans with Guidant Corp. In December of 2004, Johnson & Johnson had agreed to acquire heart medical-device maker Guidant for $76 a share or $25.4 billion. Following a wave of safety advisories and product recalls involving a large number of Guidant's heart defibrillators during 2005, Johnson & Johnson warned that they might pull out of the deal or alternatively seek to renegotiate the price of their acquisition downward. Guidant's stock dropped from the low $70s to the mid-$50s as a result until competitor Boston Scientific (BSX) came in with a $72 bid on December 5, 2005. Subsequently, Johnson & Johnson came back to fight a bidding war with Boston Scientific that drove Guidant's stock back up into the $70s by the end of 2005. By late January 2006, Guidant had agreed to be bought by Boston Scientific in a cash and stock deal valued then at $80 per share, or $27.2 billion. Johnson & Johnson walked away with a $720 million breakup fee and subsequently saw its stock recover strongly from a low of $57 in early February 2006 to a high of $69 in October of that year. Boston Scientific, on the other hand, had to wrestle with an increasing number of safety and recall problems relating to Guidant's defibrillators. Moreover, Boston Scientific had to deal with safety concerns within its own core business of drug-coated stents, used to open clogged arteries in heart disease patients. BSX's stock price continued to slide back from the low 20s at the time of the acquisition to the mid-teens by end February 2007.

Johnson & Johnson started 2005 strongly and peaked at a price of close to $70 in early April. We bought shares for the first time in that year on July 26 as Guidant-related fears mounted and at a time that the original acquisition agreement between Johnson & Johnson and Guidant remained in place. During the next 12 months, we bought and sold JNJ 27 times and netted $1,507 before Johnson & Johnson's share price broke away into levels at which we were no longer comfortable. Our trading in JNJ is detailed in the following table. Each roundtrip purchase and sale was of 100 shares as follows:

Bought 7/26/05 at $62.72	Sold 7/27/05 at $63.37	Profit = $45
Bought 8/16/05 at $62.94	Sold 8/17/05 at $63.58	Profit = $54
Bought 8/24/05 at $62.61	Sold 8/31/05 at $63.17	Profit = $46
Bought 9/2/05 at $62.88	Sold 9/6/05 at $63.52	Profit = $54
Bought 9/30/05 at $63.09	Sold 10/13/05 at $63.59	Profit = $40

Bought 10/5/05 at $62.31	Sold 10/13/05 at $63.40	Profit = $99
Bought 10/28/05 at $62.24	Sold 10/28/05 at $62.80	Profit = $46
Bought 11/1/05 at $62.21	Sold 11/15/05 at $63.01	Profit = $70
Bought 11/2/05 at $61.11	Sold 11/15/05 at $62.05	Profit = $84
Bought 11/21/05 at $61.99	Sold 11/28/05 at $62.78	Profit = $69
Bought 11/29/05 at $62.21	Sold 1/10/06 at $62.95	Profit = $54
Bought 12/2/05 at $61.37	Sold 12/5/05 at $61.90	Profit = $43
Bought 12/5/05 at $61.25	Sold 12/19/05 at $61.86	Profit = $51
Bought 12/6/05 at $60.55	Sold 12/16/05 at $61.17	Profit = $52
Bought 12/20/05 at $61.06	Sold 1/3/06 at $61.67	Profit = $51
Bought 1/11/06 at $62.22	Sold 7/28/06 at $62.93	Profit = $51
Bought 1/11/06 at $62.28	Sold 7/28/06 at $62.93	Profit = $51
Bought 1/20/06 at $61.22	Sold 6/21/06 at $61.83	Profit = $51
Bought 1/30/06 at $58.46	Sold 2/9/06 at $59.17	Profit = $61
Bought 2/10/06 at $58.46	Sold 2/14/06 at $59.06	Profit = $50
Bought 2/24/06 at $58.11	Sold 3/8/06 at $58.81	Profit = $50
Bought 3/9/06 at $58.37	Sold 3/10/06 at $58.97	Profit = $50
Bought 3/27/06 at $60.07	Sold 5/26/06 at $60.84	Profit = $57
Bought 4/4/06 at $59.07	Sold 5/15/06 at $59.75	Profit = $58
Bought 5/30/06 at $60.06	Sold 6/2/06 at $60.69	Profit = $53
Bought 6/22/06 at $61.07	Sold 7/21/06 at $61.93	Profit = $66
Bought 6/27/06 at $59.97	Sold 7/7/06 at $60.68	Profit = $51
Bought 2/21/07 at $65.00	Position still held at 2/28/07	
Bought 2/22/07 at $64.89	Position still held at 2/28/07	

From July 28, 2006, onward and the sale of 100 shares that had been bought January 11, 2006, we no longer bought positions in Johnson & Johnson as the stock moved sharply higher toward the end of the year. We moved back in again with a purchase of 200 JNJ at and just below $65 late February 2007 as the stock price drifted lower, having again almost touched $70 in late October 2006.

As an aside, Guidant's stock price experienced quite a seesaw movement of its own as Johnson & Johnson first sought to renegotiate its acquisition price and then battled Boston Scientific for control of the company. We took advantage of these circumstances and bought in and out of Guidant (GDT) four times near its lows of 2005, as Johnson & Johnson appeared to be pulling out of the deal and before Boston Scientific entered the fray. With 100-share lot purchases and sales each time, we netted $172 as follows:

Bought 11/3/05 at $56.62	Sold 11/3/05 at $57.13	Profit = $41
Bought 11/7/05 at $56.21	Sold 11/7/05 at $56.74	Profit = $43
Bought 11/8/05 at $56.47	Sold 11/8/05 at $56.97	Profit = $40
Bought 11/9/05 at $56.52	Sold 11/10/05 at $57.10	Profit = $48

Commerce Bancorp

Another stock that was buffeted by some external events that weighed on its stock price in the last couple of years and that we traded regularly is one that is not well known nationally. Apart from in the northeastern United States, the New Jersey-based banking company Commerce Bancorp (CBH) is probably unfamiliar to many. Commerce Bancorp has been innovative in offering additional value-add product extensions and services at their branches. Some of these include manned open teller positions seven days a week and coin counting machines for public use in branches. Commerce has claimed in its advertising that it is "America's most convenient bank." It has been a regularly rumored acquisition target, which has tended to exert upward pressure on its stock price. However, negative sentiment has been generated from the fallout of indictments handed down in 2004 and leading to convictions in late 2006 of two Commerce Bancorp executives in an influence-peddling scandal in Philadelphia, just across the Delaware River from Commerce Bancorp's Cherry Hill, New Jersey headquarters. Then on January 16, 2007, the stock took another beating as the company announced that two federal regulatory agencies, the Office of the Comptroller of the Currency and the Federal Reserve, had launched an investigation into financial transactions that had taken place between the bank and certain company insiders. The stock swooned almost $3 on January 16 finishing down 8.3 percent at $31.83. As can be seen in the second part of the following table, we bought 100 shares that day for $32.88 and sold them two weeks later for $33.61.

This stock split during 2005 and we traded 100 share lots both prior to the stock split and afterward. We netted $1,480 over the 26 months from the beginning of 2005 through 26 roundtrip trades.

Bought 1/4/05 at $61.93	Sold 1/13/05 at $64.01	Profit = $188
Bought 1/13/05 at $62.86	Sold 3/7/05 at $63.58	Profit = $52
Bought 1/14/05 at $61.51	Sold 3/1/05 at $62.48	Profit = $77

Then following a two-for-one stock split on March 8, 2005, still trading 100 shares:

Bought 3/8/05 at $31.43	Sold 3/31/05 at $32.45	Profit = $82
Bought 3/9/05 at $30.86	Sold 3/30/05 at $31.68	Profit = $62
Bought 4/4/05 at $31.16	Sold 4/4/05 at $31.71	Profit = $45
Bought 4/8/05 at $31.10	Sold 4/12/05 at $31.64	Profit = $44
Bought 4/11/05 at $30.74	Sold 4/12/05 at $31.54	Profit = $60

Bought 4/13/05 at $30.42	Sold 7/8/05 at $30.93	Profit = $41
Bought 4/13/05 at $29.25	Sold 4/13/05 at $29.79	Profit = $44
Bought 4/14/05 at $29.69	Sold 6/22/05 at $30.33	Profit = $44
Bought 6/6/05 at $27.50	Sold 6/14/05 at $28.10	Profit = $40
Bought 6/6/05 at $27.50	Sold 6/14/05 at $28.10	Profit = $46
Bought 6/24/05 at $29.50	Sold 6/30/05 at $30.20	Profit = $50
Bought 6/24/05 at $29.55	Sold 7/1/05 at $30.18	Profit = $49
Bought 9/19/05 at $31.18	Sold 11/9/05 at $31.77	Profit = $49
Bought 9/21/05 at $30.17	Sold 9/22/05 at $30.59	Profit = $32
Bought 10/4/05 at $30.16	Sold 11/2/05 at $30.68	Profit = $42
Bought 1/10/06 at $32.75	Sold 1/18/06 at $33.37	Profit = $52
Bought 1/20/06 at $32.75	Sold 1/31/06 at $33.38	Profit = $53
Bought 2/13/06 at $32.67	Sold 2/22/06 at $33.27	Profit = $50
Bought 6/19/06 at $34.52	Sold 6/29/06 at $35.33	Profit = $61
Bought 7/5/06 at $32.47	Sold 7/5/06 at $33.01	Profit = $44
Bought 7/6/06 at $32.49	Sold 7/19/06 at $33.25	Profit = $56
Bought 8/29/06 at $33.02	Sold 9/13/06 at $33.76	Profit = $54
Bought 1/8/07 at $34.61	Position still held at 2/28/07	
Bought 1/16/07 at $32.88	Sold 1/31/07 at $33.61	Profit = $63

PRICE PEGGING

As has been illustrated in these examples, the key to continuing profits from our short-term ripple trading tactics is to repeatedly buy and sell the same stock, using the buy price of the previous completed roundtrip trade to indicate the next buy signal marker. Given the nature of the short-term price ripples, that marker will typically be reset continuously as the stock fluctuates more to the upside or downside on a ripple move. However, from time to time we have found that a pattern can develop in a stock that essentially pegs a specific price as our fixed entry point that we can use over and over again. The two best examples of this price pegging in our recent record are found in our trading of Central Fund of Canada in 2005 and Genentech in 2006.

Central Fund of Canada

Central Fund of Canada (CEF) has essentially no business operations but acts as a repository for gold bullion and also some smaller volumes of silver (see Chapter 7). Therefore, it is a good stock to use as a proxy for trading the gold price without the cost and inconvenience of the trader actually holding or delivering the physical gold itself. Gold stayed within a fairly narrow range for the first 10 months of 2005 and only after that began to advance strongly from November 2005 onward. While the price of gold remained in this narrow trading range so did Central Fund of Canada stock. We traded in and out of CEF from January 3, 2005, to September 15, 2005. It quickly became apparent to us that a pegged price of $5.30 was an optimum entry point that enabled a regular in and out ripple trading pattern, always 1,000-share lots as follows:

Bought 1/3/05 at $5.39	Sold 2/14/05 at $5.46	Profit = $50
Bought 3/28/05 at $5.31	Sold 3/30/05 at $5.36	Profit = $40
Bought 4/14/05 at $5.30	Sold 4/19/05 at $5.36	Profit = $50
Bought 4/28/05 at $5.30	Sold 4/29/05 at $5.38	Profit = $56
Bought 5/2/05 at $5.30	Sold 5/3/05 at $5.36	Profit = $50
Bought 5/6/05 at $5.30	Sold 5/9/05 at $5.35	Profit = $40
Bought 5/9/05 at $5.30	Sold 5/10/05 at $5.35	Profit = $40
Bought 5/11/05 at $5.30	Sold 6/2/05 at $5.40	Profit = $90
Bought 6/10/05 at $5.30	Sold 6/10/05 at $5.35	Profit = $40
Bought 6/10/05 at $5.30	Sold 6/10/05 at $5.36	Profit = $46
Bought 6/14/05 at $5.30	Sold 6/16/05 at $5.38	Profit = $70
Bought 6/28/05 at $5.32	Sold 8/4/05 at $5.38	Profit = $42
Bought 7/15/05 at $5.22	Sold 7/21/05 at $5.28	Profit = $46
Bought 8/9/05 at $5.29	Sold 8/11/05 at $5.34	Profit = $40
Bought 8/26/05 at $5.30	Sold 9/1/05 at $5.36	Profit = $50
Bought 9/13/05 at $5.30	Sold 9/15/05 at $5.37	Profit = $60
Bought 9/13/05 at $5.30	Sold 9/15/05 at $5.38	Profit = $66

We traded 17 times in and out of CEF in 2005, buying 12 times at precisely the $5.30 pegged price point. We netted $876.

Genentech

South San Francisco, California-based biotech company Genentech (DNA) has successfully launched innovative treatments for medical conditions in the fields of biooncology, immunology, and tissue growth and repair. Genentech is the leading provider of antitumor therapeutics in the United States. For several years, Swiss pharmaceutical giant Roche Holding has held a majority stake in Genentech. In 2005, we had no established pegged price for Genentech, and traded into the stock for the first time at $51.33 after Genentech had come back down from a high of $68 in April 2004. We bought DNA in 100-share lots each time as follows:

Bought 1/11/05 at $51.33	Sold 3/14/05 at $53.98	Profit = $245
Bought 2/10/05 at $45.62	Sold 2/14/05 at $46.68	Profit = $86
Bought 3/10/05 at $44.75	Sold 3/14/05 at $53.74	Profit = $879
Bought 3/17/05 at $52.94	Sold 3/21/05 at $57.89	Profit = $476

At this point, Genentech mounted a very strong rally on the basis of positive developments relating to its breast cancer therapy Herceptin, and increasing optimism regarding the potential of Avastin, a drug that treats colorectal cancer. By November 2005 Genentech briefly touched the $100 level. Then it dropped back over the next months as investors felt that the advance had been overdone, as well as on negative news regarding patient fatalities following treatment with the non-Hodgkins lymphoma drug Rituxan marketed jointly by Genentech and Biogen Idec. We bought into Genentech again on April 24, 2006, and traded it a total of 21 times in 2006. It soon became clear to us that the trading pattern of the stock indicated a great price peg buying opportunity at $80 and we targeted precisely that price as an entry point, buying DNA whenever we noted that the stock had dipped beneath that level. The use of this price peg of $80 in the case of Genentech is well demonstrated in our trading in the stock as detailed here:

Bought 4/24/06 at $79.89	Sold 5/5/06 at $80.71	Profit = $72
Bought 5/2/06 at $75.65	Sold 5/2/06 at $76.20	Profit = $45
Bought 5/9/06 at $79.88	Sold 5/15/06 at $80.69	Profit = $71
Bought 5/15/06 at $79.68	Sold 5/26/06 at $80.93	Profit = $115
Bought 6/6/06 at $79.86	Sold 6/30/06 at $81.75	Profit = $169
Bought 7/17/06 at $79.82	Sold 7/24/06 at $80.70	Profit = $78
Bought 7/24/06 at $79.80	Sold 7/24/06 at $80.33	Profit = $43
Bought 7/31/06 at $79.96	Sold 7/31/06 at $80.51	Profit = $45
Bought 8/1/06 at $79.94	Sold 8/1/06 at $80.46	Profit = $42
Bought 8/2/06 at $79.99	Sold 8/3/06 at $80.61	Profit = $52
Bought 8/7/06 at $79.93	Sold 8/8/06 at $80.72	Profit = $69
Bought 8/8/06 at $79.94	Sold 8/9/06 at $80.83	Profit = $79
Bought 8/10/06 at $79.97	Sold 8/17/06 at $81.85	Profit = $168
Bought 8/24/06 at $79.99	Sold 8/29/06 at $80.75	Profit = $66
Bought 9/11/06 at $78.31	Sold 9/11/05 at $78.84	Profit = $43
Bought 9/11/06 at $78.35	Sold 9/14/06 at $79.04	Profit = $59
Bought 9/14/06 at $78.62	Sold 9/15/06 at $79.45	Profit = $73
Bought 9/18/06 at $78.63	Sold 9/19/06 at $79.59	Profit = $86
Bought 9/19/06 at $79.04	Sold 9/26/06 at $79.76	Profit = $62
Bought 11/14/06 at $79.99	Sold 11/15/06 at $80.72	Profit = $63
Bought 11/27/06 at $79.96	Sold 11/28/06 at $80.58	Profit = $52

It should be noted that even when we bought well below $80, such as the early September 2006 trades, we still sold once our target profit had been reached. Even in those cases where the price had not come back up to the $80 peg, the discipline of our method dictated taking the profit.

DNA broke out to the upside and moved away from the price peg after our November 27/November 28, 2006, trade, based largely on positive news regarding Lucentis, the company's new treatment for "wet" age-related macular degeneration (AMD), which can cause blindness in the elderly. We traded the stock just one more time in the period covered by this book on a dip.

Bought 12/14/06 at $81.49   Sold 1/4/07 at $82.23   Profit = $64

Buying and selling Genentech in this way earned us a trading profit of $3,302 from 26 trades, including the four roundtrips from 2005 and the last trade of late 2006/early 2007 that were not based on the price peg.

By the way, readers who are chartists or technical analysts will immediately recognize that what we are calling a price peg is pretty much the same as what they would call a support level, a level at which buyers tend to come in and cause a rally to start or resume. Technical analysis and chartism have some traits in common with our own approach to identifying buy signals because they plot historic price movements using charts in order to spot patterns that will allow them to predict future price moves. However, we feel this kind of analysis often seems to enforce a level of exactitude from what are essentially quite fluid patterns that to our mind is unrealistic. (Buy a good stock at $50 if it used to be at $65 because, after all, we would rather buy it when it is cheaper than when it is more expensive. This sums up our fairly simple approach.) Also the excessive use of jargon that is the stock in trade of technical analysis/chartism (e.g., *head and shoulders, the hanging man, shaven head*) turns us off and so we prefer to use simpler language, and in this particular case, *price peg* works just fine.

AMERICAN DEPOSITORY RECEIPTS

A different and rather interesting class of stock that we use as part of our trading strategy, and which may be less familiar to many readers, is that of foreign stocks trading in the United States as *American Depository Receipts* (ADRs). Essentially these are certificates that are issued by depository banks, especially by Citibank and Bank of New York. These certificates represent a number of underlying shares of a foreign company. Banks issue the certificates either at the request of the foreign companies concerned, in which case they are called *sponsored ADRs*, or without the specific backing of the underlying company in the case of *nonsponsored ADRs*. Foreign companies that seek to have their stock traded in the United States in the form of ADRs that they sponsor do so as they wish to see their shareholder base broadened by giving U.S.-based investors an easy way to buy their stock without having to go through the often complex process of buying and selling through foreign stock exchanges. The ADRs are traded on the New York Stock Exchange and NASDAQ like any U.S. stock. Sometimes you will read about American Depository Shares (ADS) and the two names are interchangeable for the most part. Technically, however, an ADS represents one share of the common stock in the home country of the issuing company, while an ADR is a certificate representing a bundle of them.

An investor taking a position in any specific ADR has some additional factors he needs to consider that do not affect stocks of U.S. companies. All ADS/ADRs have the element of foreign exchange risk. They are quoted and bought and sold in U.S. dollars, but the U.S. dollar price at any time effectively represents the value of the foreign stock trading in its home currency translated into dollars. As a result, theoretically, an investor can buy into an ADR because the company has great prospects, and the company's stock in its home country may rise during the period that the investor holds the position. Yet if the exchange rate of that country's currency against the U.S. dollar slides during the period, the investor could nevertheless be sitting on a loss in his U.S. dollar-denominated ADR.

A second risk that the investor takes by buying ADRs is a political one. The stock's home country may go through a period of instability. Perhaps the government may take steps to nationalize certain key industries including some successful companies such as the one the investor has selected. In such a situation, the resulting loss could be sizable and could well be up to and including all of the capital invested in the position.

The third risk is a market risk. Just as in the United States, most stocks in international markets have a tendency to move up and down together. However, international markets do not always move in the same direction as the U.S. market, and indeed countries often go through market cycles that are specific to the respective country or to the region in which they are located. This may be completely the opposite of what is happening in the U.S. domestic market at the time. A bet on a specific company that may make sense to the investor as he reviews the company's own business and prospects may turn out to be a negative move if the overall market in that country sinks, which could be caused by any one of a myriad of reasons, and our investor is again sitting on a loss.

The previous caveats make ADRs sound like a potential minefield just waiting to blow up the unfortunate investor or trader who wanders into the area. But in the same way that we have pointed traders in the direction of well-established, large-capitalization U.S. stocks, so also we point our readers with exactly the same enthusiasm towards certain kinds of ADRs. Let us explain.

First, the foreign exchange risk, while a real one and one to keep in mind, is only going to loom large if the company in question is from a country other than a major west European economy. Many European countries now share a common currency, the euro, and other countries outside of the Euro area that warrant consideration for ADR investment, the United Kingdom and Switzerland specifically, both have stable currencies of their own, the British pound and the Swiss Franc. The probability is very low that any of these currencies may lose value against the U.S. dollar to such an extent that a major loss owing to foreign exchange factors might occur. Any foreign exchange risk is in any case greater for an investor than it is for the short-term trader for whom this book is written, as exchange rate risks increase with the time that a security is held. Political risk is also mitigated by only considering ADRs from companies in major west European economies. Market risk does apply, even with regard to the developed western countries, and will always need to be factored in to any trading decision involving ADRs. This risk will be diluted to a large extent, however, by the fact that the majority of companies that seek ADR listings in the United States are the kind of companies that have business operations throughout the world, which reduces their vulnerability to a market downturn in any one country or region.

If any of our readers wish to include ADRs in their portfolios of monitored stocks, then we suggest that their attention should be focused particularly on the stocks of large United Kingdom-based companies trading in ADR form. This recommendation is not made because one of the authors happens to be British by background. Rather, large U.K. companies are an especially appropriate choice because they have very similar characteristics in terms of corporate culture and governance to U.S. companies. They are managed in ways that are familiar to the U.S. trader or investor and this is not necessarily true even of the largest and best-known companies in other western European countries.

The factors that make the U.K. corporate scene closer in many ways to that in the United States than in continental Europe or even Japan are legal, cultural, and historical in nature. Both the United States and United Kingdom have highly developed, mature equity capital markets and corporate legal structures based on common law traditions, rather than the Romano-Germanic civil law principles of France, Germany, and other continental European countries. Investing in the stock of a British company through the vehicle of an ADR, therefore, is a decision not unlike that of investing in a similar U.S. company. The investor or trader can have reasonable expectations that business decisions taken by management will be based principally on a desire to increase shareholder value, which ultimately depends on achieving an increase in the stock price, an increase in dividend payouts, or both. Indeed, it is true to say that in both the United States and the United Kingdom the general way in which company managers and the share-owning public at large view business is almost wholly conditioned by the importance of the stock market and companies' share price performance. Ask any chief executive officer of a public company in the United States or the United Kingdom to name his primary goal in running his business, and he will invariably respond that it is to maximize stockholder value. Such a reply is completely in keeping with the cultural conditioning of the U.S. and U.K. business worlds. Ask the same question of a French, German, or Japanese company chief executive or president, and the answer will undoubtedly be different and indeed more complex and nuanced. It may include a desire to grow the company in size (strengthening the balance sheet) or gaining importance and clout in the markets in which it operates (building market share) and certainly it will be to provide all of the stakeholders in the company with certain tangible benefits. These stakeholders would include employees, management, customers, bank lenders, and suppliers as well as stockholders, who typically would be some way down in the stakeholder pecking order. In Germany, this recognition of stakeholders' rights has led to legislation obligating large companies to give seats on their supervisory boards to worker representatives, something the Germans call *Mitbestimmung* or "co-determination."

Institutional investors dominate U.S. and U.K. company equity ownership today and their self-interest dictates that the principle of maximization of shareholder value is as important to them as it is to any private individual stockholder. By contrast, in France, Germany, and Japan, public company ownership tends to be heavily dominated by banks, often by those same banking institutions that provide both long and short term financing to the same companies in which they are part owners. Representing these major shareholders, bank officials also often occupy board seats and use their influence to ensure the company operates in a way that safeguards the solvency of the company and its ability to service and repay its bank loans. In Japan, a particular model of interlocking equity ownerships is in place in the *keiretsu*—horizontally integrated alliances of companies stretching through many industries and areas of the economy with such well-known names as Mitsubishi, Mitsui, and Sumitomo.[1] Generally centered around one bank, which lends money to the *keiretsu* member companies and also takes equity stakes in them, these large industrial groupings have much of the economic clout of the conglomerates that dominated the Japanese economy before World War II, the *zaibatsu*. Clearly these corporate structures with their complex interlocking and interdependent relationships lead to a very different approach to corporate decision making than the U.S. and U.K. corporate structure whose hallmark is a more straightforward striving for increased rewards to stockholder equity owners of the company through the medium of increased profitability.

Additionally, elements of statism can be seen to a much greater extent in the business world in many continental European countries and Japan. Often, major corporations maintain an extremely cozy relationship with the government which can result in their making business decisions for decidedly political reasons. There is often an executive cross-fertilization process at work between government on the one hand and industry and commerce on the other as senior civil servants leave their government jobs to start a second career in the senior executive ranks of major corporations—what the Japanese refer to as *amakudari*, or literally "descent from heaven."[2]

There is admittedly one possible general advantage in the continental European and Japanese corporate governance model with its stakeholder rather than shareholder focus. This is the tendency of major investors to be long-term partners rather than owners, who may actually trade regularly in and out of their position over a comparatively short period. (The latter engender a mentality that can seem more akin to renting than to owning.) Consequently, managers in continental Europe and Japan can find it easier to take a longer-term view without the pressure of having to make the quarterly numbers and the constant fear of "disappointing the Street." It is interesting to note as an aside that private equity firms, which have recently occupied such an important position in the ownership of large segments of the U.S. economy, also claim their freedom from the pressure of keeping "the Street" happy on a quarterly basis allows them to plan for the longer term and thereby gives their portfolio company managers strategic advantages over those who run public companies. However, from the self-interested point of view of the U.S./U.K. stockholder in a publicly traded company and his narrow interest in enhancing the market value of his stock, even short-termism can be regarded as a distinct advantage of the U.S. and U.K. corporate scene. It is especially so for the short-term trader, who by definition does not depend on the successful outcome of a long-range strategy by the company to reach his own profit goal with his trade.

Referring back to the comments on private equity firms above, and as an aside, it is interesting to note that private equity firms are increasingly taking on some of the characteristics of those conglomerates such as ITT and LTV in the United States and the United Kingdom's Hanson that were highly successful in the 1960s at a time of low interest rates, not too dissimilar to the recent past. Should large private equity firms now seek public listings, as hedge fund/private equity hybrid Fortress Investment Group did in February 2007, they would then likely operate in a remarkably similar way to the conglomerates of yesteryear. The question is whether a shift in the business climate will ultimately lead to their also moving to break themselves up, as happened to the 1960s conglomerates. But this is the subject for another book.

In conclusion, U.K. public companies just as much as U.S. public companies focus primarily on the benefit of shareholders when making business decisions. As a result, when a good company management either in the United States or the United Kingdom makes a business decision or implements a business strategy, the benefits of this tend to flow through to the shareholders and are not diluted to the benefit of all the other interested parties that the continental European or Japanese managers must keep happy. All this makes U.K. company ADRs the investment or trading vehicle of choice for those whose sole interest is seeking a return on their investment or a short-term trading profit.

The U.S.-based trader is also on somewhat familiar ground when buying shares in large British companies because these often have huge investments in the United States. Indeed, U.K. corporations own or control brands that many people in the United States assume are quintessentially American such as Dr. Pepper and 7UP, owned by Cadbury Schweppes Plc; Miller Beers, owned by SABMiller Plc; and Holiday Inn, a brand of Inter-Continental Hotels Group. As noted before, those large U.K. companies that have sought to have their stock traded in the United States through the medium of ADRs often have large U.S. operations.

An additional advantage for the trader using U.K. company ADRs is that these companies typically pay out higher dividend rates than do U.S. corporations. Not only are annual yields slightly higher than is typical in the United States, but most U.K. companies pay out a dividend just twice a year, rather than on a quarterly basis as is standard practice for U.S. companies. Therefore, each of those twice-yearly payments can be quite hefty. (See below for more detail). As a result, should your holding of a U.K. company ADR by chance coincide with a dividend record date, there can possibly be an extra-juicy payout coming your way.

To get a better picture of how these U.K. companies trading in ADR form are not necessarily as alien to a U.S. trader as it might appear at first sight, let us look at the U.K. company ADRs that we traded during 2005, 2006, and the first two months of 2007 and expand a little on what these companies do. Remember, all our trades in the time period are listed in the appendixes.

- *AstraZeneca* (AZN). A pharmaceutical giant with a large U.S. market share and some very well-known top-selling therapies such as Crestor, Prilosec, and Nexium. The dividend is paid on a semiannual basis and currently yields 4.5 percent.
- *BP Plc* (BP). Formerly known as British Petroleum, this London-based integrated oil giant has played down the British part of its roots since its acquisition of U.S. oil company Amoco in 1998, which allowed it to

become a company of true global stature. In its advertising these days the company utilizes the pun "Beyond Petroleum" to further dilute the British tradition of this company that was originally founded as the Anglo-Persian Oil Company to exploit oil deposits discovered in Iran in 1908. The company ranked fourth in the 2006 Fortune Global 2000 list of companies by revenue. The dividend yield is a little over 4 percent and dividends are paid quarterly.

- *Cadbury Schweppes Plc* (CSG). A major international confectionery and beverages company with such well-known U.S. brands in its portfolio as 7UP, Dr. Pepper, A&W Root Beer, and Trident and Dentyne chewing gum. The annual yield on this ADR is around 3.7 percent on a twice-yearly payout.
- *Diageo* (DEO). The world's largest producer and distributor of premium alcoholic drink brands, including Smirnoff, Johnnie Walker, Guinness, Baileys Irish Cream, J&B, Captain Morgan, Cuervo, and Tanqueray. The dividend payout is semiannual and the current yield is 2.5 percent annually.
- *GlaxoSmithKline Plc* (GSK). One of the world's largest pharmaceutical companies, GSK is headquartered in the United Kingdom but has its operational base in the United States and is the result of a merger in 2000 between the U.K.'s Glaxo Wellcome and SmithKline Beecham of the United States. Its products include well-known prescription pharmaceuticals such as Advair (anti-asthma), Paxil (for anxiety/depression), Flonase (anti-allergy), Levitra (for erectile dysfunction), Zantac (for acid reflux), and Zyban (to help stop smoking). Over-the-counter remedies include Nicoderm and Nicorette (both to aid the cessation of the smoking habit), Tagamet HB, and Tums (both for heartburn/indigestion). GlaxoSmithKline is also a major manufacturer of oral health products (Aquafresh and Sensodyne), as well as widely used children's vaccines. The stock currently yields 4 percent and dividends are paid quarterly.
- *Lloyds TSB Group* (LYG). One of the United Kingdom's largest commercial/retail banks or what are called there "high-street" or "clearing" banks. Although it used to have a large international presence, the bank is much more focused on the U.K. domestic market these days. In 1995 Lloyds Bank merged with the Trustee Savings Bank to form Lloyds TSB. The perennially attractive dividend yield on this stock is currently a little over 8 percent and dividend payouts are made semiannually. (Full disclosure: Coauthor Aidan was employed by the Lloyds Bank Group from 1981 to 1995.)
- *National Grid Plc* (NGG). This company operates as an international utility with electricity and natural gas distribution businesses in both the United Kingdom and the northeastern United States. In the United

Kingdom, it dominates the transmission of gas and electricity throughout the country. In the United States it is one of the 10 largest utilities, by number of customers, in the country, and has the largest electricity transmission and distribution network in the New England/New York region. It encompasses regional utilities that, prior to a recent overall re-branding as National Grid, had names such as Niagara Mohawk, Massachusetts Electric, and Granite State Electric. National Grid is currently in the process of acquiring KeySpan, a major distributor of natural gas and generator of electricity in the northeastern United States. The dividend yield at time of writing is 2.8 percent, paid on a semiannual basis.

- *Reuters* (RTRSY). Although it is U.K.-based, Reuters is a truly global company operating in over 90 countries. Reuters provides real-time financial data to financial services companies and general news information in words and pictures to print, television, and Internet-based news media worldwide. It yields a little less than 3 percent on dividends paid semiannually.

- *Unilever Plc* (UL). The company has a dual international organizational structure with Unilever Plc being London-based and Unilever NV based in The Netherlands. Each Unilever ADR represents four underlying ordinary Plc shares. Unilever is a consumer goods company that is home to many internationally known brands such as Axe deodorants, Bertolli olive oil, Dove soaps, Hellmann's mayonnaise, and Lipton teas. It offers a dividend yield of around 4.8 percent in a semiannual payout at the time of writing.

- *Vodafone Group* (VOD). Vodafone is the world's largest mobile telecommunications company, operating in 27 countries and with a significant presence in the United States, where the company owns and operates Verizon Wireless together with Verizon Communications as a joint venture. At the time of writing, Vodafone continues to hold a stake of 45 percent. VOD currently pays a dividend of 3.4 percent twice-yearly.

Although we have a strong preference for the U.K. company ADRs, that does not mean that we ignore totally ADR-listed companies from other countries. International companies other than from the United Kingdom that we traded during the period covered by our records in the appendixes were:

- *Ahold NV* (AHO). An Amsterdam-based supermarket operator with its principal areas of operations in the United States and Europe. In the United States, its supermarket brands include Stop & Shop, Giant Food, and Tops as well as Internet-based food retailer Peapod.

- *Philips Electronics Group* (PHG). An Eindhoven, Netherlands-based manufacturer of lighting products, consumer electronics, and medical systems. The Philips Norelco brand of electric razors is very well-known in the United States. In August 2006 Philips sold a controlling 80.1 percent stake in its Philips Semiconductors business to a consortium of U.S. private equity investors.
- *Repsol YPF* (REP). Spain's largest integrated oil company, formed through Madrid-based Repsol's acquisition of Argentina's YPF in 1999. It is Latin America's largest private (nonstate-controlled) oil company in terms of assets.
- *Sanofi-Aventis* (SNY). This large multinational pharmaceutical company is headquartered in Paris, but operates in 100 countries. It has in its portfolio of therapies a number that are very well known in the United States, including anticoagulant Lovenox, antithrombosis drug Plavix, and the antihistamine Allegra. In early 2007, there were media reports that Sanofi-Aventis planned to acquire Bristol-Myers Squibb, a company with which it partners in marketing Plavix, presently the second-biggest selling drug in the world, but threatened by potential future generic competition. Merger talk had the effect of pushing Bristol-Myers Squibb's stock price up but depressed Sanofi-Aventis' slightly, leading us to trade SNY in February 2007 as the price came under pressure.
- *Statoil ASA* (STO). Stavanger, Norway-based integrated oil and gas company and Norway's largest company with operations in 32 countries. On December 18, 2006, Statoil announced that it would merge with the oil and gas division of Norsk Hydro, a Norwegian conglomerate (see Chapter 7). The merged company will be the largest offshore production company in the world.
- *Teva Pharmaceutical Industries Ltd.* (TEVA). Based in Israel, Teva is one of the world's top-20 pharmaceutical companies and one of the largest generic drug companies in the world, producing generic medicines in all major treatment categories. It bolstered its leading position in the U.S. generic market with its acquisition of IVAX Corp. in January 2006.
- *UBS AG* (UBS). A global financial firm based in joint head offices in Basel and Zurich, Switzerland, one of the largest banking institutions in the world. It has major private banking, investment banking, and securities and asset management operations globally and is a retail and commercial bank in Switzerland. The bank was formed through the merger of Union Bank of Switzerland and Swiss Bank Corporation in 1998. UBS acquired the Paine Webber Group, a U.S. asset manager and brokerage house, in 2000.

We have not included in this summary those companies that we have traded that are located north of the border; Bank of Montreal, Barrick Gold, Central Fund of Canada, and Suncor Energy. This should not be taken as a failure to recognize these as non-U.S. companies. Detail on our trading in Central Fund of Canada can be found earlier in this chapter and Chapter 7 details our trading in Barrick Gold and Suncor Energy.

Special Situation Purchases

As can be expected in any market phases, bull or bear, some special situations occurred in the period covered by our record in the appendixes, where certain stocks were suddenly pushed down to much lower levels than where they had been trading just days before. These price declines made the stocks look very attractive from a contrarian perspective, sometimes just for a day or a few days, or at times over longer periods.

NEGATIVE NEWS

One such situation that can cause precipitous stock price drops is when there is highly negative news such as a product liability crisis or when some corporate misdeed (real or alleged) has been revealed. The following stocks illustrate such circumstances.

Bausch & Lomb

As stockholders of eye healthcare products manufacturer Bausch & Lomb (BOL) entered April 2006, little did they know that a major storm was on the horizon for their company. It hit early April when it was revealed that the company's ReNu eye care products were potentially linked with a severe fungal infection of the eye, *fusarium keratatis*, which in a worst-case scenario can lead to blindness.

As the stock plummeted on April 12 and 13 and left the 52-week high of $88 well behind, we bought the stock. Bausch & Lomb's continuing struggle with this crisis presented us with good trading opportunities in its stock for the rest of the year, trading 100 shares each time.

Bought 4/12/06 at $48.35	Sold 4/25/06 at $49.13	Profit = $68
Bought 4/13/06 at $45.15	Sold 4/13/06 at $46.31	Profit = $106
Bought 4/27/06 at $48.15	Sold 4/28/06 at $48.78	Profit = $53
Bought 5/1/06 at $48.06	Sold 5/2/06 at $48.67	Profit = $51
Bought 5/3/06 at $45.75	Sold 5/15/06 at $46.96	Profit = $111
Bought 5/3/06 at $44.14	Sold 5/8/06 at $45.00	Profit = $76
Bought 5/9/06 at $44.45	Sold 5/9/06 at $44.92	Profit = $37
Bought 5/12/06 at $44.31	Sold 5/15/06 at $45.88	Profit = $147
Bought 5/18/06 at $48.25	Sold 5/19/06 at $48.94	Profit = $59
Bought 6/22/06 at $48.52	Sold 6/28/06 at $49.41	Profit = $79
Bought 7/5/06 at $48.49	Sold 7/19/06 at $49.10	Profit = $51
Bought 7/20/06 at $48.23	Sold 8/30/06 at $48.90	Profit = $62
Bought 9/6/06 at $48.22	Sold 9/8/06 at $49.86	Profit = $144
Bought 11/17/06 at $48.84	Sold 11/21/06 at $49.63	Profit = $69
Bought 11/30/06 at $48.67	Sold 12/7/06 at $49.27	Profit = $50

Our trading profit on 15 roundtrips in Bausch & Lomb was $1,163. Its stock price finished 2006 at $52 and we were no longer buyers as the stock price continued to rise through the first months of 2007, retreating again with the general market at the end of February 2007 but not to as low as our previous buy levels.

American International Group

Dow 30 stock, insurance giant, and pillar of the corporate establishment, American International Group (AIG) took a tumble following then–New York Attorney General (and now New York Governor) Eliot Spitzer's opening of an investigation into the company's accounting practices as well as of its iconic chairman and CEO Maurice R. "Hank" Greenberg. A dramatic fall in the stock price on March 22, 2005, brought us into AIG stock with a buy of 100 shares at $56.93 when the stock was well off its 52-week high of $77.

Bought 3/22/05 at $56.93	Sold 3/29/05 at $58.06	Profit = $103
Bought 3/30/05 at $57.22	Sold 6/29/05 at $58.02	Profit = $70

Following a recovery that began in April 2005, which took AIG back up to the low 70s again, there came another slump in the stock price in the middle of 2006 and we came back in again to trade at that point.

Bought 6/5/06 at $60.35	Sold 6/7/06 at $60.99	Profit = $54
Bought 6/7/06 at $60.31	Sold 7/28/06 at $60.99	Profit = $58
Bought 8/1/06 at $60.33	Sold 8/11/06 at $61.48	Profit = $95

Our five 100-share lot trades in this stock netted us $380 in profit. By the end of 2006, AIG was back in the low 70s again.

UnitedHealth Group

The stock options backdating scandal that rocked boards of companies both large and small during 2006 started with a *Wall Street Journal* article, "The Perfect Payday," of March 18 of that year that examined stock options grants at six companies.[1] Stock options are awarded to senior company executives and in some companies also to executives lower down in the corporate hierarchy, as part of their overall agreed compensation packages. The award is typically made at an exercise price (the price at which the option can be exchanged for actual company stock) that is equal to the price of the stock on the day the award is made. Should the stock price subsequently climb, the option also climbs in value, as the option can be exchanged for stock at a predetermined time in the future. Should the stock price drop, then the option eventually expires worthless. The theory behind granting stock options is that it helps align the interest of senior executives with shareholders, who of course also want the stock price to go up.

The *Wall Street Journal* article pointed out that the companies studied had consistently awarded stock options at times when the stock price had been at particularly low levels and had subsequently rebounded. This was either amazingly coincidental and incredible good fortune for the executives involved, or it suggested that the stock option award dates were being decided some time afterward based on the hindsight of what would have been a particularly auspicious time for awards to be made. The options would then simply be backdated to make them appear as if they had been allocated at the award date. The chance that all these lucky breaks for the option grant participants represented pure coincidence was so infinitesimal that the *Wall Street Journal* concluded that stock options backdating was going on at these companies. Further investigation by the Securities & Exchange Commission (SEC) as well as by the companies that were themselves affected, confirmed this was the case and eventually over

130 companies had to admit that there had been improper backdating of stock options, and in some cases falsification of company documents to hide it. The SEC investigation of backdated options also uncovered a different but also troubling practice that came to be known as the granting of "spring loaded" options. In such cases, companies awarded stock options to senior executives immediately prior to the release of news that would almost certainly send the stock price up, thereby placing the newly minted options immediately "in the money."

One of the six companies to be named in the original options backdating scandal was healthcare insurance giant UnitedHealth Group (UNH). Its chairman and CEO Dr. William McGuire was eventually forced to step down as chairman of the company on October 15, 2006, and as CEO effective December 1, 2006. But the negative effect on UnitedHealth Group's stock price began with that March 18 article in the *Wall Street Journal*. UNH, which at that point had posted a 52-week high just shy of $65, dropped to a low point of $41.44 by May 24 before recovering to the low 50s by year's end. We traded in and out in the 40s as follows, 100-share lots each time:

Bought 5/4/06 at $46.14	Sold 5/4/06 at $46.67	Profit = $43
Bought 5/5/06 at $46.22	Sold 5/16/06 at $47.50	Profit = $118
Bought 5/11/06 at $44.59	Sold 5/12/06 at $45.84	Profit = $115
Bought 5/19/06 at $44.30	Sold 6/1/06 at $45.19	Profit = $79
Bought 6/19/06 at $44.11	Sold 6/22/06 at $44.70	Profit = $49
Bought 6/30/06 at $44.30	Sold 6/30/06 at $44.80	Profit = $40

Our profit from this short burst of trading in UnitedHealth Group was $444.

DETROIT BLUES

Both General Motors and Ford had their stock prices pushed down precipitously in 2005 as market share worries and profitability declines combined with concerns that legacy healthcare costs and poor automobile designs were leaving both companies unable to compete effectively in the North American automobile market.

General Motors Corporation

General Motors (GM) particularly was buffeted by the downward pressure of whispers of possible bankruptcy that had left its stock price floundering in a range between $25 and $29 by April 2005. Therefore, it was quite a surprise move by multibillionaire Kirk Kerkorian when he made a contrarian $31 per share tender offer for GM in May 2005 that had investors wondering if there was something he knew that nobody else did. (Kerkorian sold his entire stake on November 30, 2006, but by that time chairman and CEO Rick Wagoner appeared to have stabilized the company).

As General Motors came down from a 52-week high of $50, we bought and sold GM in either 100- or 200-share lots as follows:

Bought 3/17/05 (100 shares) at $28.23	Sold 3/21/05 at $29.85	Profit = $142
Bought 3/17/05 (100 shares) at $28.36	Sold 3/21/05 at $29.80	Profit = $130
Bought 3/18/05 (100 shares) at $28.15	Sold 3/21/05 at $29.67	Profit = $142
Bought 3/22/05 (200 shares) at $29.25	Sold 3/22/05 at $29.57	Profit = $55
Bought 3/22/05 (200 shares) at $29.47	Sold 4/1/05 at $30.00	Profit = $95
Bought 3/23/05 (200 shares) at $28.64	Sold 3/23/05 at $28.93	Profit = $46
Bought 3/23/05 (200 shares) at $28.67	Sold 3/24/05 at $28.99	Profit = $54
Bought 3/28/05 (200 shares) at $28.96	Sold 3/30/05 at $29.22	Profit = $42
Bought 3/28/05 (100 shares) at $28.53	Sold 3/30/05 at $29.28	Profit = $55
Bought 4/1/05 (200 shares) at $29.34	Sold 4/1/05 at $29.67	Profit = $55
Bought 4/1/05 (200 shares) at $29.39	Sold 4/4/05 at $29.82	Profit = $65
Bought 4/1/05 (100 shares) at $29.34	Sold 4/6/05 at $29.89	Profit = $41
Bought 4/4/05 (200 shares) at $29.29	Sold 4/6/05 at $29.60	Profit = $42
Bought 4/8/05 (200 shares) at $29.55	Sold 5/4/05 at $30.37	Profit = $155
Bought 4/11/05 (200 shares) at $28.85	Sold 4/11/05 at $29.13	Profit = $42
Bought 4/14/05 (100 shares) at $26.99	Sold 5/3/05 at $27.61	Profit = $42
Bought 4/14/05 (200 shares) at $28.13	Sold 5/4/05 at $31.57	Profit = $674

Kirk Kerkorian made his $31 per share tender offer on May 4, 2005. After selling our 400-share position on that same day, we did not trade in General Motors again until the price had dropped to where it had previously been trading under $30.

Bought 10/5/05 (100 shares) at $29.60	Sold 10/17/05 at $31.05	Profit = $135
Bought 10/18/05 (100 shares) at $29.50	Sold 6/30/06 at $30.15	Profit = $55
Bought 11/10/05 (100 shares) at $23.38	Sold 11/11/05 at $23.95	Profit = $47
Bought 11/15/05 (100 shares) at $23.11	Sold 11/18/05 at $23.80	Profit = $59
Bought 11/15/05 (100 shares) at $22.82	Sold 11/18/05 at $23.37	Profit = $41
Bought 11/21/05 (100 shares) at $23.36	Sold 1/30/06 at $24.33	Profit = $87

We traded in and out of General Motors a total of 23 times in 2005 and 2006, netting $2,301.

Ford Motor Company

Noting a 52-week high of over $16, we bought into Ford Motor Company (F) on April 12, 2005 at $10.14. Our subsequent trades were as follows, all in 300-share lots:

Bought 4/12/05 at $10.14	Sold 5/4/05 at $10.34	Profit = $50
Bought 5/5/05 at $9.89	Sold 5/9/05 at $10.07	Profit = $44
Bought 5/10/05 at $9.78	Sold 5/18/05 at $9.97	Profit = $43
Bought 5/10/05 at $9.83	Sold 5/19/05 at $10.01	Profit = $44
Bought 5/25/05 at $9.87	Sold 5/27/05 at $10.11	Profit = $62
Bought 8/30/05 at $9.69	Sold 8/31/05 at $9.90	Profit = $43
Bought 9/1/05 at $9.69	Sold 9/2/05 at $9.87	Profit = $44
Bought 9/15/05 at $9.87	Position still held at 2/28/07	

We bought in and out of Ford seven times in 2005, netting $330. At the end of February 2007 we were left with 300 shares unsold and the price stood at $7.91 having fallen back again with the general overall stock price downdraft that took place at the end of that month.

NEGATIVE EARNINGS ANNOUNCEMENTS

Another potential cause of a sudden and dramatic stock price decline can be the very negative sentiment that is created by a quarterly earnings announcement that "surprises the Street" with unexpected negative news. There were occasions where such powerful earnings-related pullbacks caused us, as a result, to add new stocks to our "portfolio" of monitored stocks and immediately jump in with a contrarian first-time buy. Four examples are Electronic Arts, Dell Inc., Legg Mason, and Black & Decker.

Electronic Arts

The Redwood City, California–based video game developer Electronic Arts (ERTS) announced on May 3, 2006 that its fourth quarter profit was sharply lower and that it expected both a steep decline in revenue and a loss in the current first quarter. The negative outlook stunned those analysts who follow ERTS as it went way beyond their already somewhat negative short-term projections. The stock opened 11 percent down the next day on May 4 at $48.69, a 52-week low. As the stock price gyrated early that day, we bought 100 shares for $49.09. As it turned out, the stock fell further both that day and over the next two months, dropping to a low of $39.99 before recovering sharply. We sold the first 100 shares on August 2 for $49.83. This trade and others over the next months were as follows, 100-share lots each time.

Bought 5/4/06 at $49.09	Sold 8/2/06 at $49.83	Profit = $63
Bought 8/14/06 at $49.01	Sold 8/15/06 at $50.42	Profit = $121
Bought 8/23/06 at $49.91	Sold 8/30/06 at $50.56	Profit = $55

After Electronic Arts hit a 52-week high of $59.85 on November 3, 2006, and then again fell back to lower levels, we bought again in December.

Bought 12/6/06 at $54.40	Position still held at 2/28/07	
Bought 12/12/06 at $51.95	Sold 12/13/06 at $52.74	Profit = $59
Bought 12/20/06 at $51.92	Sold 1/3/07 at $52.56	Profit = $54
Bought 1/3/07 at $50.55	Sold 1/3/07 at $51.08	Profit = $43
Bought 1/17/07 at $50.58	Sold 1/19/07 at $51.28	Profit = $60
Bought 1/19/07 at $50.58	Sold 2/2/07 at $54.04	Profit = $336
Bought 2/5/07 at $50.42	Sold 2/20/07 at $51.56	Profit = $104

Our nine completed roundtrip trades in ERTS netted us $895 in profit.

Dell Inc.

The Round Rock, Texas–based personal computer manufacturer Dell Inc. (DELL) gave a profit warning on the evening of May 8, 2006. It announced that its earnings for the first fiscal quarter would be below previously released guidance numbers as a result of the company's having instituted price cuts to counter competitive pressures, especially from a newly resurgent Hewlett-Packard. The announcement focused attention on the fact that Dell's previously highly successful direct to consumer sales model, and exclusive reliance on Intel microprocessors were causing distribution and pricing rigidities. Dell's competitors such as HP and Lenovo now appeared to be better positioned with their strong distribution channel relationships with electronics retailers such as Best Buy and Circuit City, and component sourcing from Advanced Micro Devices as well as Intel. When the market opened May 9, 2006, Dell stock tumbled almost 7 percent to open at $24.65. As Dell stock bounced around that morning, we bought 200 DELL at $24.55, then sold them for $24.94, then bought them back for $24.68 and then sold them for $24.98. We traded DELL a few times more over the next few months of weakness until the stock started to recover in the last couple of months of the year, 200 shares each trade.

Bought 5/9/06 at $24.55	Sold 5/9/06 at $24.94	Profit = $68
Bought 5/9/06 at $24.68	Sold 5/9/06 at $24.98	Profit = $50
Bought 5/11/06 at $24.63	Sold 5/30/06 at $25.13	Profit = $90
Bought 6/16/06 at $24.37	Sold 6/30/06 at $24.76	Profit = $68
Bought 6/30/06 at $24.28	Sold 6/30/06 at $24.54	Profit = $42
Bought 7/5/06 at $24.27	Sold 10/16/06 at $24.60	Profit = $56

From mid-October onward, Dell advanced and ended 2006 trading at $25.09. However, after an early positive showing in 2007, the stock fell back to the low 20s again as some of the same worries regarding the competitiveness of Dell's business model remained in place. CEO Kevin Rollins resigned January 31, 2007, and company founder and Chairman Michael Dell reassumed the CEO position. With Dell having fallen back into our targeted buy territory, we kept in mind those well-known recovery stories where a founder had returned to reinvigorate his company. Steve Jobs had done this at Apple and Charles Schwab also returned to turn around his eponymous online brokerage firm. At the same time, we tried not to think too hard about Ted Waitt's not so successful return to Gateway. We bought into Dell twice more in the period covered by this book, 200 shares each time, our last purchase being made on February 27 during the market meltdown of that day.

| Bought 2/12/07 at $23.52 | Sold 2/14/07 at 23.92 | Profit = $70 |
| Bought 2/27/07 at $23.46 | Position still held at 2/28/07 | |

With our seven roundtrip trades we made $444 in profit.

Legg Mason Inc.

The Baltimore, Maryland–based asset management firm Legg Mason (LM) reported on October 10, 2006, after the closing bell that its earnings for the second quarter would fall short of analysts' expectations. Having already surprised the Street on the negative side in earlier quarters, the shares took a beating, opening 13 percent lower on October 11 and losing an additional 5 percent during that day to close at $87.15. We bought 100 shares of Legg Mason early on the morning of October 12 at $87.36, then sold them within a couple of hours for $88.04. We then bought them back for $87.55 and sold them again on the same day for $88.15. Our third purchase of LM stock on October 12 for $87.66 had to be held for two weeks to achieve a profit. We sold those on October 26 for $88.30. We netted a total of $162 from these three roundtrips, two of which took place entirely on October 12. By the end of 2006, Legg Mason was trading at $95 and by the end of February 2007 was trading in the low $100s, despite a pull-back along with the overall market at the end of that month.

Black & Decker Corp.

Another Maryland company, Towson-based Black & Decker (BDK), the well-known manufacturer of power tools and accessories and home improvement products, announced before the market's open on the morning of December 15, 2006, that it was significantly lowering its fourth quarter guidance below the consensus estimates of analysts following the stock. This development was viewed as a direct and very negative reflection of the dramatic slowdown that was taking hold in new housing starts and home sales. Black & Decker stock was pummeled, closing December 15 at $78.26, a drop of 10 percent from the previous day's close. On the morning of the following Monday, December 18, we bought 100 shares at $77.93 and sold them later that day for $78.76. We then bought them back again on that same day at $78.40 and unwound that position nine days later on December 27 for $79. Our profit on the two roundtrips was $123. By the end of January 2007, Black & Decker stock was trading around $87, higher than it had been prior to the December 15 announcement.

INDUSTRIAL ACTION: THREATENED OR ACTUAL

A move that could certainly be considered counterintuitive and classically contrarian would be to buy the stock of a company that is threatened or hit by industrial action. In late 2006, the United Steelworkers Union threatened Goodyear Tire & Rubber Co. (GT) with strikes in a dispute over planned plant closings. As strike calls mounted and then took effect October 5 at 16 plants in the United States and Canada, Goodyear's share price came under pressure and the uncertainty of the situation led to extreme share price volatility. We bought and sold Goodyear stock eight times during the week the strike was called with the stock price fluctuating around $14 and change. Price weakness lasted just a couple of weeks into the three month strike, however, as it became clear that the company was well prepared to weather a prolonged bout of industrial action. For most of the time that the strike was actually taking place, Goodyear's stock rallied and continued to do so after the dispute was settled in early January, touching $25 on January 9, 2007, before falling back at the end of February to $24.62.

ACQUISITIONS

Another common cause of a sudden drop in a stock's price that can represent a buying opportunity occurs following the announcement by a company of a planned acquisition. Typically, when one company announces its intention to acquire another company, the stock of the acquiring company drops regardless of whether the acquisition is done on a friendly or a hostile basis. There are several reasons for this phenomenon. The acquiring company more often than not needs to pay a premium to the target's current market price to secure the purchase. Moreover, the acquisition can often be expected to dilute the acquirer's earnings, at least over the short term and often increase net debt, making the company more highly leveraged. Also, there is always some element of doubt that the acquisition can be made to work in terms of post-merger integration of the two companies. There is a risk of potential management distraction as well as a fear that on a long-term view the acquirer may have over-valued its prize and is overpaying. Finally, there is the simple statistical fact that many if not most mergers and acquisitions do not add value over time.

From the viewpoint of the shareholders in the company being acquired, however, the news is normally nothing but positive. The acquiring company buys out the stockholders at a premium price over what the stock was trading for preannouncement. There is also the possible additional upside should the company now become "in play" and spark a bidding war between several suitors. (See the story of the Johnson & Johnson/Boston Scientific/Guidant saga in Chapter 6 as an illustration of this.)

For a trader seeking ripple price fluctuations, acquisitions provide two opportunities for profit. The first is by using acquisition arbitrage. The second is by taking advantage of the typical drop in price that affects an acquiring company as it announces its move.

Arbitrage involves the profitable exploitation of price disparities between two markets, but in a merger/acquisition situation, various kinds of arbitrage opportunity can be opened up when one company bids for another. In a hostile takeover, arbitrageurs can take a position betting that a bid will have to be raised to ensure the snaring of the target, or that a bidding war may ensue, now that the target is seen to be "in play." This can be risky because the bid may be called off with the result that the so-called bid premium will disappear, driving the target company's stock price back to where it was before the bid was first made, a losing proposition for the arbitrageur.

A situation more to our liking is where a bid is agreed upon at a certain price, but for regulatory or other reasons the deal can only be completed at a later date, often several months later. The element of doubt in investors' minds—that the deal will, in fact, successfully close—means that the stock of the target company typically trades at a discount to the agreed acquisition price. Later, as the date of the deal's closing nears, the price trends upwards towards the agreed price. There is risk here, too, that the deal may ultimately fall through. That is why the price disparity exists. But in an agreed bid the risk is less than it is when the bid is hostile or contested, and in many cases can be well worth the risk. It is worthwhile taking a look at one example of this from our own trading record, involving specialist credit card issuer MBNA Corp.

MBNA Corp.

We first bought 200 shares of MBNA Corp. (stock symbol at that time KRB) rather fortuitously for $21.58 on June 16, 2005, just two weeks before Bank of America agreed to buy MBNA in a $35 billion cash and stock deal. However, the deal was set to complete only by January 1, 2006, after all necessary approvals from each company's shareholders as well as regulatory green lights had been obtained. On the day the bid was announced, June 30, 2005, we sold our 200 shares for $26.60, netting a profit of $993. Nevertheless, following the pop that came with the merger announcement, the stock price fell back later that day as further consideration was given to the possibility of the deal not receiving its necessary regulatory approvals. There were also fears that Bank of America's stock price could dip under the pressure of the acquisition, thus lessening the theoretical value of the deal owing to its stock component—something which did indeed occur over the next few months. As MBNA's stock retreated on June 30, we bought back our 200 shares at $26.33 and on the following day, July 1, we bought an additional 200 MBNA shares at $25.74. These last were sold on July 13 at $26.04, but bought back again July 19 for $25.74. The stock price remained under pressure until it became clear that the deal would indeed go through and after Bank of America had recouped all of the stock price losses that had occurred during the months of July to October following the deal announcement. The 400 shares we still held in November 2005 were sold for $26.04 and $26.59 on November 9 and November 21, respectively. Our overall trading profit on these four roundtrips in MBNA was $1,115 of which $122 resulted from arbitrage trades based on purchases made after the deal had been announced.

Other arbitrage situations we played trading the stock of an acquisition target company in 2005 and 2006 were in the cases of Guidant (GDT—$172 profit from four round trips—see Chapter 4) and Univision (UNV—$207 profit from three round trip trades).

For contrarians who look for a price drop as an impetus to buy, the acquirer in an M&A transaction can also look interesting as a potential purchase because the price decline that typically affects it at the time the acquisition is announced is often reversed later on. This is not just because the deal may turn out to be a fundamentally sound one and the price being paid is perfectly rational for the assets being acquired, but a recovery in the acquirer's stock price can also subsequently occur even in those cases where the merits of the deal do turn out to be less than stellar. The fact is that a big corporation's prospects are based on so much more than just the outcome of one transaction. Yet, when a big deal is in the news, it tends to drown out all other considerations affecting the acquirer's prospects.

One case in point was the Bank of America/MBNA transaction, which we outlined earlier, where Bank of America's stock was pressured downward by the pending acquisition for most of the six months prior to final closing of the deal. We took advantage of this decline in price, buying and selling Bank of America (BAC) twice during the period its MBNA acquisition was pending, with two trades netting $97. Here follow three more examples that aptly illustrate how a stock price decline relating to an acquisition that a company is making can prompt us to initiate trading in that stock. These three separate takeover situations involved Anadarko Petroleum Corporation, CVS Corp., and Norway's Statoil ASA.

Anadarko Petroleum Corporation

Anadarko Petroleum Corporation (APC) is an oil and gas producer based in The Woodlands, Texas. On Friday, June 23, 2006, the company announced two major acquisitions in the oil and gas sector. APC agreed to acquire Kerr-McGee Corporation and Western Gas Resources for $21.1 billion in cash and the assumption of $2.2 billion in debt. Anadarko paid a steep premium for both purchases and announced a program of asset sales to pay down debt, but concerns regarding the acquirer's debt levels initially resulted in an immediate 7 percent drop in APC's stock price on the day the deals were announced. Anadarko's stock price closed at $44.90 on that day. We bought 100 APC on Monday, June 26, 2006, at $43.91, and then traded 100-share lots as follows over subsequent months.

Bought 6/26/06 at $43.91	Sold 6/28/06 at $44.57	Profit = $55
Bought 7/17/06 at $43.70	Sold 7/18/06 at $44.45	Profit = $55
Bought 7/18/06 at $43.66	Sold 7/26/06 at $44.46	Profit = $60
Bought 9/12/06 at $43.86	Sold 9/13/06 at $44.70	Profit = $74
Bought 9/14/06 at $44.00	Sold 9/18/06 at $44.80	Profit = $70
Bought 9/19/06 at $43.87	Sold 9/28/06 at $44.47	Profit = $46
Bought 9/19/06 at $43.96	Sold 10/16/06 at $44.68	Profit = $52
Bought 9/20/06 at $42.68	Sold 9/27/06 at $43.35	Profit = $71
Bought 9/27/06 at $42.66	Sold 9/27/06 at $43.35	Profit = $59

Bought 10/3/06 at $42.09	Sold 10/10/06 at $43.14	Profit = $95
Bought 12/18/06 at $43.91	Position still held at 2/28/07	
Bought 12/22/06 at $42.43	Sold 12/27/06 at $43.13	Profit = $60
Bought 1/3/07 at $42.63	Sold 1/22/07 at $43.24	Profit = $51
Bought 1/22/07 at $42.63	Sold 1/23/07 at $43.23	Profit = $50
Bought 1/25/07 at $42.52	Sold 1/31/07 at $43.30	Profit = $68
Bought 2/6/07 at $42.14	Sold 2/7/07 at $42.83	Profit = $59
Bought 2/7/07 at $42.09	Position still held at 2/28/07	

The 15 completed roundtrip trades in Anadarko netted us $925 in trading profit.

CVS Corporation

Woonsocket, Rhode Island–based CVS Corporation (CVS), which operates one of the country's largest chains of retail pharmacy stores, announced on November 1, 2006 an all-stock bid worth around $21.2 billion for Caremark Rx, a leading pharmacy benefit management company based in Nashville, Tennessee. CVS stock dropped 7.4 percent to close at $29.06 on the news. We bought 100 CVS shares November 3 for $28.93 and then traded five additional 100-share lots as follows thereafter.

Bought 11/3/06 at $28.93	Sold 11/6/06 at $29.55	Profit = $52
Bought 11/9/06 at $28.99	Sold 11/16/06 at $29.58	Profit = $49
Bought 11/9/06 at $28.60	Sold 11/13/06 at $29.21	Profit = $51
Bought 11/17/06 at $28.91	Sold 12/5/06 at $29.57	Profit = $56
Bought 11/27/06 at $27.70	Sold 11/29/06 at $28.30	Profit = $50
Bought 11/27/06 at $27.32	Sold 11/29/06 at $27.92	Profit = $50

Then on December 18 came the announcement of a competing and higher bid by Express Scripts, also a pharmacy benefit management company and a direct rival of Caremark Rx. We bought 100 shares of CVS early on in the day that the rival bid was announced in the belief that CVS share price would likely be pushed up on the news. We closed the roundtrip trade three days later.

Bought 12/18/06 at $29.94	Sold 12/21/06 at $30.65	Profit = $61

Our total profit from trading CVS seven times following its bid announcement was $369.

Statoil ASA

Statoil (STO) is the largest oil and gas company in Scandinavia and is Norway's largest company. Although the stock is publicly listed on both the Oslo and the New York stock exchanges, the Norwegian government maintains a controlling stake of 70.9 percent. The company produces oil and natural gas from Norway's continental shelf in the North Sea, where it is the biggest producer, as well as from many other production operations around the world. Statoil also operates around 2,000 gas stations in nine European countries. On December 18, 2006, Statoil announced that it would acquire the oil and gas operations of Norwegian conglomerate Norsk Hydro. The announcement initially caused a 4 percent drop in Statoil's share price with the New York-quoted ADR closing at $26.74 on December 18. But in the next weeks the stock price moved further south, reaching a low on January 10, 2007 of $23.66. We bought STO for the first time December 19, 2006 buying 200 shares at $26.33 and selling them that same day at $26.60. Our trades in the stock—200 shares each time—ran as follows:

Bought 12/19/06 at $26.33	Sold 12/19/06 at $26.60	Profit = $44
Bought 12/20/06 at $26.68	Sold 1/31/07 at $27.01	Profit = $56
Bought 1/10/07 at $24.02	Sold 1/12/07 at $24.36	Profit = $58
Bought 1/17/07 at $23.96	Sold 1/17/07 at $24.29	Profit = $56
Bought 2/8/07 at $25.74	Sold 2/8/07 at $26.00	Profit = $42
Bought 2/12/07 at $25.72	Sold 2/13/07 at $26.03	Profit = $52
Bought 2/20/07 at $25.47	Sold 2/21/07 at $25.78	Profit = $52
Bought 2/27/07 at $25.41	Position still held at 2/28/07	

The last of these purchases was made during the strong market fall-back of February 27, 2007. Our profit on the seven roundtrip trades was $360.

A CASE STUDY IN NEGATIVITY: WM. WRIGLEY JR. CO.

Not all events that drive stocks down are so dramatic that they cause a precipitous price drop from one day to the next, or as in the case of Statoil above, over the course of a few weeks. Sometimes a stock undergoes a veritable Chinese water torture of persistent price declines over many months. When this has gone on for some time, negative press coverage can gather momentum, spreading the perception that the company has serious problems, and the company and its stock begin to appear to be numbered among the "walking wounded" of the stock market. Often this perception is completely wrong. Yet once it tarnishes the stock, many institutional investors will not touch the stock with the proverbial 10-foot pole and the continuing slide takes on the appearance of a self-fulfilling prophecy. There are quite a number of examples that we could choose to illustrate such price action, but one that stands out for us as being particularly apposite is that of Wm. Wrigley Jr. Co. (WWY).

The Chicago-based chewing gum manufacturer was founded in 1891 by William Wrigley Jr., a soap salesman who hit on the idea of offering free baking powder with the soap he sold. When he found that the baking powder was more popular than the soap he began to sell the baking powder and gave away free chewing gum with each can of baking powder. You can probably guess what happened next.

Four generations of Wrigleys built the company to become the preeminent manufacturer and distributor of chewing gum around the world. The founder's great-grandson, Bill Wrigley, chairman and CEO of the company since 1999, made the bold decision to diversify into other lines of candy beyond the chewing gum that had dominated the company's business since its founding. Following an abortive attempt to buy chocolate maker Hershey Co. in 2002, Wrigley in late 2004 purchased Kraft Foods' Life Savers and Altoids brands as well as other confectionery brands for $1.48 billion. By late 2005, however, it became clear that integration of these new product lines was going to be more difficult than Wrigley's management had originally bargained. Meanwhile, Wrigley felt increasing competitive pressures in its core gum business from Cadbury Schweppes, the U.K.-based confectioner, which invested heavily in its own gum brands Trident and Dentyne that it had acquired when it purchased Pfizer's Adams confectionery unit. Wrigley's stock price that had almost hit $60 in October 2005 started a long and painful slide to an intraday low of $4,300 on July 25, 2006.

We became increasingly aware of the drumbeat of bad press relating to Wrigley's strategy and the performance of the embattled Chairman and CEO as the stock price hit the low 40s. Sentiment regarding Wrigley's prospects was almost uniformly negative. But it seemed to us that a company that had dominated the chewing gum business for over 100 years, not just domestically but internationally, was being beaten up unfairly. We bought 100 shares on July 25 for $43.05, a hair above the low of the day and of the year and we sold them later that day for $43.76. Over the next few months, we traded Wrigley as follows, 100-share lots each time:

Bought 7/25/06 at $43.05	Sold 7/25/06 at $43.76	Profit = $51
Bought 7/26/06 at $44.19	Sold 7/27/06 at $45.29	Profit = $100
Bought 8/1/06 at $45.20	Sold 8/2/06 at $46.02	Profit = $72
Bought 8/9/06 at $45.83	Sold 8/10/06 at $46.50	Profit = $57
Bought 8/23/06 at $46.42	Sold 10/23/06 at $50.70	Profit = $418
Bought 9/6/06 at $45.95	Sold 10/20/06 at $46.68	Profit = $53

Our six trades in Wrigley netted a profit of $751. Our final closing trade in the stock with our sale on October 23 netted such a big profit because it was announced on that day that Bill Wrigley would relinquish the CEO position to William Perez, who had shortly before been forced out of that same role at Nike Inc. by Nike cofounder Phil Knight after just 13 months (see Chapter 6). Clearly investors liked what they saw in the appointment of Perez to the head of the company. Prior to his unhappy time at Nike he had spent 34 years at SC Johnson, the privately held household cleaning products company, including eight years as president and CEO there. His experience in managing a company with a collection of major brands was undoubted.

With the announcement of Perez's appointment as CEO—with Bill Wrigley remaining Executive Chairman—Wrigley's stock soared 14 percent, reaching a high of $54.37 on October 23 before falling back to close the day at $53.23. Wrigley ended 2006 at $51.72, 13 percent less than its all-time high of $59.48 on October 3, 2005, but a solid 20 percent above the year's low of $43.

EXTERNAL EVENTS THAT SEND STOCKS FALLING

We mentioned in Chapter 4 the old cliché much used on Wall Street, "Don't catch a falling knife," which warns the trader from being tempted to buy a stock that is falling sharply. Recall that the thinking behind this is that a plunging stock can go knifing through the buyer's hands and continue its descent. We are not believers that this adage always holds true. There are many pressures on professional investors that discourage them from buying or force them into selling stocks that are on a precipitous fall. This helps to accelerate the drop and removes support levels that might bring the fall to a floor or start a reversal until the stock price has overshot any kind of logical price level. The Wrigley story above illustrates this well. For the trader who likes to buy when merchandise is "on sale," however, this is often a great time to buy. This tendency to overshoot on the downside in reaction to sudden unexpected bad news is true not only for individual stocks where negative events relate to that specific company or its industry. It is also true when shocking and calamitous news hits outside of the worlds of business and finance. Sometimes the kinds of events in the news that cause such a sharp drop are truly momentous. Certainly the appalling attacks on the United States of September 11, 2001, qualify for this description. The stock market reaction to the attacks came when the markets reopened Monday, September 17, having been closed for the four trading days of September 11 to 14. The market experienced an immediate selling rout and the Dow dropped 685 points September 17 and then suffered an additional 685 point loss during the rest of that week, bringing the Dow to 8,236 on Friday, September 21 representing a 14.3 percent drop for the week. With hindsight, this presented investors and traders with a great buying opportunity, given that the Dow ended 2001 at 10,022. This holds true even though the markets did dip even lower than the 8,000 level for more normal cyclical business and economic reasons a year later.

The reaction of the market to the September 11 events with a wave of panic selling was the most dramatic of recent years. However, events external to the financial world that generate fear and concern causing a brief market drop are actually not that unusual. One that we can illustrate from our recent trading record of the last couple of years covered in Appendixes A through C was also caused by an act of terrorism, this time the bombings of three tube (subway) trains and one bus in London on July 7, 2005. Following these horrific attacks, markets around the world fell significantly, only to retrace their steps relatively quickly. Stock prices fell close to 100 points in New York on July 7 almost immediately from the opening bell, indicating a wave of selling and a tendency for potential buyers to sit on their hands and wait to see what would develop. As the market plunged we jumped in as buyers, picking up several companies' stocks at prices that were significantly lower than the previous day and then selling them very quickly as the market rebounded and our price targets were reached. The stocks we bought were the following:

100 United Tech. bought 7/7/05 at $50.02	Sold 7/7/05 at $50.64	Profit = $41
200 Microsoft bought 7/7/05 at $24.62	Sold 7/8/05 at $24.99	Profit = $54
200 Bell South bought 7/7/05 at $26.39	Sold 7/8/05 at $26.71	Profit = $44
100 General Electric bought 7/7/05 at $34.18	Sold 7/8/05 at $34.70	Profit = $42
100 Lloyds TSB bought 7/7/05 at $33.09	Sold 7/11/05 at $34.35	Profit = $105
100 JP Morgan Chase bought 7/7/05 at $34.45	Sold 7/11/05 at $35.05	Profit = $40

Our trades from purchases made on July 7, 2005, netted us $326 in profit and the longest we held on to positions bought that day was four days. Interestingly, following the near 100-point drop in the Dow early in the morning, the Dow actually finished the day up 32.

There are a couple of points worth emphasizing here. Firstly, the drop in prices that takes place when bad news hits in this way does not occur because the institutional investors who drive the market do not understand that typically following such a panic stocks bounce back. It is rather a result of those institutional investors knowing that the bad news will make the market drop, who take action by selling some of their holdings immediately so that they will be less affected by the drop to come. They are aware that they will be buyers at a lower level. It is also caused and exaggerated by institutional investors not wishing to be seen as buyers when stocks are dropping sharply, so not wanting to "catch a falling knife." Unlike contrarian buyers such as ourselves, they do not wish to buy into stocks that are moving down because this would mean that they would necessarily be buying into instant losing positions. They will typically wait for the market to stabilize at a bottom or support level and to see that the selling pressure has dissipated before making their move. Both tendencies mean that a sharp drop in prices as a result of the bad news is inevitable—again essentially a self-fulfilling prophecy.

Secondly, we would not agree with some who might say that making profits from market moves that are caused by tragic events bringing death and destruction is in some way amoral or unethical. The buying and selling of stocks hinges on buyers and sellers striking a price through the medium of the market. The decision to buy, sell, or hold is made based on the desire of all market participants to maximize their return and is affected by all events, economic, political, financial, or in business that take place around the country and around the world. This is true, however distasteful and abhorrent political or terrorism-related events such as those mentioned above truly may be. We believe that it is the continuing ability of smoothly functioning markets to bring together willing buyers and sellers of equities, financial instruments, commodities, and the like, that helps to hammer home the strength and robustness of our system even faced with adversity and terror attack.

BUY THE RUMOR, SELL THE NEWS ... OR BUY THE NEWS?

Another of those well-worn Wall Street adages and one that has a good pedigree goes, "Buy the rumor, sell the news." Stocks often enjoy a good upward run based on chatter among market professionals regarding forthcoming news, such as strong quarterly numbers. Often the so-called "whisper number" circulating among the professionals is higher than the number that stock analysts have arrived at in consensus based on guidance from senior executives at the company. Once the actual numbers are announced, should they come in below the whisper number, then this news hits the Street as if the chief executive had just announced the CFO had disappeared after embezzling all the company's cash—the stock swoons. It does not matter if these numbers are essentially sound or even good.

Interestingly, even if the whisper number is reached, the stock often still falls back sharply as those who had bought into it now sell and take their profits. In both cases, such a drop in a stock's price inspired by an announcement (which hits the stock out of the gate at the opening bell, should the results have been announced the previous evening or that morning before the bell), can take several dollars off the stock price and bring it to a level that puts it squarely in buy territory under our trading technique, so in such cases we are buyers of the news. Typically, following the initial sharp drop, the stock tends to come back during the rest of the day as value-oriented investors and traders perceive value and buy. As the day progresses, the stock often seesaws as traders come in at low prices, but take profits each time there is an upswing. As a result, the ripple trader can buy and sell several times in the same day and make a handsome profit.

One good example of this comes courtesy of Nike Inc. (NKE). We bought and sold Nike twice on December 21, 2005, when it followed precisely this pattern. Its quarterly earnings were above expectations, but a relative weakness in future orders was perceived by analysts. The stock fell $4.48 or around 5 percent at the open and we bought 100 shares for $84 even. It then climbed back up to $84.56 at which point we sold, only to buy again shortly afterward for $84.31 with a final sale later that day at $84.98. We made $103 with the stock on that day. Why were investors in such turmoil over Nike? The quarterly profits announced were 15 cents higher than the $1.03 consensus forecast. Go figure!

STOCKS THAT MAY BE BOUGHT WHEN MARKETS ARE UP

Remember that it is a discipline of our trading strategy that stocks are at least initially bought at times when prices are down on the day overall (measured by the Dow Jones Industrial Average) and the stock being purchased is also down for the day. However, there are certain stocks that regularly move in the opposite direction to the overall market. This is particularly true of gold mining stocks and energy (oil and gas) stocks. While gold mining stocks are shares in corporations and therefore react to their own specific company news, their stock price movements typically follow the gold price. Gold-mining companies' production costs are fixed, so any increase in the gold price flows through to their bottom line (and profits are equally crimped by a fall in the gold price). As a rising gold price is a harbinger of inflationary pressures, it tends to rise when stocks overall are under pressure and fall when the stock market is up on the day.

What this means in our trading strategy is that on a day when stocks in general are higher and we are not looking to buy most stocks, we may nevertheless buy gold stocks. This is true as long as the gold stocks are lower on that day and should the usual basis on which we make a purchase hold true—the stock in question is relatively close to the low part of its 52-week range. Additionally, as far as gold stocks are concerned, we watch the historical gold price and only buy when gold is in a relatively low part of its own trading range. This is factored in with the gold stock price we are looking at.

In 2005 and 2006, we traded one gold mining stock only—Barrick Gold (ABX)—and also bought in and out of a specialty gold vehicle called Central Fund of Canada (CEF) (see Chapter 6).

Gold Mining

Barrick Gold, formerly known as American Barrick, is a Toronto-based precious metals mining company with predominantly gold mining interests in a number of countries around the world, including large mines in the United States and Canada. We traded in and out of Barrick Gold as follows in 2005 and 2006, 200 shares each time except where noted:

Bought 1/6/05 at $22.24	Sold 1/11/05 at $22.64	Profit = $60
Bought 1/13/05 at $22.26	Sold 1/24/05 at $22.85	Profit = $98
Bought 1/25/05 at $22.26	Sold 2/10/05 at $22.46	Profit = $25
Bought 2/1/05 at $21.65	Sold 2/2/05 at $21.96	Profit = $42
Bought 2/3/05 at $21.59 (170 shares)	Sold 2/3/05 at $21.94	Profit = $46
Bought 2/3/05 at $21.64	Sold 2/10/05 at $22.46	Profit = $149
Bought 2/8/05 at $21.39 (180 shares)	Sold 2/9/05 at $21.73	Profit = $47
Bought 5/13/05 at $21.69	Sold 5/18/05 at $21.94	Profit = $40
Bought 5/20/05 at $21.67	Sold 5/23/05 at $21.93	Profit = $42
Bought 11/4/05 at $24.69	Sold 11/4/05 at $24.99	Profit = $50

As the overall market generally weakened in the second half of 2005, the gold price and thus gold stock prices were strong—true to the pattern of an opposite correlation between the stock market and gold. However, in 2006 this opposite correlation was discontinued as both gold markets and the stock market went higher. The dip in Barrick Gold's price in the second half of 2005, which spurred the one brief trade on November 4 was a fallback caused by Barrick's announced bid for fellow Canadian gold miner Placer Dome.

In 2006, faced with gold stocks priced above our comfort level, we only traded Barrick Gold twice on a dip from previous highs close to $30.

| Bought 3/23/06 at $25.77 | Sold 3/24/06 at $26.09 | Profit = $52 |
| Bought 3/23/06 at $25.77 | Sold 3/24/06 at $26.16 | Profit = $64 |

Our overall trading profit from twelve roundtrips in Barrick Gold over 2005 and 2006 was $715.

Toronto–based Central Fund of Canada (CEF) is a specialized investment holding company that essentially sits on a large quantity of bullion, mostly gold, but also some silver. As it has no operations as such, the value of the stock is entirely driven by precious metals prices—that is, by the price of gold. We traded CEF a total of seventeen times in 2005 and not at all in 2006. Details are provided in the Price Pegging section of Chapter 6.

Our one other foray into a mining company stock was a purchase and sale of Freeport-McMoRan Copper & Gold (FCX) on January 5, 2007, as mining stocks sold off amid sharply lower metals prices. Freeport was our target as it was hit by the "double whammy" of lower gold and significantly lower copper prices over the course of a few days. We bought 100 FCX at $49.98 and sold them the same day for $50.60, netting a profit of $52.

Oil and Gas

Another group of stocks that very often move in the opposite direction to the overall market on any given day are oil and gas stocks. Oils have the same reverse correlation with the rest of the stock market as gold mining stocks. As oil prices rise, they pinch profitability at other companies as higher oil prices increase those companies' production and distribution cost bases. The companies that make money when oil prices rise are the oil companies themselves. The very strong upward trend in the oils in 2005 and much of 2006, based on factors such as increased demand in Asia, the tightening of supplies caused by various hurricanes that hit the southern United States including Katrina, and continuing political strife in the Middle East, found them generally too pricey overall to fit our strategy during much of the period, except for certain dips. In late 2006, however, as the oil and gas sectors dropped back, not to bargain levels, but to levels significantly cheaper than where they had been, we bought and sold Exxon Mobil (XOM), ConocoPhillips (COP), BP Plc (BP), Anadarko Petroleum Corporation (APC), Repsol YPF (REP), and Suncor Energy (SU) as noted in the next section. We also traded the major coal producer Peabody Energy (BTU), which follows the fortunes of the oil and gas companies fairly closely, but tends to move with wider swings, something that we as ripple traders find very attractive. As mentioned earlier in this chapter, we also traded Statoil of Norway as an acquirer play late in 2006 and early 2007.

THE PEAK OIL DEBATE AND STOCKS

It is worth mentioning that the cost of energy, and particularly oil, has a huge effect on stock prices. When oil prices are relatively benign, as they were for much of the 1990s, people often tend to forget or overlook the link between the strength of the stock market and relatively low oil prices. When oil spikes, as it did in 2005 and early 2006, then everyone sits up and takes notice of the correlation. A debate on the subject of peak oil has emerged during the times of oil price spikes over the last couple of years. While this debate is still largely confined to academics, scientists and economists who are expert in the energy field, it percolates down with regularity through the mainstream media whenever energy prices shoot dramatically higher. In the media, the issue is often articulated through screaming headlines informing us that oil, our principal form of energy, is running out. Alternatively, the debate focuses on a perceived "dependence on foreign oil," which the Bush administration has picked up as a prime policy theme.

The crux of the peak oil debate is whether we have reached or are soon to reach a point at which new oil production for the first time fails to keep up with the rate of decline in existing oil fields. If the scenario of imminent peak oil is a valid one, then it would seem clear to us that investors should ditch all their stocks except for their oil company investments and then watch as oil stocks become pretty much the only ones of value. But we continue to trade both nonenergy and energy stocks alike based on the strong belief that peak oil is not imminent and if it does ever come that will be so many years from now that today's markets should not reflect it. We do not believe that it is alternative fuel sources—such as solar, wave, geothermal energy, or biofuels such as corn- or sugar-based ethanol that have been much in the news—that stave off peak oil. We believe that peak oil will not occur in the foreseeable future owing to both new oil discoveries in places where exploration in the past has seemed too risky or expensive or where the environment for exploration and drilling has seemed very harsh, such as some regions of Russia. We also consider that it is the continuing development of new technologies that allow oil companies to exploit already discovered but expensive to develop sources of bituminous oil such as the Alberta oil sands in Canada and extra-heavy oil in Venezuela that will provide much of our new oil supply in the decades to come.

The oil sands of Alberta, Canada, are particularly interesting, especially as these deposits are situated in a country that is very politically secure and friendly to the United States, attributes that are relatively uncommon in major oil-producing countries. Alberta's oil sand deposits are second only in size to Saudi Arabia's oil reserves and could, theoretically, alone satisfy the world's demand for petroleum for many decades. The oil, which is heavy and viscous, is difficult to extract and refine, but technological advances continue to make economic extraction more and more practical. The debate regarding the feasibility of commercial extraction from the oil sands reminds us of the way North Sea oil was considered prior to the oil shocks of the 1970s—known to be plentiful but considered too expensive and technologically difficult to recover. Yet huge quantities of North Sea oil have been extracted in the last decades using technology that was largely developed to resolve the specific difficulties of the hostile North Sea drilling environment.

We are bullish on the prospect of relatively plentiful oil for many decades to come, although short-term shortages as well as gluts will continue as ever to be part of the picture. As a result we are traders in oil stocks in the same way that we are with others based on our contrarian approach—we look to buy them when they are at relatively cheap levels, but we do not chase them as they become more expensive. We do confess to a particular bullish disposition toward the Alberta oil sands development, however, and we have in our own trading used the stock of one particular oil company that is very active in that region as a proxy for the overall development of the resource. That stock is Suncor Energy (SU).

Suncor Energy

This is an integrated energy company based in Calgary, Alberta, Canada, with a special operating focus on development of Canada's Athabasca oil sands. It markets petroleum and petrochemical products in Canada and the United States, including from its own network of Phillips 66 branded retail gas stations in Colorado. The company also has wind-power and ethanol alternative-energy operations.

We traded this stock just once in 2005 as energy stocks enjoyed an overall robust market that year, but fell back sharply in May. SU itself appeared particularly attractive at the time coming off a 52-week high of $42.

Bought 5/18/05 at $37.12	Sold 5/25/05 at $37.79	Profit = $57

Following this brief drop, energy stocks took off again, and SU even more than most. By April 19, 2006, the stock reached a high of $89.88. Subsequent to this, Suncor in common with other energy stocks backed off sharply from its highs and by mid-June 2006 we were ready to go back into SU at a price that was 23 percent down from that April 19 high.

Bought 6/19/06 at $69.55	Sold 6/21/06 at $70.26	Profit = $51

Suncor bounced back up to the mid and high $80 levels from late June through early August. Then there was another drop back in energy stocks that also included Suncor Energy. We entered a phase of regular trading in that stock, along with a number of other energy stocks, during the latter months of 2006 as the overall stock market rose strongly but the countercyclical energy stocks essentially remained in a flat trading range. This situation was perfect for short-term ripple trading profits to be harvested. Indeed, the following detail probably provides the very best example from our record of successful short-term trading of the ripples in a stock.

Bought 9/6/06 at $75.71	Sold 9/7/06 at $76.44	Profit = $63
Bought 9/7/06 at $74.82	Sold 9/7/06 at $75.48	Profit = $56
Bought 9/8/06 at $74.71	Sold 10/16/06 at $75.33	Profit = $52
Bought 9/22/06 at $67.21	Sold 9/26/06 at $67.94	Profit = $63
Bought 10/3/06 at $65.82	Sold 10/4/06 at $66.57	Profit = $65
Bought 10/4/06 at $64.94	Sold 10/4/06 at $65.62	Profit = $58
Bought 10/18/06 at $73.67	Sold 10/19/06 at $74.48	Profit = $71
Bought 10/23/06 at $74.85	Sold 10/23/06 at $75.40	Profit = $45
Bought 10/23/06 at $74.75	Sold 10/24/06 at $75.71	Profit = $86
Bought 10/30/06 at $74.85	Sold 10/31/06 at $75.67	Profit = $72
Bought 10/31/06 at $74.80	Sold 10/31/06 at $75.42	Profit = $52
Bought 11/1/06 at $74.20	Sold 11/1/06 at $75.01	Profit = $71
Bought 11/1/06 at $74.38	Sold 11/1/06 at $75.45	Profit = $102
Bought 11/1/06 at $74.90	Sold 11/2/06 at $75.51	Profit = $51
Bought 11/2/06 at $74.73	Sold 11/3/06 at $76.20	Profit = $137
Bought 11/17/06 at $74.66	Sold 11/17/06 at $75.37	Profit = $61
Bought 11/17/06 at $74.45	Sold 11/17/06 at $75.23	Profit = $68
Bought 1/3/07 at $75.34	Sold 1/23/07 at $75.98	Profit = $54
Bought 1/10/07 at $70.73	Sold 1/11/07 at $71.39	Profit = $56
Bought 1/11/07 at $70.24	Sold 1/12/07 at $70.98	Profit = $64
Bought 1/24/07 at $74.89	Sold 1/24/07 at $75.47	Profit = $48
Bought 1/25/07 at $74.67	Sold 1/25/07 at $75.32	Profit = $55
Bought 1/25/07 at $74.73	Sold 1/26/07 at $76.05	Profit = $122
Bought 1/26/07 at $74.85	Position still held at 2/28/07	

Our final roundtrip purchase and sale of Suncor in the period covered by our record in this book was made on February 28, 2007, the day after the market's 413 drop, as the market came part way back with a 52-point recovery.

Bought 2/28/07 at $70.46	Sold 2/28/07 at $71.11	Profit = $55

On 26 roundtrip trades in 2005, 2006, and the beginning of 2007, always in 100-share lots, we made a trading profit of $1,735 on SU. No fewer than 17 of those trades and $1,173 of the profit came in the trading burst of the 72-day period from September 6 to November 17, 2006.

CHAPTER 8

On Self-Discipline

Some Concluding Thoughts

It should be clear to the reader now that for our contrarian short-term ripple trading method to work, a good measure of self-discipline is needed. Our strategy itself is a relatively simple one. Almost anybody with some basic knowledge of a few companies that make up corporate America can theoretically understand and put these concepts to practical use. The initial buy technique itself involves nothing more complicated than making comparisons of current stock prices to their 52-week highs and lows. Lower ranges then dictate the buying decisions, with the proviso that both the overall market and the price of the stock in question are lower on the day. Alternatively, when "riding the ripples," the signal to buy is given when the natural ripple fluctuation of the stock has driven it back to the level of the trader's previous buy. The sell decision with our method is even simpler. There is no agonizing over whether to let profits ride or whether this may be risking a pullback in price. The sale is made if and when the trader's predetermined profit has been achieved. Even without the inflexibility of limit orders being placed, a self-disciplined approach of taking action to make the sale once the profit target has been broken through is necessary.

However simple the foregoing may sound, it would be wrong to say that traders can follow this method successfully unless they have the temperament that allows them to maintain a high level of self-control to resist the emotional pressures that such a strategy entails. These emotional pressures arise from the fact that this strategy is contrarian. The following of contrarian disciplines is always tough because we are psychologically wired to feel comfortable when following the crowd and, conversely, to feel uncomfortable when doing something opposite of perceived wisdom. When you buy a stock at a point where it is toward its lower levels of the year, you are bucking the general opinion on the prospects for that stock. It can take nerves of steel to go with that purchase when you look at the stock's chart and see a recent downward trend line. Each time we bought General Motors stock during 2005 and 2006, 23 times in all, our purchases flew in the face of extraordinary negativity surrounding that stock and the future of the company.

The decision is only made more difficult because our initial buying is done on those days when both the overall market and the individual stock that we buy are down on the day. That is a day when investors are gloomy about the market in general. This negativity can be based on events in the geopolitical, economic, or financial spheres, or it may just be an indefinable "tiredness" of the market. There can be many reasons that a market takes on a gloomy disposition. What is certain is that the gloom feeds on itself.

It takes strong self-discipline on the part of the trader to choose precisely this moment when doom and gloom, or even just a general undercurrent of negativity is the prevailing market sentiment, to step up to the plate and buy. Equally, when a profit has been made and it is time to sell, by definition the trader's stock will be trending upward and nobody likes to sell a stock while it is going up. What if it goes up another two bucks? Think of the money that will be left on the table! Riding your profits is a perfectly sensible strategy for many investors and indeed traders. The strategy that we outline depends on achieving very short-term profits by taking advantage of the constant, natural, short-term ripple fluctuation in stock prices—and it works as you will see in Appendixes A through C. So if this is a strategy that works for you, then regular harvesting of your profits as they present themselves to be taken is the order of the day. This allows you to come back in again once the stock drops back to your original purchase price.

The trader cannot allow fear or greed, especially when it is displayed by others, to rub off and make him or her unwilling to follow the buy signal presented by a target stock falling lower on a down day in the market—or to sell when a stock has reached a profit target but is still on its way up. Warren Buffett once stated that his goals are "to be fearful when others are greedy and to be greedy only when others are fearful."[1]

Even for those investors who can intellectually understand that buying a stock when it is "on sale" makes more sense than buying it at a point where it has already become more expensive, it is still tough to make the buy decision at that point. Why? Perhaps traders and investors crave the endorphin rush that comes with buying a stock on the rise and having the instant gratification of seeing it rise further. Perhaps they love that feeling that their intelligence has been validated when they buy a stock and it then goes up—something that can only be achieved on a regular basis through the buying of stocks that are already moving north. Buying a stock that is falling only to see it continue to drop, even for a short time, has the opposite effect on the trader unless he or she is well steeled for this to happen. Selling a stock only to watch it rise further can also be a huge downer for a trader, especially for one who is not easily able to detach himself from the feeling of still being invested in the stock after it has been sold. To some extent the more ice water that flows through your veins, and the less need you feel for immediate self- and peer-approval for your buying and selling decisions, the better you can make this technique work for you.

Self-discipline is sorely tested for traders following our technique when the market pushes strongly upward over a period of weeks or months. This was the case in the last five months of 2006 and into the start of 2007. This was a time when many of the stocks that we bought and sold at lower levels were now being traded at prices that were significantly higher. It is natural to think in these circumstances of money potentially having been left on the table. To combat this feeling it is always best if the trader can recognize that he is only invested in a stock during the time that he actually owns it. For example, if he sold 100 Bausch & Lomb (BOL) shares as we did on April 13, 2006, for $46.31, having bought them for $45.15 just hours earlier on that same day, he should feel pleased with himself. The trader has locked in a profit of over $100 in one day (the actual amount depending on brokerage commission levels), so he should not get upset if the stock several months later rises above the $50 mark (as indeed it did), leaving him fixated on whether he did the right thing in selling at $46.31. It is helpful if the trader can recognize that the rise in Bausch & Lomb stock on any day, or over any weeks or months that he does not own it, is no different from the price rise that takes place in the same time period of the many thousands of other stocks that he did not own and maybe never owned (or maybe never even heard of). If our stock should continue higher after we have sold it, and that is what naturally often happens as we are by definition selling into a climbing trend, we do not cry over the spilt milk of any additional price rise forgone.

One other valuable advantage that is bestowed on a user of our technique is that he tends to be largely invested in stocks when the market is relatively weak and mostly in cash when the market is strong. This comes about as an automatic effect of a technique that has the trader make his initial purchase of any stock at a point where it—and typically the market overall, are priced toward the lower part of their trading range for the year. The effect is further enhanced by the riding of the ripples, where a stock is bought at the same price or one that is lower than where it was purchased in the previous roundtrip trade. As the market rises, the opportunities to make these low trading range purchases recedes as prices generally move higher and buy signals therefore become less and less common. At the same time, a rising market also allows those stocks that were bought at some point in the recent past under our contrarian principles to be sold as most come back up to their profit target under our method. The combination of these two factors means that in a rising market the contrarian ripple trader tends automatically to reduce the stock positions he holds through sales, while cash balances increase as opportunities to buy become fewer and fewer. In a falling market, on the other hand, the opposite occurs as positions already held tend to be pushed down from their selling targets while new buying signals for stocks tend to increase as more and more come down to attractive lower-range prices. The upshot is that as the market weakens, the amount of stock we hold pending a profitable sale increases and there is a simultaneous reduction in our cash balances. Heavy in stocks and light in cash in a weak market and heavy in cash and light in stocks in a strong market—that is exactly how our contrarian principles tell us we want to be.

From our own recent experience, the contrast between late 2005 and late 2006 is striking. As the market came to the end of a listless and slightly down year in 2005, we sat on very little cash, having been prompted by our buying signals to buy strongly throughout 2005, but especially in the last months of the year. By the end of 2006, on the other hand, we had relatively low stock holdings. Those we did have were largely dominated by energy stocks that had been pushed down from their highs toward the end of 2006. We were as a result, at the end of 2006, mainly in cash, and this did not start to change until the market dropped back and then tumbled at the end of February 2007. The cliché is buy low and sell high. Our discipline tends to make us buy low and sell higher than that. There is certainly no reason to sniff at the profits that derive from a strategy such as this.

RISING MARKETS ARE ALWAYS GOOD?

Traders who choose to follow our contrarian ripple trading method will be beneficiaries of a fringe benefit that they are freed from the tyranny of the "markets going up are good—markets going down are bad" syndrome. It is typical in the financial press and TV business news to hear talk of a good day on the market when stocks are up and, in solemn tones, a bad day on the market when the Dow is down. This view of the markets is shared by most of the investing public and by professionals as well. It comes about because most investors and traders are firmly on the long side and, having bought into their stock positions, they now only feel smart if these go up. Conversely, they can feel dumb if the stock they bought at $50 goes down to $48. This view of up equals good and down equals bad is irrational. The only people who should feel good about a market going up are those who are fully invested and waiting to sell their positions. For anyone who has cash and wishes to invest it, a falling market should be a welcome sight. For most people, however, this is an alien mindset.

By the very nature of our trading strategy and philosophy, we tend only to be fully invested in stocks following a fairly long period of market weakness and we are absolutely never fully in cash. As a result, a market moving up makes us feel good about the fact that we can take profits on some of the stocks we have bought in recent days. However, a market moving down also makes us feel good about the purchases that the downward movement opens up under our method. This even holds true when the market takes a major tumble, such as that of February 27, 2007. On that day, the Dow dropped 413 points or over 3 percent, but intraday was showing a loss of 543 points owing to trading-volume-related technical glitches that affected the computers that calculate and feed the Dow index numbers to market participants. We are content in such a market pull-back to let our riding of the ripples pull us back into stock positions where buy signals flash as those stocks that we have previously sold drop back to the last purchase price. In the case of the February 27, 2007, market drop, we did exactly this, ripple trading back into eight stock positions on that day that we had previously sold in the preceding days or weeks, including one, Weatherford International (WFT) that we bought, sold and bought back that day. The one stock we bought that day that was not a ripple trade was Texas Instruments (TXN). (See the appendixes for details.) Meanwhile, it was positive news for us that the market was finally making a significant move downwards, allowing us to ripple trade back into these stocks.

One market scenario that can give us the blahs is the listless one where the market moves sideways for long periods and stocks in general are going nowhere, neither up nor down. Luckily this happens only quite rarely. Even in a year such as 2005, when the market did indeed go mostly sideways, there were fluctuations within that narrow trading range that provided good ripple trading opportunities. A good fluctuating market is always the one that best suits our trading method. A market that goes up or down strongly for a long period—such as the bullish market of the last half of 2006 and the beginning of 2007 that topped out February 20—is also not a favorite of ours, as the opportunities to trade the ripples are much reduced as a result. However, no market is ever completely without short-term fluctuations, and you will find us buying to some extent in every market phase.

SELLING SHORT

One of the big differences between books that set out to help readers invest and books that concentrate on trading strategies is that the latter often provide great detail on short selling and may treat this technique as an integral part of an overall trading method and strategy. Selling short is the practice in which instead of buying a stock with the hope of selling it later at a profit, a stock is first sold and then subsequently bought back, hopefully at a lower price than the selling price, thus generating a profit on the trade. The ability to sell a stock that the trader does not own is based on a service provided by brokers whereby a stock held on behalf of other clients is loaned to the short-seller in order for the short sale to be made. At some point the stock that has been "borrowed" in this way has to be returned or, as the old adage has it, "He who sells what isn't his'n must buy it back or go to prison."

It should be noted that shorting of large-capitalization stocks and the subsequent buying back of the stocks shorted are not particularly difficult. Where smaller company stocks are involved, however, those who short them can sometimes run the serious risk of a "short squeeze." This is a situation where short sellers need to buy back the stock to square their position as the price of the stock is climbing, and therefore going against them, but find that there is simply not enough stock available to meet the demand of all short-sellers wishing to cover. This drives the price much higher still and can increase the short-seller's losses significantly.

On the face of it, the selling short of large-cap stocks (to avoid the short squeeze predicament) would appear to be a reasonable tool for the short-term trader to generate returns. Some readers looking at our technique may think to themselves that if we can consistently buy stocks from a contrarian perspective, that is when the price is relatively low, and are then able to sell quickly at a profit, surely we could do equally well selling short when the opposite circumstances occur. It would seem only natural for us to spot a stock that is toward the upper level of its 52-week range and then, on a day that both the market and the individual stock have risen, sell it short, wait for the inevitable downturn, and then buy the stock back at a profit.

Unfortunately, selling short is not the mirror image of buying into a long position, and this is for a number of reasons. The most important of these comes from the fact that the general trend of the market over time is upwards. It is for this reason that buy and hold is not in any sense a strategy that we would ever reject out of hand. While not every stock is destined to increase in value and earn a decent return for its holder, companies are in business to make a profit and earn a return for their shareholders and most established, well-capitalized companies with good business models and management, do exactly that. We mentioned earlier that in buying stocks we normally have the benefit of a wind at our backs. This is true for all who are long stocks. For those who go short, however, there is always a similar headwind against them, and so right from the get-go this impairs their odds of success in this kind of trading. The fact that a short-seller has to pay out, rather than receive any dividends that are paid on the stock he has sold short, only adds to the negative effect of this headwind. As if that were not enough for the short-seller to contend with, the practice is also covered by the so-called "uptick rule" instituted by the Securities and Exchange Commission (SEC) following the 1929 market crash for which short-sellers were unfairly given much of the blame. The rule stipulates that you can only sell a stock short at the point that its price trend is upwards. This is no different from the way we would want it to be using our contrarian principles should we be interested in shorting stocks, but it does indicate how the dice have been loaded against the short-seller. There is no equivalent rule on the long side that says that you are only allowed to buy a stock that is going down.

Another reason why selling short is not a good fit specifically for our trading technique is the fact that the short-seller is betting a little against a lot. Should the short-seller mimic our technique on the long side, he may gain $50 to $100 if the stock falls and he takes his profit as we prescribe. But should the stock not fall back and instead climb further, or should the company receive a takeover offer from another company, which would likely drive up its price significantly, the losses could be very large indeed—the risk-to-reward ratio is completely out of sync. While our policy is to hold positions that do not quickly make our desired profit, and sometimes even to buy an additional number of shares after the stock has dropped a point or two, such an approach on the short side would be expensive and might wreck the entire trading strategy. Keep in mind that on the long side, the worst that can happen (and it is not very likely if you stick to good, well-established companies) is that your company goes bust and you lose your entire investment. On the short side, however, your risk if the position goes against you and you hold on is theoretically infinite.

Very few people are clever enough to win at the short game. Some like Jim Chanos have become well known Wall Street icons for their skill with this technique. Hedge funds, which have been around for decades, but recently have become one of the most important groups of alternative investment pools operating in the financial markets, have successfully used short selling as one of their trading and hedging tools. For the man in the street and for those we have targeted as our readers, we strongly caution that selling short is much too risky a proposition to consider as part of what we consider our essentially risk-averse trading strategy.

For any contrarian, however, the temptation to engage in at least some limited short selling will be especially strong at times when a very frothy bull market is under way, especially such as the one that became a veritable bubble towards the end of the 1990s. The problem with taking the plunge with the shorting technique in such circumstances is that no matter how right you may be about the market being in bubble territory and the inevitability of an eventual retrenchment, the correct timing of your move is extremely difficult to pinpoint as bubble markets can continue to defy gravity for much longer than seems rational or possible. As John Maynard Keynes shrewdly observed, "Markets can remain irrational for longer than you can remain solvent."

If our warnings on the subject of shorting stocks still do not steer the trader away from this technique, then we suggest that one sector that holds less risk than most for some very limited shorting is the airline sector. This may seem a strange choice, especially as the airlines have at the time of writing been going through something of a consolidation phase, with stock prices rising to reflect the merger activity and speculation on future deals. (Then again, this is precisely what should make a contrarian considering a short position sit up and take notice.) In a historical context, however, major airlines are a *terrible* business to be in, with huge fixed costs in aircraft and staffing (and post-9/11 all those additional security measures) that have to be covered whatever the business environment. Airlines are also particularly vulnerable to high oil prices, which spike with unceasing regularity and have often helped push the major airlines into the red. Even though dozens of airlines have come and gone since the passing of the United States Airlines Deregulation Act of 1978, the majors have over the years become adept at rebooting themselves in the bankruptcy courts, with the result that there are still too many of them around to be seriously competitive. This is unlikely to change even after the current merger cycle is complete. The airline business is simply too glamorous for new entrants not to want to come in and there are few barriers to entry in the U.S. market following the 1978 Act. For those that also operate in international skies, the overcrowding of the market is even more daunting as every country wants to run its own, often government-owned or controlled flag-carrier, whatever kind of sinkhole for taxpayers' money that might represent. There have been a few exceptions (such as Southwest Airlines) to the remark usually credited to Virgin Atlantic Airways founder Sir Richard Branson that "the best way to become a millionaire is to start as a billionaire and then buy an airline." But Warren Buffett probably had the measure of the intrinsically poor quality of the airline business when he made this wry comment; "If I'd been at Kitty Hawk in 1903 when Orville Wright took off, I would have been farsighted enough, and public-spirited enough—I owe this to future capitalists—to shoot him down." This came from the same investing genius who struggled mightily with an investment in US Airways that led him to quip in 1997; "Those who have watched my moves in this investment know that I have compiled a record that is unblemished by success." All told a strategy of selling short a big airline company such as AMR Corp. (owner of American Airlines, stock symbol AMR) or Continental Airlines (CAL) when oil prices are relatively low and buying the stock back when the inevitable oil price rise comes around and depresses the stock might work well for someone determined to try his luck with short selling. Again, we ourselves do not recommend this risk-laden technique to anybody. Indeed, as we put the finishing touches to this chapter, the salutary lesson of what can go wrong with even a well-thought-through trading strategy on the short side was made apparent when rumors surfaced and were reported on in *Business Week* that British Airways and Goldman Sachs were considering a joint bid for AMR. The alleged target stock jumped almost 5 percent at market open on February 16, 2007. It subsequently appeared that such a combination might be fanciful, especially as current rules limit foreign ownership of any U.S. airline's voting stock to 25 percent. But the simple fact that it could be aired as a serious possibility shows that shorting, even of an airline stock, is always a risky strategy.

CHECKING THE FUTURES

One habit worth following each day is to check in with the TV financial news in the early morning to see the Dow Jones futures price, reflecting the market price of the standard futures contracts on the Dow Jones Industrial Average that are traded on the Chicago Board of Trade (CBOT). Futures contracts are agreements to buy or sell a specific amount of a commodity or financial instrument at a stipulated future date. Futures contracts can be sold at any time before the settlement date. Futures can be used for hedging (to offset other related risk positions) or for speculation, (to make a bet on the direction of future prices to obtain a profit). Standard contracts in the Dow futures run for set three-month periods. Their quoted price, along with those for the S&P and NASDAQ 100 futures prices can be seen on CNBC as part of the financial information they display on the screen in a "bug" throughout their early morning reopening market coverage. These futures contracts trade around the clock, with activity in Asia and Europe while the United States is asleep. The CBOT offers electronic trading in the Dow futures between the hours of 6:15 P.M. and 7:00 A.M. (CST) and the CBOT trading floor itself commences open auction trading at 7:20 A.M. (CST). As with the underlying indices themselves, we think the Dow Jones Industrial Average futures number is the one deserving of the closest attention, as it relates to the index that we perceive as the closest market proxy in existence, whether that status is based on logic or not (see Chapter 5).

Any morning of the week, the Dow Jones Industrial Average futures price can be checked to see if it is up or down from the previous day. Should the number show a strong change to the plus or minus side, this represents a good indicator of likely market sentiment at the opening of the stock market itself. Please note that a small plus or minus change is not an indication that the market will open in that direction. A strong upside futures movement, however, indicating strong buying interest of the futures in Asia and Europe as well as an optimistic frame of mind on the part of early U.S. futures traders, bodes well for a stock market opening on the upside at 9:30 A.M. EST. A strongly negative futures number equally presages a lower opening of the stock market. The futures number therefore provides a very good indicator of whether the contrarian short-term trader should be poised to sell (into strength) or buy (into weakness) soon after the market opens.

Interestingly, the indicators given by a strong futures index number have a very strong correlation with the market open, but not so much with the trading session overall. So the value of checking this number in the morning is probably greatest for the short-term trader. It will probably only be helpful to him if he has the opportunity to check the market and act on the market action soon after the open. Be aware, however, that buying right at the open is not usually a good idea as individual stocks can take a few minutes following their first trade to settle a little and start trading with normal spreads between bid and ask prices. Right at the open there is a tendency for the trader to be hit by both the broader spread and a greater likelihood of "slippage," where the price achieved for a buy or sell order may not be as good as that posted at the time he places his order to trade with his online broker. Our best advice is to be sensitive to the signs that the Dow futures may have given you regarding the likely direction of opening prices, but not to rush to buy or sell in the first three or four minutes of market trading.

RECORDKEEPING

At this point a word on the keeping of trading records might be helpful. In order to be able to take advantage of the trading technique we use and have found successful, it is very important that the trader keeps good records of each trade. Depending on your personality, adeptness with spreadsheets, or other factors, this may involve records kept on a spreadsheet on your PC, or you may make do with simple handwritten records. Either way, the information that you need to keep comprises the number of shares and the identity of the stock bought, purchase date and cost per share and the cost of the purchases in dollars net of commissions paid. It should be clear from your records that the position is open until it is in fact sold, at which time the date of sale, the selling price per share and the total proceeds net of brokerage commissions should be entered next to the purchase, as well as profit made on the trade net of commissions. The records should be easily accessible in such a way that on a day and at a time that the market is solidly up, you can quickly look at each open position to verify whether it has reached the set price target for it to be sold. Equally, the information should be set out in such a way that on a day and at a time when the market is showing a significant decline, you can refer back to positions that you previously bought and then sold, to see which stocks have fallen back to a previous buy price and so are again primed for purchase.

THE GUESTS WHO WON'T GO HOME

This book has used as its foundation our trading record for the 26 months that ended February 28, 2007. Details of all completed trades, 1,225 of them and all profitable, are laid out in Appendixes A through C. Trading profit figures are in all cases net of brokerage commissions so represent a true trading profit before taxes, and exclude dividends received. As we have indicated in our explanation of our trading technique, it is no surprise that none of our trades were loss-makers as we hold on to positions until they turn around and reach their profitability target and are then sold. Appendix D contains full details on all stocks we bought in the 26 months covered by this book but that remained unsold at the end of February 2007, of which there were a total of 48 positions, or 50 when Viacom's split into Viacom and CBS is counted. We would consider those that were purchased from August 2006 onward to represent those that fit into our typical trading patterns in which we fully accept that around half of our stock purchases need to be held longer than a week to close the trade. However, if we look back at the 17 stock positions that we purchased prior to August 1, 2006, or seven months prior to the closing date of our record for this book, then you can perhaps see why we would consider the 13 companies behind these 17 open positions to be *guests who won't go home.* You should recognize the allusion to dinner party hosts who find that there are always guests who, for whatever reason, cannot understand that the party is over and it is time that they follow the example of the other guests and leave. It doesn't matter how many hints are dropped, there they sit comfortable with that last cup of coffee. If you look at our guests that won't go home in Appendix D, and compare to our record of completed trades in the other appendixes, you will see that for several of these tardy guests, Wal-Mart Stores, Tyco International, Juniper Networks, Intel, and The Cheesecake Factory, the purchases that were made in them were followed by other roundtrip trades (sometimes many others) in the same stocks at lower levels. In the case of certain of these still-open positions, such as Viacom, Ford, Gateway,

Yahoo!, and Qualcomm, the open position was one that came after a series of profitable trades in each stock at levels similar to or higher than this specific purchase. Then there are the trades that stand alone, one-time buys that have not yet come back to the target price that would see them sold at our targeted profit; Fannie Mae and Fifth Third Bancorp.

Holding on to losing positions for a longer period of time in the hope that they will eventually recover is often cited as an example of one of the classic mistakes made by the nonprofessional investor. Clearly we are guilty of it in the case of each of the 13 companies' stocks, although keeping things in perspective, the longest held is Fannie Mae at just over 25 months. So why would we continue to hold these positions and await a profitable outcome, rather than accept defeat, sell them, and take the capital loss tax deduction? The reason is simple. In each and every case, we believe that the 13 companies are buys at *current* levels and not sells, this being based on the market price today and not the market price we paid. While it would be nice to admit we got these 13 wrong and then to be able to sell them for the exact amount we paid for them, this is not the way it works. With the 20/20 vision afforded by hindsight, we recognize that our purchases were made too early. But if the stocks were contrarian buys when we bought into them, they became even more so as their stock prices were pushed down further by internal corporate or market developments. This would include unfolding accounting scandals at Fannie Mae (FNM), resulting in investigations by the Securities Exchange Commission (SEC) and the Office of Federal Housing Enterprise Oversight (OFHEO), as well as serious management problems exacerbated by a poorly digested acquisition resulting in regulatory sanctions from the Federal Reserve at Fifth Third Bancorp (FITB). Sure, we would have preferred to have bought Fannie Mae at its low of $41 in October 2005, or Fifth Third Bancorp at its low of $36 in July 2006, but we fully expect both stocks, as well as all of the other guests that won't go home, to be sold for our requisite profit at some stage in the near to medium-term future. This would include even Gateway, which as of February 28, 2007, had lost 30 percent of its value since we bought it in December 2005, but which had been successfully ripple traded by us nine times previous to that during October and November 2005 for a profit of $860.

[Authors' postscript added in June 2007: As of May 31, 2007, 7 of the lingering 17 guests had finally decided to call it a night and make their way home. We closed them out as profitable roundtrip trades in a strongly up-trending market. This included Fifth Third Bancorp, sold for $41.97 on May 23. An additional 21 other open positions from February 28, 2007, as detailed in Appendix D, were closed out profitably in that same three-month period.]

FINAL THOUGHTS

It is our hope that this book will prove useful to people on a number of different levels. There may be those who will look at our trading results for a 26-month period as laid out in the appendixes and will be motivated to follow the principles of our trading method as closely as possible so as to have a chance to replicate the kind of trading record that is evidenced there. Of course, in the words of the classic disclaimer, "Past performance is no guarantee of future results." It must be understood that all we can do in this book is to set out some tried-and-tested (by us) techniques together with trading records to show that they have worked. The techniques basically revolve around stock buys prompted by the stock in question having moved to a position close to its 52-week low and paying close attention to the fluctuations that are a defining characteristic of markets generally and the stock market specifically. We have found it to be a valuable technique for short-term trading to use the fluctuations of the market over a typical two to three day period, buying when the market and the stock being targeted have trended downward—thereby being in some sense on sale. We have also espoused a discipline whereby profits are taken essentially as soon as the desired level of profit has been reached, with a view to being able to "ride the ripples," buying and selling the same targeted stocks over and over again, a profit being taken on each roundtrip. If you do follow our method, good luck to you!

Please recognize that we have not, and indeed are not able to, put in place a trading system on "autopilot." Whether this technique works well or badly for you depends on three things. First, you need to have the necessary self-discipline to follow what is a thoroughly contrarian trading strategy with all the emotional and psychological resistance that brings with it. Second, you need to put together for yourself a list or "portfolio" of company stocks that you can monitor for the requisite contrarian buy signals, but ensure that you have enough knowledge of your monitored companies to know that being "on sale" means good ripple trading profits are available at lower levels in the stock price rather than a swift plunge into bankruptcy. If you are a bad stock-picker because you are easily taken by flights of fancy about some stocks, especially those that are "hot" for a short period of time, you will probably not do well with this technique. Neither will you if you have the tendency to buy a stock simply because you see it written up in the press, or touted by a TV pundit. Third, never forget the importance of luck. While not a casino, the stock market can often be seen to bestow its favors on those who deserve them least and at the same time has a tendency often to bite the more deserving in a part of the anatomy where sitting ability may be impaired in future.

There will be those whose take-away from this book is a nugget of information on a stock or two that we have mentioned, or maybe some insight into a subject such as ADRs or selling short. If this is you, good luck to you as well. You may find that even that tidbit of information may have been worth the cost of buying the book.

For those who put this book down and say it serves them in no way at all, good luck to you also. There are as many ways to approach investing and trading as there are people who do it, and if a technique is not for you, then do not despair—just find one that does works for you. But never lose sight of one thing. The money that you win or lose in your stock market trading and/or investing is real money. Do not use money that you can ill-afford to lose should things turn against you.

Happy trading!

Trading Record for 2005 (Net of All Commissions)

Stock	Date Sold	Date Purchased	Proceeds	Cost	Profit	Percent Profit Annualized
300 Corning Inc.	1/3/2005	12/28/2004	$3,583	$3,532	$51	88%
100 Viacom	1/3/2005	12/29/2004	$3,740	$3,691	$49	97%
200 Intel	1/3/2005	12/30/2004	$4,720	$4,664	$56	110%
100 Viacom	1/5/2005	12/27/2004	$3,773	$3,730	$43	47%
200 SBC Communications	1/5/2005	1/4/2005	$5,145	$5,102	$43	308%
100 AstraZeneca	1/5/2005	1/4/2005	$3,636	$3,589	$47	478%
100 CIT Group	1/6/2005	1/6/2005	$4,256	$4,211	$45	390%
100 CIT Group	1/6/2005	1/6/2005	$4,260	$4,206	$54	469%
100 3M Co.	1/7/2005	1/4/2005	$8,263	$8,196	$67	99%
300 Corning Inc.	1/7/2005	12/28/2004	$3,563	$3,532	$31	32%
200 Barrick Gold	1/11/2005	1/6/2005	$4,518	$4,458	$60	98%
100 Commerce Bancorp	1/13/2005	1/4/2005	$6,391	$6,203	$188	123%
300 Advanced Micro Devices	1/13/2005	1/12/2005	$4,553	$4,516	$37	299%
300 Corning Inc.	1/18/2005	1/3/2005	$3,572	$3,532	$40	28%
100 Viacom	1/18/2005	5/6/2004	$3,907	$3,867	$40	2%
200 Barrick Gold	1/24/2005	1/13/2005	$4,560	$4,462	$98	73%
100 Coca-Cola Co.	1/27/2005	1/4/2005	$4,180	$4,136	$44	17%
100 AstraZeneca	1/27/2005	12/21/2004	$3,745	$3,673	$72	19%
100 AstraZeneca	1/27/2005	12/21/2004	$3,727	$3,667	$60	16%
100 AstraZeneca	1/27/2005	1/14/2005	$3,745	$3,576	$169	133%
100 Qualcomm	1/31/2005	1/24/2005	$3,723	$3,682	$41	58%
100 State Street Corp.	1/31/2005	1/26/2005	$4,470	$4,430	$40	66%
200 SBC Communications	1/31/2005	1/28/2005	$4,776	$4,734	$42	108%
				Subtotal	**$1,417**	
200 News Corporation	2/2/2005	1/19/2005	$3,560	$3,504	$56	42%
100 Wal-Mart Stores	2/2/2005	1/28/2005	$5,294	$5,243	$51	71%
200 Barrick Gold	2/2/2005	2/1/2005	$4,382	$4,340	$42	353%

(Continues)

Stock	Date Sold	Date Purchased	Proceeds	Cost	Profit	Percent Profit Annualized
170 Barrick Gold	2/3/2005	2/3/2005	$3,723	$3,677	$46	457%
200 News Corporation	2/4/2005	2/3/2005	$3,518	$3,468	$50	526%
100 Clear Channel Comms.	2/7/2005	1/3/2005	$3,389	$3,335	$54	17%
100 CIT Group	2/7/2005	1/20/2005	$4,191	$4,129	$62	30%
100 Intl. Game Technology	2/7/2005	1/28/2005	$3,142	$3,097	$45	53%
100 Qualcomm	2/7/2005	2/1/2005	$3,734	$3,679	$55	91%
200 Intel	2/8/2005	1/3/2005	$4,682	$4,644	$38	8%
300 Corning Inc.	2/8/2005	1/20/2005	$3,594	$3,520	$74	40%
300 Corning Inc.	2/8/2005	1/21/2005	$3,557	$3,511	$46	27%
100 Tyco International	2/8/2005	2/3/2005	$3,453	$3,401	$52	112%
200 Pfizer Inc.	2/8/2005	1/20/2005	$5,070	$4,988	$82	32%
180 Barrick Gold	2/9/2005	2/8/2005	$3,904	$3,857	$47	445%
200 Barrick Gold	2/10/2005	1/25/2005	$4,487	$4,462	$25	13%
200 Barrick Gold	2/10/2005	2/3/2005	$4,487	$4,338	$149	179%
1000 Central Fund of Canada	2/14/2005	1/3/2005	$5,450	$5,400	$50	8%
200 Micron Technology	2/14/2005	1/7/2005	$2,333	$2,284	$49	21%
200 Micron Technology	2/14/2005	1/11/2005	$2,317	$2,255	$62	30%
100 Qualcomm	2/14/2005	2/7/2005	$3,676	$3,629	$47	68%
100 CIT Group	2/14/2005	2/8/2005	$4,166	$4,120	$46	68%
200 News Corporation	2/14/2005	2/9/2005	$3,516	$3,472	$44	93%
100 Intl. Game Technology	2/14/2005	2/9/2005	$3,143	$3,096	$47	111%
100 Eli Lilly	2/14/2005	2/9/2005	$5,568	$5,522	$46	61%
300 Corning Inc.	2/14/2005	2/9/2005	$3,566	$3,526	$40	83%
100 Tyco International	2/14/2005	2/10/2005	$3,405	$3,350	$55	150%
100 Genentech	2/14/2005	2/10/2005	$4,658	$4,572	$86	172%
100 Intel	2/14/2005	12/31/2004	$2,403	$2,340	$63	22%
100 Wal-Mart Stores	2/15/2005	2/10/2005	$5,277	$5,236	$41	57%
100 Eli Lilly	2/15/2005	2/15/2005	$5,560	$5,515	$45	298%
300 Corning Inc.	2/16/2005	2/16/2005	$3,565	$3,523	$42	435%
300 Corning Inc.	2/16/2005	2/16/2005	$3,566	$3,511	$55	572%
100 Reuters	2/16/2005	2/19/2004	$4,717	$4,627	$90	2%
100 Tyco International	2/16/2005	2/16/2005	$3,360	$3,319	$41	451%
200 Avaya Inc.	2/17/2005	2/9/2005	$2,725	$2,684	$41	70%
200 Pfizer Inc.	2/18/2005	2/16/2005	$5,034	$4,976	$58	213%
200 Bristol-Myers Squibb	2/22/2005	1/13/2005	$4,951	$4,909	$42	8%
200 Bristol-Myers Squibb	2/23/2005	1/13/2005	$4,956	$4,912	$44	8%
200 Avaya Inc.	2/23/2005	2/22/2005	$2,693	$2,652	$41	564%
200 Intel	2/24/2005	2/23/2005	$4,707	$4,654	$53	416%
100 Qualcomm	2/25/2005	2/16/2005	$3,652	$3,620	$32	36%
100 Eli Lilly	2/25/2005	2/17/2005	$5,573	$5,519	$54	45%
100 Tyco International	2/25/2005	2/16/2005	$3,381	$3,336	$45	55%
100 Reuters	2/25/2005	2/18/2004	$4,809	$4,761	$48	1%
200 Micron Technology	2/25/2005	2/24/2005	$2,323	$2,280	$43	688%
100 Wal-Mart Stores	2/28/2005	2/25/2005	$5,192	$5,128	$64	152%
				Subtotal	**$2,488**	
100 Commerce Bancorp	3/1/2005	1/14/2005	$6,238	$6,161	$77	10%
100 Qualcomm	3/1/2005	2/28/2005	$3,659	$3,615	$44	444%
100 Biogen Idec	3/1/2005	3/1/2005	$4,106	$4,062	$44	395%
100 CIT Group	3/1/2005	2/22/2005	$4,128	$4,088	$40	51%
100 State Street Corp.	3/2/2005	2/17/2005	$4,467	$4,419	$48	30%
100 CIT Group	3/2/2005	2/22/2005	$4,141	$4,092	$49	55%
200 News Corporation	3/2/2005	2/22/2005	$3,486	$3,444	$42	56%

Stock	Date Sold	Date Purchased	Proceeds	Cost	Profit	Percent Profit Annualized
300 Time Warner	3/2/2005	2/24/2005	$5,315	$5,242	$73	85%
100 Qualcomm	3/2/2005	3/2/2005	$3,660	$3,603	$57	577%
100 Chiron	3/2/2005	10/8/2004	$3,904	$3,684	$220	15%
100 Wal-Mart Stores	3/3/2005	2/22/2005	$5,295	$5,223	$72	56%
250 Corning Inc.	3/3/2005	2/22/2005	$2,933	$2,887	$46	65%
100 CIT Group	3/4/2005	3/2/2005	$4,161	$4,092	$69	308%
100 Commerce Bancorp	3/7/2005	1/13/2005	$6,348	$6,296	$52	6%
100 Qualcomm	3/7/2005	3/3/2005	$3,627	$3,558	$69	177%
100 Qualcomm	3/7/2005	3/3/2005	$3,632	$3,585	$47	120%
100 Qualcomm	3/9/2005	3/9/2005	$3,661	$3,604	$57	577%
300 Time Warner	3/10/2005	3/9/2005	$5,289	$5,239	$50	348%
100 Clear Channel Comms.	3/11/2005	3/9/2005	$3,373	$3,330	$43	236%
100 Clear Channel Comms.	3/11/2005	3/9/2005	$3,368	$3,327	$41	225%
100 Genentech	3/14/2005	1/11/2005	$5,388	$5,143	$245	28%
100 Genentech	3/14/2005	3/10/2005	$5,364	$4,485	$879	1788%
100 Chiron	3/14/2005	3/11/2005	$3,714	$3,665	$49	163%
300 Time Warner	3/15/2005	3/14/2005	$5,303	$5,242	$61	425%
300 Corning Inc.	3/15/2005	3/8/2005	$3,467	$3,421	$46	70%
100 Viacom	3/17/2005	2/16/2005	$3,845	$3,683	$162	55%
100 Viacom	3/17/2005	2/22/2005	$3,845	$3,619	$226	99%
100 Genentech	3/21/2005	3/17/2005	$5,780	$5,304	$476	819%
100 General Motors	3/21/2005	3/17/2005	$2,975	$2,833	$142	457%
100 General Motors	3/21/2005	3/17/2005	$2,973	$2,843	$130	417%
100 General Motors	3/21/2005	3/18/2005	$2,962	$2,820	$142	613%
200 Bristol-Myers Squibb	3/22/2005	3/21/2005	$4,997	$4,837	$160	1207%
200 General Motors	3/22/2005	3/22/2005	$5,910	$5,855	$55	343%
100 CIT Group	3/23/2005	3/18/2005	$3,905	$3,862	$43	81%
200 General Motors	3/23/2005	3/23/2005	$5,781	$5,735	$46	293%
100 IBM	3/24/2005	3/16/2005	$9,114	$9,072	$42	21%
100 Clear Channel Comms.	3/24/2005	3/22/2005	$3,370	$3,324	$46	253%
100 CIT Group	3/24/2005	3/23/2005	$3,883	$3,843	$40	380%
200 General Motors	3/24/2005	3/23/2005	$5,793	$5,739	$54	343%
200 SBC Communications	3/28/2005	3/17/2005	$4,718	$4,674	$44	31%
100 AIG	3/29/2005	3/22/2005	$5,801	$5,698	$103	94%
100 IBM	3/29/2005	3/29/2005	$9,086	$9,044	$42	170%
100 Commerce Bancorp	3/30/2005	3/9/2005	$3,158	$3,096	$62	35%
100 Qualcomm	3/30/2005	3/24/2005	$3,672	$3,601	$71	120%
200 General Motors	3/30/2005	3/28/2005	$5,839	$5,797	$42	132%
1000 Central Fund of Canada	3/30/2005	3/28/2005	$5,355	$5,315	$40	137%
100 General Motors	3/30/2005	3/28/2005	$2,918	$2,863	$55	351%
100 Commerce Bancorp	3/31/2005	3/8/2005	$3,235	$3,153	$82	41%
100 State Street Corp.	3/31/2005	3/23/2005	$4,376	$4,336	$40	42%
300 Time Warner	3/31/2005	3/29/2005	$5,290	$5,237	$53	185%
100 IBM	3/31/2005	3/29/2005	$9,089	$9,040	$49	99%
				Subtotal	**$4,967**	
200 General Motors	4/1/2005	3/22/2005	$5,994	$5,899	$95	59%
200 General Motors	4/1/2005	4/1/2005	$5,928	$5,873	$55	342%
100 United Technologies	4/1/2005	4/1/2005	$10,097	$10,063	$34	123%
100 State Street Corp.	4/1/2005	3/23/2005	$4,388	$4,334	$54	51%
200 General Motors	4/4/2005	4/1/2005	$5,953	$5,888	$65	134%

(Continues)

Stock	Date Sold	Date Purchased	Proceeds	Cost	Profit	Percent Profit Annualized
100 Commerce Bancorp	4/4/2005	4/4/2005	$3,166	$3,121	$45	526%
100 CIT Group	4/5/2005	3/31/2005	$3,847	$3,795	$52	100%
100 Verizon	4/5/2005	3/31/2005	$3,578	$3,531	$47	97%
300 Time Warner	4/5/2005	4/1/2005	$5,280	$5,239	$41	71%
300 Corning Inc.	4/6/2005	3/15/2005	$3,495	$3,418	$77	37%
100 Chiron	4/6/2005	3/16/2005	$3,734	$3,658	$76	38%
100 Lloyds TSB Group	4/6/2005	4/4/2005	$3,625	$3,572	$53	271%
200 General Motors	4/6/2005	4/4/2005	$5,910	$5,868	$42	131%
100 General Motors	4/6/2005	4/1/2005	$2,982	$2,941	$41	102%
100 Lloyds TSB Group	4/7/2005	3/29/2005	$3,643	$3,600	$43	48%
100 United Technologies	4/7/2005	4/4/2005	$10,100	$10,039	$61	74%
300 Corning Inc.	4/8/2005	2/18/2005	$3,630	$3,523	$107	23%
200 Microsoft	4/8/2005	3/16/2005	$5,008	$4,958	$50	17%
200 Intel	4/8/2005	3/31/2005	$4,694	$4,652	$42	41%
100 Merck	4/8/2005	10/6/2004	$3,350	$3,315	$35	2%
200 General Motors	4/11/2005	4/11/2005	$5,819	$5,777	$42	265%
100 Tyco International	4/12/2005	3/31/2005	$3,433	$3,392	$41	37%
100 Commerce Bancorp	4/12/2005	4/8/2005	$3,159	$3,115	$44	129%
100 Commerce Bancorp	4/12/2005	4/11/2005	$3,144	$3,084	$60	710%
100 Morgan Stanley	4/12/2005	4/12/2005	$5,451	$5,409	$42	283%
100 United Technologies	4/12/2005	4/12/2005	$10,022	$9,977	$45	165%
300 Corning Inc.	4/12/2005	4/12/2005	$3,556	$3,515	$41	426%
100 Eli Lilly	4/13/2005	3/14/2005	$5,576	$5,484	$92	20%
100 Commerce Bancorp	4/13/2005	4/13/2005	$2,974	$2,930	$44	548%
100 Adobe Systems	4/18/2005	4/18/2005	$5,458	$5,407	$51	344%
100 State Street Corp.	4/19/2005	4/8/2005	$4,453	$4,292	$161	124%
1000 Central Fund of Canada	4/19/2005	4/14/2005	$5,355	$5,305	$50	69%
100 Nike Inc.	4/19/2005	4/15/2005	$7,752	$7,636	$116	139%
100 Coca-Cola	4/19/2005	4/18/2005	$4,234	$4,088	$146	1304%
100 JP Morgan Chase	4/20/2005	3/24/2005	$3,546	$3,497	$49	19%
300 Corning Inc.	4/20/2005	4/13/2005	$3,690	$3,523	$167	247%
100 United Technologies	4/21/2005	4/14/2005	$10,088	$10,042	$46	24%
100 Colgate-Palmolive	4/21/2005	4/20/2005	$5,185	$5,146	$39	277%
100 General Electric	4/21/2005	4/20/2005	$3,598	$3,557	$41	421%
100 Nike Inc.	4/21/2005	4/20/2005	$7,801	$7,635	$166	794%
300 Time Warner	4/22/2005	4/15/2005	$5,285	$5,233	$52	52%
200 Intel	4/25/2005	4/11/2005	$4,681	$4,639	$42	24%
100 Verizon	4/29/2005	4/11/2005	$3,553	$3,513	$40	23%
100 United Technologies	4/29/2005	4/27/2005	$10,086	$10,031	$55	100%
1000 Central Fund of Canada	4/29/2005	4/28/2005	$5,366	$5,310	$56	385%
200 Intel	4/29/2005	4/28/2005	$4,692	$4,650	$42	330%
100 Nike Inc.	4/29/2005	4/29/2005	$7,677	$7,621	$56	268%
				Subtotal	**$2,941**	
100 Anheuser-Busch	5/2/2005	4/29/2005	$4,725	$4,680	$45	117%
100 General Motors	5/3/2005	4/14/2005	$2,751	$2,709	$42	30%
1000 Central Fund of Canada	5/3/2005	5/2/2005	$5,355	$5,305	$50	344%
100 Adobe Systems	5/3/2005	5/2/2005	$5,755	$5,704	$51	326%
200 General Motors	5/4/2005	4/8/2005	$6,069	$5,914	$155	37%
200 General Motors	5/4/2005	4/14/2005	$6,307	$5,633	$674	218%
300 Ford Motor	5/4/2005	4/12/2005	$3,097	$3,047	$50	27%
200 Tyco International	5/4/2005	5/4/2005	$5,749	$5,699	$50	320%
100 Morgan Stanley	5/5/2005	5/2/2005	$5,049	$5,003	$46	112%
100 Adobe Systems	5/6/2005	5/5/2005	$5,737	$5,695	$42	269%

Stock	Date Sold	Date Purchased	Proceeds	Cost	Profit	Percent Profit Annualized
300 Ford Motor	5/9/2005	5/5/2005	$3,016	$2,972	$44	135%
1000 Central Fund of Canada	5/9/2005	5/6/2005	$5,345	$5,305	$40	92%
100 Lazard	5/10/2005	5/9/2005	$2,351	$2,303	$48	761%
1000 Central Fund of Canada	5/10/2005	5/9/2005	$5,345	$5,305	$40	275%
100 Procter & Gamble	5/10/2005	5/10/2005	$5,506	$5,462	$44	294%
100 Morgan Stanley	5/12/2005	5/10/2005	$5,009	$4,966	$43	158%
100 Colgate-Palmolive	5/16/2005	5/13/2005	$4,914	$4,873	$41	102%
100 Procter & Gamble	5/16/2005	5/13/2005	$5,515	$5,460	$55	123%
100 Qualcomm	5/18/2005	4/1/2005	$3,641	$3,598	$43	9%
100 JP Morgan Chase	5/18/2005	5/12/2005	$3,549	$3,488	$61	106%
200 Barrick Gold	5/18/2005	5/13/2005	$4,383	$4,343	$40	67%
100 Lloyds TSB Group	5/18/2005	5/17/2005	$3,423	$3,382	$41	442%
300 Ford Motor	5/18/2005	5/10/2005	$2,984	$2,941	$43	67%
300 Time Warner	5/19/2005	4/25/2005	$5,266	$5,194	$72	21%
300 Time Warner	5/19/2005	4/26/2005	$5,272	$5,219	$53	16%
300 Ford Motor	5/19/2005	5/10/2005	$2,998	$2,954	$44	60%
100 Anheuser-Busch	5/19/2005	5/10/2005	$4,722	$4,681	$41	36%
100 Morgan Stanley	5/19/2005	5/13/2005	$4,983	$4,932	$51	63%
100 CIT Group	5/23/2005	3/9/2005	$4,170	$4,079	$91	11%
200 Bell South	5/23/2005	5/5/2005	$5,334	$5,282	$52	20%
200 Barrick Gold	5/23/2005	5/20/2005	$4,381	$4,339	$42	118%
100 Exxon Mobil	5/23/2005	5/20/2005	$5,449	$5,409	$40	90%
100 Morgan Stanley	5/23/2005	5/10/2005	$5,027	$4,976	$51	29%
100 Anheuser-Busch	5/24/2005	5/24/2005	$4,713	$4,668	$45	352%
100 Suncor Energy	5/25/2005	5/18/2005	$3,774	$3,717	$57	80%
100 Morgan Stanley	5/25/2005	5/24/2005	$4,970	$4,922	$48	356%
200 Intel	5/26/2005	7/2/2004	$5,430	$5,377	$53	1%
200 Intel	5/26/2005	7/2/2004	$5,445	$5,365	$80	2%
300 Ford Motor	5/27/2005	5/25/2005	$3,028	$2,966	$62	381%
100 Lloyds TSB Group	5/27/2005	5/26/2005	$3,368	$3,333	$35	383%
				Subtotal	**$2,705**	
100 Goldman Sachs	6/1/2005	5/25/2005	$9,899	$9,838	$61	32%
100 Goldman Sachs	6/1/2005	6/1/2005	$9,837	$9,788	$49	183%
100 Morgan Stanley	6/1/2005	5/31/2005	$4,952	$4,908	$44	327%
100 Morgan Stanley	6/1/2005	5/31/2005	$4,968	$4,905	$63	469%
100 Lloyds TSB Group	6/1/2005	5/26/2005	$3,369	$3,328	$41	75%
1000 Central Fund of Canada	6/2/2005	5/11/2005	$5,395	$5,305	$90	28%
100 Reuters	6/2/2005	5/23/2005	$4,307	$4,266	$41	35%
100 Goldman Sachs	6/2/2005	6/2/2005	$9,831	$9,786	$45	168%
100 State Street Corp.	6/3/2005	7/6/2004	$4,984	$4,923	$61	1%
100 Goldman Sachs	6/7/2005	6/2/2005	$9,901	$9,781	$120	90%
100 Morgan Stanley	6/7/2005	6/3/2005	$4,936	$4,894	$42	78%
100 Reuters	6/7/2005	6/3/2005	$4,380	$4,261	$119	255%
100 Lloyds TSB Group	6/8/2005	5/31/2005	$3,399	$3,342	$57	78%
200 Pfizer Inc.	6/10/2005	6/9/2005	$5,555	$5,509	$46	305%
1000 Central Fund of Canada	6/10/2005	6/10/2005	$5,345	$5,305	$40	275%
1000 Central Fund of Canada	6/10/2005	6/10/2005	$5,353	$5,307	$46	316%
100 Goldman Sachs	6/10/2005	6/10/2005	$9,925	$9,878	$47	174%
100 Goldman Sachs	6/13/2005	6/13/2005	$9,946	$9,875	$71	262%
100 Commerce Bancorp	6/14/2005	6/6/2005	$2,800	$2,760	$40	66%

(Continues)

Stock	Date Sold	Date Purchased	Proceeds	Cost	Profit	Percent Profit Annualized
100 Commerce Bancorp	6/14/2005	6/6/2005	$2,803	$2,757	$46	76%
100 Wal-Mart Stores	6/15/2005	4/1/2005	$5,006	$4,950	$56	6%
200 News Corporation	6/15/2005	4/14/2005	$3,480	$3,434	$46	8%
100 Goldman Sachs	6/15/2005	6/15/2005	$9,864	$9,823	$41	152%
100 Lazard	6/16/2005	5/11/2005	$2,354	$2,310	$44	19%
100 Goldman Sachs	6/16/2005	5/12/2005	$10,290	$10,190	$100	10%
1000 Central Fund of Canada	6/16/2005	6/14/2005	$5,375	$5,305	$70	241%
100 Colgate-Palmolive	6/20/2005	6/2/2005	$5,061	$4,988	$73	30%
100 Colgate-Palmolive	6/20/2005	6/2/2005	$5,031	$4,984	$47	19%
300 Time Warner	6/21/2005	5/31/2005	$5,269	$5,228	$41	14%
100 Commerce Bancorp	6/22/2005	4/14/2005	$3,023	$2,979	$44	8%
100 FedEx Corp	6/27/2005	6/24/2005	$8,050	$8,005	$45	68%
100 United Technologies	6/28/2005	6/24/2005	$5,233	$5,188	$45	79%
100 Procter & Gamble	6/28/2005	6/27/2005	$5,321	$5,281	$40	276%
100 FedEx Corp	6/28/2005	6/27/2005	$8,040	$8,000	$40	183%
100 Reuters	6/28/2005	6/27/2005	$4,257	$4,217	$40	346%
100 AIG	6/29/2005	3/30/2005	$5,797	$5,727	$70	5%
200 Bell South	6/29/2005	6/27/2005	$5,323	$5,282	$41	142%
200 MBNA	6/30/2005	6/16/2005	$5,314	$4,321	$993	599%
100 Commerce Bancorp	6/30/2005	6/24/2005	$3,010	$2,960	$50	103%
				Subtotal	**$3,095**	
100 Commerce Bancorp	7/1/2005	6/24/2005	$3,011	$2,962	$49	86%
200 Microsoft	7/5/2005	7/5/2005	$4,984	$4,942	$42	310%
100 United Technologies	7/7/2005	7/7/2005	$5,053	$5,012	$41	299%
100 Commerce Bancorp	7/8/2005	4/13/2005	$3,088	$3,047	$41	6%
100 IBM	7/8/2005	4/15/2005	$7,934	$7,887	$47	3%
100 Wal-Mart Stores	7/8/2005	6/16/2005	$4,992	$4,950	$42	14%
200 Microsoft	7/8/2005	7/7/2005	$4,988	$4,934	$54	399%
200 Bell South	7/8/2005	7/7/2005	$5,332	$5,288	$44	304%
100 General Electric	7/8/2005	7/7/2005	$3,465	$3,423	$42	448%
200 Micron Technology	7/11/2005	3/2/2005	$2,320	$2,270	$50	6%
190 Micron Technology	7/11/2005	3/2/2005	$2,224	$2,160	$64	8%
100 Procter & Gamble	7/11/2005	7/6/2005	$5,370	$5,263	$107	148%
100 Reuters	7/11/2005	7/6/2005	$4,263	$4,213	$50	87%
100 Lloyds TSB Group	7/11/2005	7/7/2005	$3,424	$3,319	$105	289%
100 JP Morgan Chase	7/11/2005	7/7/2005	$3,495	$3,455	$40	106%
100 Procter & Gamble	7/12/2005	6/23/2005	$5,430	$5,384	$46	16%
200 Walt Disney Co.	7/12/2005	7/5/2005	$5,050	$5,010	$40	42%
300 Avaya	7/13/2005	6/6/2005	$2,755	$2,686	$69	25%
200 News Corporation	7/13/2005	6/29/2005	$3,489	$3,445	$44	33%
200 Adobe Systems	7/13/2005	6/30/2005	$5,774	$5,734	$40	20%
200 MBNA	7/13/2005	7/1/2005	$5,198	$5,158	$40	24%
100 Procter & Gamble	7/14/2005	6/10/2005	$5,505	$5,452	$53	10%
100 Anheuser-Busch	7/14/2005	7/6/2005	$4,604	$4,564	$40	40%
200 Intel	7/15/2005	6/25/2004	$5,618	$5,577	$41	1%
100 United Technologies	7/19/2005	6/30/2005	$5,240	$5,189	$51	19%
100 Qualcomm	7/21/2005	1/20/2005	$3,892	$3,851	$41	9%
200 Microsoft	7/21/2005	2/15/2005	$5,248	$5,190	$58	3%
100 Qualcomm	7/21/2005	6/9/2005	$3,871	$3,641	$230	55%
100 Reuters	7/21/2005	7/20/2005	$4,229	$4,175	$54	472%
1000 Central Fund of Canada	7/21/2005	7/15/2005	$5,273	$5,227	$46	54%
100 Colgate-Palmolive	7/22/2005	4/25/2005	$5,180	$5,140	$40	3%
100 Washington Mutual	7/22/2005	6/1/2004	$4,317	$4,275	$42	1%
100 Washington Mutual	7/25/2005	6/1/2004	$4,339	$4,275	$64	1%

Stock	Date Sold	Date Purchased	Proceeds	Cost	Profit	Percent Profit Annualized
100 Morgan Stanley	7/25/2005	4/13/2005	$5,429	$5,384	$45	3%
200 Intel	7/27/2005	7/25/2005	$5,389	$5,341	$48	164%
100 Johnson & Johnson	7/27/2005	7/26/2005	$6,327	$6,282	$45	261%
100 Eli Lilly	7/28/2005	7/25/2005	$5,523	$5,482	$41	91%
				Subtotal	**$2,036**	
100 Biogen Idec	8/1/2005	3/3/2005	$4,026	$3,960	$66	4%
100 Clear Channel Comms.	8/1/2005	4/27/2005	$3,285	$3,240	$45	5%
200 Microsoft	8/1/2005	7/25/2005	$5,181	$5,141	$40	41%
100 Reuters	8/1/2005	7/27/2005	$4,143	$4,058	$85	153%
200 Adobe Systems	8/2/2005	8/2/2005	$5,653	$5,565	$88	577%
200 Sara Lee	8/3/2005	6/14/2005	$4,028	$3,982	$46	8%
1000 Central Fund of Canada	8/4/2005	6/28/2005	$5,370	$5,328	$42	8%
300 Time Warner	8/5/2005	6/23/2005	$5,287	$5,228	$59	10%
200 Microsoft	8/5/2005	11/16/2004	$5,534	$5,458	$76	2%
200 Tyco International	8/10/2005	8/2/2005	$5,623	$5,575	$48	39%
200 News Corporation	8/10/2005	8/3/2005	$3,485	$3,439	$46	70%
100 Morgan Stanley	8/10/2005	8/5/2005	$5,309	$5,266	$43	60%
100 United Technologies	8/11/2005	8/1/2005	$5,055	$5,010	$45	33%
1000 Central Fund of Canada	8/11/2005	8/9/2005	$5,335	$5,295	$40	138%
200 Walt Disney Co.	8/11/2005	8/10/2005	$5,137	$5,097	$40	286%
100 UBS	8/11/2005	8/10/2005	$8,375	$8,268	$107	472%
200 Intel	8/11/2005	8/11/2005	$5,335	$5,287	$48	331%
100 Procter & Gamble	8/11/2005	8/11/2005	$5,359	$5,314	$45	309%
100 United Technologies	8/12/2005	7/19/2005	$5,225	$5,183	$42	12%
100 Procter & Gamble	8/15/2005	8/12/2005	$5,377	$5,335	$42	96%
100 Morgan Stanley	8/15/2005	8/12/2005	$5,347	$5,282	$65	150%
100 Dow Jones & Co.	8/16/2005	2/17/2005	$4,090	$3,964	$126	6%
100 Johnson & Johnson	8/17/2005	8/16/2005	$6,353	$6,299	$54	313%
100 Procter & Gamble	8/18/2005	8/17/2005	$5,387	$5,334	$53	363%
100 Procter & Gamble	8/22/2005	8/4/2005	$5,516	$5,443	$73	27%
100 Dow Jones & Co.	8/22/2005	8/17/2005	$4,143	$3,969	$174	320%
100 UBS	8/22/2005	8/18/2005	$8,320	$8,245	$75	83%
100 Johnson & Johnson	8/31/2005	8/24/2005	$6,312	$6,266	$46	38%
100 iStar Financial	8/31/2005	8/26/2005	$4,168	$4,126	$42	74%
100 Nike Inc.	8/31/2005	8/30/2005	$7,886	$7,835	$51	238%
300 Ford Motor	8/31/2005	8/30/2005	$2,960	$2,917	$43	538%
				Subtotal	**$1,895**	
100 National Grid	9/1/2005	7/5/2005	$4,838	$4,725	$113	15%
100 UBS	9/1/2005	8/23/2005	$8,309	$8,269	$40	20%
1000 Central Fund of Canada	9/1/2005	8/26/2005	$5,355	$5,305	$50	57%
100 Lloyds TSB Group	9/2/2005	8/16/2005	$3,449	$3,339	$110	71%
300 Ford Motor	9/2/2005	9/1/2005	$2,956	$2,912	$44	552%
100 Anheuser-Busch	9/6/2005	7/27/2005	$4,539	$4,496	$43	9%
100 Eli Lilly	9/6/2005	8/3/2005	$5,537	$5,480	$57	11%
100 Eli Lilly	9/6/2005	8/3/2005	$5,533	$5,486	$47	9%
100 Citigroup	9/6/2005	8/23/2005	$4,425	$4,379	$46	27%
200 Bristol-Myers Squibb	9/6/2005	8/23/2005	$4,949	$4,891	$58	31%
100 United Technologies	9/6/2005	8/26/2005	$5,084	$5,037	$47	31%
100 General Electric	9/6/2005	8/30/2005	$3,358	$3,310	$48	76%
100 Johnson & Johnson	9/6/2005	9/2/2005	$6,347	$6,293	$54	78%
100 Lloyds TSB Group	9/7/2005	4/15/2005	$3,612	$3,572	$40	3%

(Continues)

Stock	Date Sold	Date Purchased	Proceeds	Cost	Profit	Percent Profit Annualized
100 Reuters	9/7/2005	8/3/2005	$4,117	$4,014	$103	27%
100 Juniper Networks	9/7/2005	8/18/2005	$2,378	$2,340	$38	30%
200 Tyco International	9/7/2005	9/7/2005	$5,603	$5,551	$52	342%
100 Nike Inc.	9/9/2005	9/2/2005	$7,895	$7,808	$87	58%
100 Anheuser-Busch	9/9/2005	9/8/2005	$4,530	$4,487	$43	350%
100 FedEx Corp.	9/12/2005	9/8/2005	$8,041	$7,998	$43	49%
100 Morgan Stanley	9/14/2005	9/13/2005	$5,300	$5,260	$40	278%
1000 Central Fund of Canada	9/15/2005	9/13/2005	$5,365	$5,305	$60	206%
1000 Central Fund of Canada	9/15/2005	9/13/2005	$5,373	$5,307	$66	227%
200 Adobe Systems	9/16/2005	8/3/2005	$5,709	$5,643	$66	10%
300 Time Warner	9/16/2005	8/16/2005	$5,587	$5,537	$50	11%
100 Bank of America	9/16/2005	9/14/2005	$4,322	$4,265	$57	244%
100 JP Morgan Chase	9/16/2005	8/12/2005	$3,489	$3,448	$41	12%
100 FedEx Corp.	9/21/2005	9/13/2005	$8,212	$8,000	$212	121%
100 Nike Inc.	9/22/2005	9/20/2005	$8,117	$8,046	$71	161%
100 Commerce Bancorp	9/22/2005	9/21/2005	$3,054	$3,022	$32	386%
100 Nike Inc.	9/23/2005	9/23/2005	$8,057	$7,997	$60	274%
200 Adobe Systems	9/26/2005	9/20/2005	$5,681	$5,599	$82	89%
100 ADP	9/28/2005	9/7/2005	$4,310	$4,242	$68	28%
200 Microsoft	9/28/2005	9/22/2005	$5,111	$5,067	$44	53%
100 Reuters	9/28/2005	9/26/2005	$3,982	$3,940	$42	195%
100 Biogen Idec	9/28/2005	9/27/2005	$3,865	$3,816	$49	469%
100 Morgan Stanley	9/29/2005	8/16/2005	$5,343	$5,301	$42	7%
100 Morgan Stanley	9/29/2005	9/14/2005	$5,304	$5,262	$42	19%
100 Biogen Idec	9/29/2005	9/29/2005	$3,853	$3,800	$53	509%
200 Walt Disney Co.	9/30/2005	9/15/2005	$4,845	$4,804	$41	21%
100 Juniper Networks	9/30/2005	9/19/2005	$2,379	$2,334	$45	64%
200 Tyco International	9/30/2005	9/29/2005	$5,575	$5,535	$40	264%
850 Gateway Inc.	9/30/2005	9/21/2005	$2,279	$2,234	$45	82%
				Subtotal	**$2,511**	
1000 Gateway Inc.	10/3/2005	9/21/2005	$2,755	$2,695	$60	68%
200 Walt Disney Co.	10/4/2005	10/3/2005	$4,851	$4,803	$48	365%
100 General Electric	10/7/2005	9/28/2005	$3,381	$3,339	$42	51%
100 United Technologies	10/7/2005	10/6/2005	$4,994	$4,959	$35	258%
100 Reuters	10/10/2005	10/6/2005	$3,942	$3,855	$87	206%
100 Johnson & Johnson	10/13/2005	9/30/2005	$6,354	$6,314	$40	18%
100 Johnson & Johnson	10/13/2005	10/5/2005	$6,335	$6,236	$99	72%
200 Adobe Systems	10/13/2005	10/13/2005	$5,639	$5,599	$40	261%
100 United Technologies	10/14/2005	10/5/2005	$5,141	$5,045	$96	77%
100 General Motors	10/17/2005	10/5/2005	$3,100	$2,965	$135	138%
100 Morgan Stanley	10/17/2005	10/12/2005	$5,250	$5,206	$44	62%
1000 Gateway Inc.	10/19/2005	10/11/2005	$2,710	$2,650	$60	103%
900 Gateway Inc.	10/19/2005	10/12/2005	$2,441	$2,392	$49	107%
100 United Technologies	10/19/2005	10/18/2005	$5,094	$5,019	$75	545%
100 Morgan Stanley	10/19/2005	10/19/2005	$5,182	$5,140	$42	298%
100 Exxon Mobil	10/19/2005	10/19/2005	$5,642	$5,587	$55	359%
100 JP Morgan Chase	10/21/2005	8/12/2005	$3,505	$3,456	$49	7%
100 UBS	10/21/2005	10/18/2005	$8,324	$8,267	$57	84%
100 Exxon Mobil	10/21/2005	10/20/2005	$5,593	$5,552	$41	270%
1000 Gateway Inc.	10/21/2005	10/20/2005	$2,722	$2,640	$82	1134%
900 Gateway Inc.	10/21/2005	10/20/2005	$2,450	$2,392	$58	885%
100 Bank of America	10/24/2005	9/21/2005	$4,299	$4,259	$40	10%
100 DuPont	10/24/2005	10/3/2005	$3,948	$3,907	$41	18%
100 Reuters	10/24/2005	10/20/2005	$3,868	$3,827	$41	98%

Stock	Date Sold	Date Purchased	Proceeds	Cost	Profit	Percent Profit Annualized
100 UBS	10/24/2005	10/21/2005	$8,317	$8,270	$47	69%
100 Exxon Mobil	10/24/2005	10/21/2005	$5,603	$5,541	$62	136%
100 Lloyds TSB Group	10/25/2005	10/10/2005	$3,257	$3,213	$44	33%
200 Alcoa	10/26/2005	10/3/2005	$4,843	$4,799	$44	15%
200 Microsoft	10/26/2005	10/4/2005	$5,053	$4,995	$58	19%
200 Pfizer Inc.	10/28/2005	10/21/2005	$4,289	$4,245	$44	54%
1000 Gateway Inc.	10/28/2005	10/27/2005	$2,755	$2,635	$120	1662%
1000 Gateway Inc.	10/28/2005	10/27/2005	$2,743	$2,587	$156	2201%
100 Abbott Laboratories	10/28/2005	10/28/2005	$4,270	$4,233	$37	319%
100 Caterpillar	10/28/2005	10/28/2005	$5,047	$5,003	$44	321%
100 Exxon Mobil	10/28/2005	10/28/2005	$5,608	$5,567	$41	269%
100 UBS	10/28/2005	10/28/2005	$8,315	$8,270	$45	199%
100 Johnson & Johnson	10/28/2005	10/28/2005	$6,275	$6,229	$46	270%
100 Avery Dennison	10/31/2005	8/10/2005	$5,659	$5,603	$56	4%
100 Wal-Mart Stores	10/31/2005	8/19/2005	$4,721	$4,681	$40	4%
200 Walt Disney Co.	10/31/2005	10/6/2005	$4,841	$4,797	$44	13%
200 Alcoa	10/31/2005	10/27/2005	$4,820	$4,776	$44	84%
				Subtotal	**$2,388**	
100 Juniper Networks	11/1/2005	10/3/2005	$2,380	$2,333	$47	25%
100 Commerce Bancorp	11/2/2005	10/4/2005	$3,063	$3,021	$42	17%
100 Reuters	11/2/2005	10/28/2005	$3,888	$3,815	$73	140%
100 Qualcomm	11/2/2005	10/31/2005	$4,053	$3,995	$58	265%
100 Guidant Corp.	11/3/2005	11/3/2005	$5,708	$5,667	$41	264%
200 Barrick Gold	11/4/2005	11/4/2005	$4,993	$4,943	$50	369%
100 Weyerhaeuser	11/7/2005	11/4/2005	$6,305	$6,257	$48	93%
100 Guidant Corp.	11/7/2005	11/7/2005	$5,669	$5,626	$43	279%
100 Colgate-Palmolive	11/8/2005	11/3/2005	$5,242	$5,193	$49	69%
100 Guidant Corp.	11/8/2005	11/8/2005	$5,692	$5,652	$40	258%
200 MBNA	11/9/2005	7/19/2005	$5,198	$5,158	$40	3%
100 Commerce Bancorp	11/9/2005	9/19/2005	$3,172	$3,123	$49	11%
300 El Paso Corp.	11/9/2005	11/9/2005	$3,346	$3,293	$53	587%
200 Walt Disney Co.	11/10/2005	8/24/2005	$5,144	$5,102	$42	4%
100 Morgan Stanley	11/10/2005	11/3/2005	$5,331	$5,266	$65	64%
100 Guidant Corp.	11/10/2005	11/9/2005	$5,705	$5,657	$48	310%
100 Weyerhaeuser	11/11/2005	11/8/2005	$6,238	$6,190	$48	94%
100 General Motors	11/11/2005	11/10/2005	$2,390	$2,343	$47	732%
100 Johnson & Johnson	11/15/2005	11/1/2005	$6,296	$6,226	$70	29%
100 Johnson & Johnson	11/15/2005	11/2/2005	$6,200	$6,116	$84	39%
200 Tyco International	11/16/2005	10/5/2005	$5,592	$5,532	$60	9%
300 El Paso Corp.	11/17/2005	11/15/2005	$3,412	$3,299	$113	625%
200 AT&T	11/18/2005	3/3/2004	$4,058	$4,019	$39	1%
100 General Electric	11/18/2005	6/23/2005	$3,545	$3,539	$6	0%
100 General Electric	11/18/2005	8/2/2005	$3,545	$3,436	$109	11%
100 General Motors	11/18/2005	11/15/2005	$2,375	$2,316	$59	310%
100 General Motors	11/18/2005	11/15/2005	$2,330	$2,289	$41	218%
200 MBNA	11/21/2005	6/30/2005	$5,313	$5,271	$42	2%
100 iStar Financial	11/21/2005	11/16/2005	$3,611	$3,571	$40	82%
100 General Electric	11/21/2005	6/23/2005	$3,618	$3,542	$76	5%
200 Intel	11/23/2005	8/12/2005	$5,341	$5,289	$52	3%
100 National Grid	11/23/2005	9/30/2005	$4,767	$4,724	$43	6%
200 News Corporation	11/23/2005	10/20/2005	$3,172	$3,132	$40	14%
100 Juniper Networks	11/23/2005	11/15/2005	$2,376	$2,335	$41	80%
100 Coca-Cola Co.	11/23/2005	11/16/2005	$4,267	$4,226	$41	51%
200 Vodafone Group Plc	11/23/2005	11/21/2005	$4,381	$4,339	$42	177%
100 Dow Jones & Co.	11/23/2005	11/22/2005	$3,430	$3,386	$44	474%

(Continues)

Stock	Date Sold	Date Purchased	Proceeds	Cost	Profit	Percent Profit Annualized
1000 Gateway Inc.	11/23/2005	11/22/2005	$3,005	$2,955	$50	618%
100 Johnson & Johnson	11/28/2005	11/21/2005	$6,273	$6,204	$69	58%
100 Anheuser-Busch	11/29/2005	9/22/2005	$4,464	$4,404	$60	7%
				Subtotal	**$2,104**	
100 Juniper Networks	12/5/2005	11/30/2005	$2,338	$2,288	$50	160%
100 Johnson & Johnson	12/5/2005	12/2/2005	$6,185	$6,142	$43	85%
200 Vodafone Group Plc	12/6/2005	11/28/2005	$4,383	$4,333	$50	53%
100 Lloyds TSB Group	12/6/2005	11/30/2005	$3,339	$3,287	$52	96%
200 Cisco Systems	12/7/2005	12/5/2005	$3,587	$3,503	$84	438%
100 Lloyds TSB Group	12/7/2005	9/26/2005	$3,402	$3,360	$42	6%
100 Lloyds TSB Group	12/8/2005	9/26/2005	$3,412	$3,358	$54	8%
100 National Grid	12/8/2005	11/28/2005	$4,789	$4,724	$65	50%
200 Intel	12/12/2005	12/7/2005	$5,295	$5,243	$52	72%
100 Nike Inc.	12/12/2005	12/9/2005	$8,751	$8,557	$194	276%
100 Eli Lilly	12/13/2005	9/19/2005	$5,538	$5,473	$65	5%
100 Pfizer Inc.	12/13/2005	12/6/2005	$2,175	$2,122	$53	130%
100 Unilever	12/13/2005	12/6/2005	$4,050	$3,984	$66	86%
100 Abbott Laboratories	12/14/2005	11/23/2005	$3,963	$3,910	$53	24%
200 Cisco Systems	12/15/2005	12/9/2005	$3,555	$3,505	$50	87%
100 Johnson & Johnson	12/16/2005	12/6/2005	$6,112	$6,060	$52	31%
200 Bristol-Myers Squibb	12/19/2005	11/28/2005	$4,555	$4,427	$128	50%
100 Johnson & Johnson	12/19/2005	12/5/2005	$6,181	$6,130	$51	22%
100 Nike Inc.	12/20/2005	12/19/2005	$8,802	$8,745	$57	238%
100 Carnival Corp.	12/20/2005	12/19/2005	$5,363	$5,302	$61	420%
100 Kellogg Co.	12/21/2005	12/5/2005	$4,474	$4,425	$49	25%
100 Avery Dennison	12/21/2005	12/19/2005	$5,634	$5,584	$50	163%
100 Nike Inc.	12/21/2005	12/21/2005	$8,451	$8,405	$46	200%
100 Nike Inc.	12/21/2005	12/21/2005	$8,493	$8,436	$57	247%
100 ConocoPhillips	12/23/2005	12/23/2005	$5,882	$5,841	$41	256%
200 Cendant	12/28/2005	12/14/2005	$3,369	$3,325	$44	35%
100 Cadbury Schweppes	12/28/2005	12/15/2005	$3,831	$3,780	$51	38%
200 Cablevision Systems	12/28/2005	12/20/2005	$4,667	$4,615	$52	51%
				Subtotal	**$1,712**	
				Total	**$30,259**	

Trading Record for 2006 (Net of All Commissions)

Stock	Date Sold	Date Purchased	Proceeds	Cost	Profit	Percent Profit Annualized
200 Vodafone Group Plc	1/3/2006	12/19/2005	$4,401	$4,311	$90	51%
100 Johnson & Johnson	1/3/2006	12/20/2005	$6,162	$6,111	$51	22%
100 Unilever	1/3/2006	12/20/2005	$4,051	$3,998	$53	35%
100 Exxon Mobil	1/3/2006	12/22/2005	$5,763	$5,701	$62	33%
100 Diageo	1/3/2006	12/23/2005	$5,915	$5,863	$52	29%
100 ConocoPhillips	1/3/2006	12/27/2005	$5,892	$5,841	$51	46%
100 iStar Financial	1/3/2006	12/27/2005	$3,649	$3,599	$50	72%
100 Lloyds TSB Group	1/3/2006	12/27/2005	$3,475	$3,424	$51	78%
200 Microsoft	1/3/2006	12/29/2005	$5,311	$5,261	$50	69%
100 Kellogg Co.	1/3/2006	12/30/2005	$4,393	$4,335	$58	122%
100 Anheuser-Busch	1/3/2006	12/30/2005	$4,356	$4,304	$52	110%
100 Lloyds TSB Group	1/3/2006	12/30/2005	$3,423	$3,371	$52	141%
200 Intel	1/3/2006	1/3/2006	$5,069	$4,995	$74	541%
100 Avery Dennison	1/3/2006	1/3/2006	$5,560	$5,523	$37	245%
100 Cadbury Schweppes	1/4/2006	12/13/2005	$3,932	$3,862	$70	30%
200 Cisco Systems	1/4/2006	12/16/2005	$3,569	$3,515	$54	30%
100 Exxon Mobil	1/4/2006	12/19/2005	$5,843	$5,790	$53	21%
200 Cablevision	1/4/2006	1/3/2006	$4,670	$4,607	$63	499%
100 Abbott Laboratories	1/5/2006	12/30/2005	$4,002	$3,950	$52	80%
200 Intel	1/6/2006	12/19/2005	$5,295	$5,241	$54	21%
100 Coca-Cola Co.	1/6/2006	12/27/2005	$4,126	$4,074	$52	47%
100 Kellogg Co.	1/6/2006	12/27/2005	$4,431	$4,380	$51	42%
100 Juniper Networks	1/6/2006	1/3/2006	$2,203	$2,152	$51	288%
100 Anheuser-Busch	1/6/2006	1/5/2006	$4,356	$4,304	$52	441%
100 Abbott Laboratories	1/9/2006	11/14/2005	$4,237	$4,139	$98	15%
100 Nike Inc.	1/9/2006	12/30/2005	$8,737	$8,685	$52	22%
100 Nike Inc.	1/9/2006	1/6/2006	$8,651	$8,576	$75	106%
100 Johnson & Johnson	1/10/2006	11/29/2005	$6,285	$6,231	$54	8%
200 Walt Disney Company	1/10/2006	12/15/2005	$5,029	$4,953	$76	22%

(Continues)

Stock	Date Sold	Date Purchased	Proceeds	Cost	Profit	Percent Profit Annualized
300 El Paso Corp.	1/10/2006	12/27/2005	$3,736	$3,683	$53	38%
100 Juniper Networks	1/10/2006	1/9/2006	$2,200	$2,149	$51	866%
96 Intl. Game Technology	1/11/2006	2/17/2005	$3,009	$2,971	$38	1%
100 Coca-Cola Co.	1/11/2006	12/12/2005	$4,172	$4,131	$41	12%
100 Wal-Mart Stores	1/11/2006	1/5/2006	$4,636	$4,560	$76	101%
100 Intl. Game Technology	1/12/2006	2/17/2005	$3,149	$3,096	$53	2%
100 Kraft Foods	1/12/2006	12/23/2005	$2,893	$2,819	$74	48%
100 Nike Inc.	1/13/2006	1/13/2006	$8,607	$8,559	$48	205%
100 Commerce Bancorp	1/18/2006	1/10/2006	$3,332	$3,280	$52	72%
100 Diageo	1/18/2006	1/17/2006	$5,921	$5,871	$50	311%
100 Yahoo! Inc.	1/18/2006	1/18/2006	$3,587	$3,499	$88	918%
200 Vodafone Group Plc	1/23/2006	1/19/2006	$4,339	$4,275	$64	137%
100 Yahoo! Inc.	1/24/2006	1/19/2006	$3,509	$3,453	$56	118%
200 Intel	1/24/2006	1/23/2006	$4,305	$4,253	$52	446%
100 Abbott Laboratories	1/25/2006	1/11/2006	$4,195	$4,126	$69	44%
100 Wal-Mart Stores	1/25/2006	1/13/2006	$4,604	$4,553	$51	34%
100 Colgate-Palmolive	1/25/2006	1/20/2006	$5,490	$5,376	$114	155%
200 Vodafone Group Plc	1/25/2006	1/24/2006	$4,267	$4,215	$52	450%
100 Yahoo! Inc.	1/25/2006	1/25/2006	$3,484	$3,441	$43	456%
100 Juniper Networks	1/25/2006	1/25/2006	$2,156	$2,088	$68	1189%
200 Bristol-Myers Squibb	1/25/2006	1/25/2006	$4,301	$4,257	$44	377%
100 Coca-Cola Co.	1/26/2006	1/18/2006	$4,122	$4,072	$50	56%
100 Citigroup Inc.	1/26/2006	1/20/2006	$4,663	$4,598	$65	86%
100 Yahoo! Inc.	1/26/2006	1/25/2006	$3,497	$3,446	$51	540%
200 Intel	1/26/2006	1/25/2006	$4,307	$4,249	$58	498%
100 Coca-Cola Co.	1/27/2006	12/12/2005	$4,187	$4,134	$53	10%
100 Carnival Corp.	1/27/2006	1/27/2006	$5,296	$5,243	$53	369%
100 AT&T Inc. (200 SBC)	1/27/2006	1/5/2005	$5,155	$5,098	$57	1%
100 General Motors	1/30/2006	11/21/2005	$2,428	$2,341	$87	19%
100 Juniper Networks	1/30/2006	1/27/2006	$1,793	$1,706	$87	620%
190 Microsoft	1/31/2006	10/11/2004	$5,364	$5,354	$10	0%
100 Commerce Bancorp	1/31/2006	1/20/2006	$3,333	$3,280	$53	54%
100 3M Co.	1/31/2006	1/30/2006	$7,316	$7,265	$51	256%
				Subtotal	**$3,602**	
300 Time Warner	2/1/2006	12/8/2005	$5,461	$5,405	$56	7%
100 iStar Financial	2/1/2006	1/30/2006	$3,604	$3,549	$55	283%
100 iStar Financial	2/1/2006	1/30/2006	$3,599	$3,558	$41	210%
300 Tyson Foods Inc.	2/1/2006	1/31/2006	$4,354	$4,283	$71	605%
100 3M Co.	2/1/2006	2/1/2006	$7,250	$7,208	$42	213%
100 Carnival Corp.	2/2/2006	1/30/2006	$5,294	$5,241	$53	123%
300 Time Warner	2/6/2006	9/20/2005	$5,608	$5,528	$80	4%
300 Time Warner	2/6/2006	9/20/2005	$5,564	$5,518	$46	2%
100 Coca-Cola Co.	2/7/2006	2/3/2006	$4,130	$4,080	$50	112%
100 HJ Heinz Co.	2/8/2006	12/23/2005	$3,439	$3,394	$45	10%
200 LaBranche & Co.	2/9/2006	10/14/2003	$2,708	$2,631	$77	1%
100 Johnson & Johnson	2/9/2006	1/30/2006	$5,912	$5,851	$61	38%
300 Tyson Foods Inc.	2/9/2006	2/3/2006	$4,333	$4,283	$50	71%
100 Wal-Mart Stores	2/9/2006	2/6/2006	$4,571	$4,521	$50	135%
100 Coca-Cola Co.	2/9/2006	2/7/2006	$4,132	$4,077	$55	246%
100 3M Co.	2/10/2006	2/2/2006	$7,277	$7,226	$51	32%
100 Colgate-Palmolive	2/14/2006	2/7/2006	$5,430	$5,375	$55	53%
100 Johnson & Johnson	2/14/2006	2/10/2006	$5,901	$5,851	$50	78%
100 Cadbury Schweppes	2/14/2006	2/13/2006	$3,886	$3,834	$52	495%
100 Coca-Cola Co.	2/14/2006	2/13/2006	$4,129	$4,076	$53	475%
100 Citigroup	2/15/2006	2/2/2006	$4,625	$4,569	$56	34%
100 Carnival Corp.	2/15/2006	2/3/2006	$5,290	$5,240	$50	29%

Stock	Date Sold	Date Purchased	Proceeds	Cost	Profit	Percent Profit Annualized
100 Kellogg Co.	2/15/2006	2/7/2006	$4,357	$4,304	$53	56%
100 DuPont	2/16/2006	1/12/2006	$4,135	$4,065	$70	18%
100 Boston Scientific Corp.	2/16/2006	1/17/2006	$2,455	$2,405	$50	25%
100 Kellogg Co.	2/16/2006	1/17/2006	$4,440	$4,380	$60	17%
200 Vodafone Group Plc	2/16/2006	1/31/2006	$4,283	$4,203	$80	43%
300 Goodyear Tire	2/16/2006	2/16/2006	$4,450	$4,394	$56	465%
300 Goodyear Tire	2/17/2006	2/16/2006	$4,459	$4,400	$59	489%
100 Kellogg Co.	2/21/2006	12/21/2005	$4,485	$4,432	$53	7%
100 JM Smucker Co.	2/21/2006	2/17/2006	$3,837	$3,779	$58	140%
100 JM Smucker Co.	2/21/2006	2/17/2006	$3,853	$3,789	$64	154%
100 Carnival Corp.	2/21/2006	2/21/2006	$5,185	$5,128	$57	406%
100 Carnival Corp.	2/21/2006	2/21/2006	$5,168	$5,125	$43	306%
100 Nike Inc.	2/22/2006	1/17/2006	$8,624	$8,572	$52	6%
100 Fortune Brands Inc.	2/22/2006	2/13/2006	$7,841	$7,782	$59	31%
100 Commerce Bancorp	2/22/2006	2/13/2006	$3,322	$3,272	$50	62%
300 Goodyear Tire	2/22/2006	2/21/2006	$4,456	$4,400	$56	465%
100 Nike Inc.	2/23/2006	1/12/2006	$8,714	$8,661	$53	5%
100 Dow Jones & Co.	2/24/2006	9/19/2005	$4,019	$3,968	$51	3%
100 Fortune Brands Inc.	2/27/2006	2/24/2006	$7,828	$7,767	$61	96%
100 Fortune Brands Inc.	2/27/2006	2/24/2006	$7,821	$7,770	$51	80%
				Subtotal	**$2,335**	
100 DuPont	3/1/2006	2/27/2006	$4,070	$4,009	$61	278%
100 Fortune Brands Inc.	3/1/2006	2/28/2006	$7,830	$7,774	$56	263%
200 News Corporation	3/2/2006	8/24/2005	$3,497	$3,443	$54	3%
200 Vodafone Group Plc	3/3/2006	2/21/2006	$4,309	$4,197	$112	97%
100 Carnival Corp.	3/3/2006	3/2/2006	$5,196	$5,145	$51	362%
100 Nike Inc.	3/3/2006	3/2/2006	$8,649	$8,594	$55	234%
100 Nike Inc.	3/3/2006	3/2/2006	$8,637	$8,596	$41	174%
200 Cisco Systems	3/6/2006	8/3/2004	$4,276	$4,219	$57	1%
100 Clear Channel Comms.	3/6/2006	2/13/2006	$2,919	$2,863	$56	34%
100 Fortune Brands Inc.	3/6/2006	3/6/2006	$7,826	$7,773	$53	249%
100 Nike Inc.	3/7/2006	3/7/2006	$8,515	$8,471	$44	190%
100 Molson Coors Brewing	3/8/2006	1/18/2006	$6,730	$6,668	$62	7%
100 Johnson & Johnson	3/8/2006	2/24/2006	$5,871	$5,821	$50	26%
100 3M Co.	3/8/2006	3/6/2006	$7,265	$7,210	$55	139%
100 Nike Inc.	3/9/2006	3/7/2006	$8,510	$8,457	$53	114%
100 Coca-Cola Co.	3/10/2006	12/7/2005	$4,280	$4,224	$56	5%
100 Peabody Energy Corp.	3/10/2006	3/9/2006	$4,624	$4,549	$75	602%
100 Johnson & Johnson	3/10/2006	3/9/2006	$5,892	$5,842	$50	312%
100 Washington Mutual	3/10/2006	3/9/2006	$4,249	$4,195	$54	470%
200 Cendant	3/15/2006	1/20/2006	$3,375	$3,325	$50	10%
100 General Electric	3/15/2006	1/20/2006	$3,405	$3,353	$52	10%
100 Carnival Corp.	3/15/2006	3/7/2006	$5,073	$5,005	$68	62%
100 3M Co.	3/15/2006	3/9/2006	$7,325	$7,229	$96	81%
100 Anheuser-Busch	3/16/2006	1/12/2006	$4,339	$4,255	$84	11%
100 Wal-Mart Stores	3/16/2006	3/2/2006	$4,603	$4,511	$92	53%
100 Abbott Laboratories	3/17/2006	9/13/2005	$4,513	$4,464	$49	2%
200 Comcast Corp.	3/21/2006	3/7/2006	$5,425	$5,375	$50	24%
100 Peabody Energy Corp.	3/21/2006	3/21/2006	$4,594	$4,539	$55	442%
200 Bristol-Myers Squibb	3/22/2006	9/21/2005	$5,147	$4,883	$264	11%

(Continues)

Stock	Date Sold	Date Purchased	Proceeds	Cost	Profit	Percent Profit Annualized
100 Peabody Energy Corp.	3/22/2006	3/21/2006	$4,584	$4,536	$48	386%
200 Catalina Marketing	3/22/2006	3/21/2006	$4,643	$4,591	$52	413%
100 Peabody Energy Corp.	3/22/2006	3/21/2006	$4,588	$4,537	$51	410%
200 Barrick Gold	3/24/2006	3/23/2006	$5,213	$5,161	$52	368%
200 Barrick Gold	3/24/2006	3/23/2006	$5,225	$5,161	$64	453%
200 Catalina Marketing	3/28/2006	3/27/2006	$4,645	$4,593	$52	413%
200 Catalina Marketing	3/28/2006	3/27/2006	$4,691	$4,611	$80	633%
200 Vodafone Group Plc	3/29/2006	3/28/2006	$4,239	$4,183	$56	489%
200 Repsol YPF	3/30/2006	3/27/2006	$5,713	$5,659	$54	116%
100 Nike Inc.	3/30/2006	3/27/2006	$8,577	$8,529	$48	68%
				Subtotal	**$2,512**	
100 Nike Inc.	4/3/2006	3/30/2006	$8,575	$8,525	$50	54%
92 Nike Inc.	4/3/2006	3/30/2006	$7,888	$7,842	$46	54%
200 Repsol YPF	4/3/2006	3/31/2006	$5,715	$5,661	$54	116%
200 Bristol-Myers Squibb	4/3/2006	3/31/2006	$4,983	$4,931	$52	128%
100 Procter & Gamble	4/4/2006	3/28/2006	$5,822	$5,771	$51	46%
200 Catalina Marketing	4/4/2006	3/31/2006	$4,649	$4,591	$58	115%
200 Catalina Marketing	4/4/2006	3/31/2006	$4,653	$4,595	$58	115%
200 Vodafone Group Plc	4/4/2006	3/31/2006	$4,289	$4,193	$96	209%
200 Repsol YPF	4/4/2006	4/4/2006	$5,699	$5,659	$40	258%
100 Unilever Plc	4/5/2006	3/27/2006	$4,122	$4,073	$49	49%
100 Eli Lilly	4/5/2006	4/4/2006	$5,537	$5,486	$51	339%
100 3M Co.	4/6/2006	4/15/2005	$8,164	$8,099	$65	1%
300 El Paso Corp.	4/6/2006	3/6/2006	$3,739	$3,692	$47	15%
200 Comcast Corp.	4/6/2006	3/21/2006	$5,445	$5,367	$78	33%
100 Marshall & Ilsley Corp.	4/7/2006	3/24/2006	$4,483	$4,425	$58	34%
100 Fortune Brands Inc.	4/11/2006	4/7/2006	$7,904	$7,823	$81	94%
100 Bausch & Lomb Inc.	4/13/2006	4/13/2006	$4,626	$4,520	$106	856%
100 St. Jude Medical Inc.	4/17/2006	4/13/2006	$3,628	$3,573	$55	140%
300 Time Warner	4/18/2006	3/28/2006	$5,086	$5,039	$47	16%
300 El Paso Corp.	4/18/2006	4/7/2006	$3,742	$3,692	$50	45%
100 Marshall & Ilsley Corp.	4/18/2006	4/7/2006	$4,476	$4,426	$50	37%
200 Repsol YPF	4/18/2006	4/11/2006	$5,809	$5,661	$148	136%
100 Fortune Brands Inc.	4/18/2006	4/11/2006	$7,874	$7,822	$52	35%
100 General Electric	4/18/2006	4/17/2006	$3,390	$3,340	$50	546%
100 Nike Inc.	4/18/2006	4/17/2006	$8,207	$8,154	$53	237%
200 Bristol-Myers Squibb	4/19/2006	4/3/2006	$4,993	$4,927	$66	31%
100 Coca-Cola Co.	4/19/2006	4/11/2006	$4,186	$4,129	$57	63%
100 Unilever Plc	4/19/2006	4/12/2006	$4,120	$4,068	$52	67%
100 Intl. Game Technology	4/20/2006	7/8/2004	$3,798	$3,740	$58	1%
100 Intl. Game Technology	4/20/2006	7/13/2004	$3,771	$3,677	$94	1%
300 Intel	4/20/2006	4/3/2006	$5,914	$5,864	$50	18%
100 St. Jude Medical Inc.	4/20/2006	4/11/2006	$3,829	$3,709	$120	131%
100 Procter & Gamble	4/20/2006	4/17/2006	$5,673	$5,623	$50	108%
200 Bristol-Myers Squibb	4/20/2006	4/19/2006	$4,975	$4,925	$50	371%
300 Time Warner	4/20/2006	4/20/2006	$5,077	$5,033	$44	319%
200 Catalina Marketing	4/24/2006	4/6/2006	$4,679	$4,589	$90	40%
200 Catalina Marketing	4/24/2006	4/6/2006	$4,669	$4,601	$68	30%
100 Procter & Gamble	4/24/2006	4/21/2006	$5,678	$5,627	$51	110%
100 Kraft Foods Inc.	4/25/2006	9/7/2005	$3,121	$3,071	$50	3%

Stock	Date Sold	Date Purchased	Proceeds	Cost	Profit	Percent Profit Annualized
100 Bausch & Lomb Inc.	4/25/2006	4/12/2006	$4,908	$4,840	$68	39%
200 Bristol-Myers Squibb	4/25/2006	4/24/2006	$4,969	$4,917	$52	386%
100 Anheuser-Busch	4/26/2006	11/30/2005	$4,467	$4,415	$52	3%
300 Tyson Foods Inc.	4/26/2006	2/22/2006	$4,330	$4,280	$50	7%
100 Kellogg Co.	4/26/2006	3/31/2006	$4,494	$4,411	$83	26%
100 Anheuser-Busch	4/26/2006	4/7/2006	$4,440	$4,279	$161	72%
100 Procter & Gamble	4/27/2006	4/5/2006	$5,822	$5,767	$55	16%
200 Pfizer Inc.	4/27/2006	4/7/2006	$5,026	$4,976	$50	18%
100 Marshall & Ilsley Corp.	4/27/2006	4/19/2006	$4,484	$4,425	$59	61%
300 Intel	4/27/2006	4/20/2006	$5,959	$5,861	$98	87%
300 Time Warner	4/27/2006	4/21/2006	$5,118	$5,044	$74	89%
300 Tyson Foods Inc.	4/27/2006	4/27/2006	$3,997	$3,908	$89	831%
100 Nike Inc.	4/28/2006	4/26/2006	$8,209	$8,154	$55	123%
100 Abbott Laboratories	4/28/2006	4/11/2006	$4,240	$4,187	$53	27%
100 Abbott Laboratories	4/28/2006	4/11/2006	$4,221	$4,172	$49	25%
100 Bausch & Lomb Inc.	4/28/2006	4/27/2006	$4,873	$4,820	$53	401%
				Subtotal	**$3,546**	
100 Nike Inc.	5/1/2006	4/28/2006	$8,213	$8,153	$60	90%
100 ADP	5/1/2006	4/28/2006	$4,451	$4,365	$86	240%
100 Wal-Mart Stores	5/1/2006	4/28/2006	$4,601	$4,512	$89	240%
100 Bausch & Lomb Inc.	5/2/2006	5/1/2006	$4,862	$4,811	$51	387%
100 Genentech	5/2/2006	5/2/2006	$7,615	$7,570	$45	217%
100 Clear Channel Comms.	5/3/2006	4/11/2006	$2,931	$2,864	$67	39%
100 Procter & Gamble	5/3/2006	5/3/2006	$5,609	$5,567	$42	275%
200 Avaya Inc.	5/4/2006	3/15/2005	$2,602	$2,552	$50	2%
200 Tyco International	5/4/2006	1/13/2006	$5,645	$5,595	$50	3%
200 Cablevision Systems	5/4/2006	5/1/2006	$4,011	$3,959	$52	160%
300 Goodyear Tire	5/4/2006	2/23/2006	$4,402	$4,349	$53	6%
600 Ahold NV	5/4/2006	5/3/2006	$4,909	$4,853	$56	421%
100 UnitedHealth Group	5/4/2006	5/4/2006	$4,662	$4,619	$43	340%
100 Genentech	5/5/2006	4/24/2006	$8,066	$7,994	$72	30%
100 Dow Jones & Co.	5/8/2006	4/18/2006	$3,781	$3,730	$51	25%
100 Nike Inc.	5/8/2006	5/3/2006	$8,200	$8,150	$50	45%
98 Nike Inc.	5/8/2006	5/3/2006	$7,999	$7,956	$43	39%
300 Intel	5/8/2006	5/1/2006	$5,929	$5,864	$65	58%
100 Bausch & Lomb Inc.	5/8/2006	5/3/2006	$4,495	$4,419	$76	126%
100 Procter & Gamble	5/9/2006	5/4/2006	$5,652	$5,588	$64	84%
200 Dell	5/9/2006	5/9/2006	$4,983	$4,915	$68	505%
200 Dell	5/9/2006	5/9/2006	$4,991	$4,941	$50	369%
100 Bausch & Lomb Inc.	5/9/2006	5/9/2006	$4,487	$4,450	$37	303%
100 UnitedHealth Group	5/12/2006	5/11/2006	$4,579	$4,464	$115	940%
100 Johnson & Johnson	5/15/2006	4/4/2006	$5,970	$5,912	$58	9%
100 Bausch & Lomb Inc.	5/15/2006	5/3/2006	$4,691	$4,580	$111	74%
100 Genentech	5/15/2006	5/9/2006	$8,064	$7,993	$71	54%
100 Bausch & Lomb Inc.	5/15/2006	5/12/2006	$4,583	$4,436	$147	403%
100 Abbott Laboratories	5/15/2006	5/12/2006	$4,213	$4,155	$58	170%
100 iStar Financial	5/15/2006	5/15/2006	$3,742	$3,697	$45	444%
100 UnitedHealth Group	5/16/2006	5/5/2006	$4,745	$4,627	$118	85%
200 Bristol-Myers Squibb	5/16/2006	5/11/2006	$4,977	$4,917	$60	89%
100 Nike Inc.	5/16/2006	5/15/2006	$8,195	$8,141	$54	242%
600 Ahold NV	5/16/2006	5/15/2006	$4,977	$4,865	$112	840%
100 Morgan Stanley	5/18/2006	5/17/2006	$6,049	$5,994	$55	335%
600 Ahold NV	5/18/2006	5/17/2006	$4,933	$4,865	$68	510%

(Continues)

Stock	Date Sold	Date Purchased	Proceeds	Cost	Profit	Percent Profit Annualized
100 Morgan Stanley	5/18/2006	5/18/2006	$6,043	$5,996	$47	286%
200 Tyco International	5/19/2006	5/17/2006	$5,443	$5,389	$54	183%
100 Morgan Stanley	5/19/2006	5/18/2006	$6,050	$5,998	$52	316%
100 Bank of Montreal	5/19/2006	5/18/2006	$5,502	$5,451	$51	341%
100 Bausch & Lomb Inc.	5/19/2006	5/18/2006	$4,889	$4,830	$59	446%
100 ADP	5/22/2006	4/28/2006	$4,521	$4,459	$62	21%
100 Cadbury Schweppes Plc	5/22/2006	5/19/2006	$3,877	$3,803	$74	237%
100 Morgan Stanley	5/22/2006	5/22/2006	$5,888	$5,845	$43	269%
100 Unilever Plc	5/23/2006	5/17/2006	$4,070	$4,016	$54	82%
100 Procter & Gamble	5/23/2006	5/19/2006	$5,458	$5,406	$52	88%
100 Microsoft	5/23/2006	5/22/2006	$2,318	$2,257	$61	986%
100 Bank of Montreal	5/23/2006	5/22/2006	$5,515	$5,455	$60	401%
200 Repsol YPF	5/24/2006	5/17/2006	$5,473	$5,405	$68	66%
200 Repsol YPF	5/25/2006	5/12/2006	$5,605	$5,557	$48	24%
100 St. Jude Medical Inc.	5/25/2006	5/22/2006	$3,487	$3,435	$52	184%
200 Tyco International	5/25/2006	5/23/2006	$5,439	$5,387	$52	176%
100 Morgan Stanley	5/25/2006	5/24/2006	$5,954	$5,828	$126	789%
200 Repsol YPF	5/25/2006	5/24/2006	$5,539	$5,405	$134	905%
100 Bank of Montreal	5/25/2006	5/24/2006	$5,549	$5,442	$107	718%
100 Johnson & Johnson	5/26/2006	3/27/2006	$6,074	$6,017	$57	6%
100 Genentech	5/26/2006	5/15/2006	$8,088	$7,973	$115	48%
200 Bristol-Myers Squibb	5/26/2006	5/16/2006	$4,983	$4,925	$58	43%
100 Morgan Stanley	5/26/2006	5/22/2006	$6,055	$5,965	$90	138%
200 Dell	5/30/2006	5/11/2006	$5,021	$4,931	$90	35%
600 Ahold NV	5/31/2006	5/19/2006	$4,895	$4,847	$48	30%
100 Morgan Stanley	5/31/2006	5/30/2006	$5,973	$5,912	$61	377%
100 Weyerhaeuser	5/31/2006	5/30/2006	$6,434	$6,366	$68	390%
100 Morgan Stanley	5/31/2006	5/31/2006	$5,950	$5,908	$42	259%
				Subtotal	$4,277	
100 UnitedHealth Group	6/1/2006	5/19/2006	$4,514	$4,435	$79	50%
200 Bristol-Myers Squibb	6/1/2006	5/30/2006	$4,973	$4,919	$54	200%
100 Weyerhaeuser	6/1/2006	5/31/2006	$6,429	$6,365	$64	367%
100 Reuters	6/1/2006	6/1/2006	$4,226	$4,180	$46	402%
600 Ahold NV	6/1/2006	6/1/2006	$4,861	$4,823	$38	288%
100 Nike Inc.	6/2/2006	5/16/2006	$8,202	$8,130	$72	19%
100 Qualcomm	6/2/2006	5/17/2006	$4,761	$4,687	$74	36%
100 Cablevision Systems	6/2/2006	5/22/2006	$2,016	$1,969	$47	79%
100 Johnson & Johnson	6/2/2006	5/30/2006	$6,064	$6,011	$53	107%
100 Cadbury Schweppes Plc	6/2/2006	6/1/2006	$3,880	$3,804	$76	729%
100 Cheesecake Factory	6/2/2006	6/1/2006	$2,938	$2,884	$54	683%
200 Tyco International	6/6/2006	6/6/2006	$5,434	$5,390	$44	298%
100 Molson Coors Brewing	6/7/2006	5/11/2006	$6,717	$6,665	$52	11%
100 Morgan Stanley	6/7/2006	6/5/2006	$5,931	$5,877	$54	168%
100 AIG	6/7/2006	6/5/2006	$6,094	$6,040	$54	163%
100 Cadbury Schweppes Plc	6/7/2006	6/6/2006	$3,843	$3,794	$49	471%
100 Procter & Gamble	6/8/2006	6/2/2006	$5,471	$5,404	$67	75%
100 Cheesecake Factory	6/9/2006	6/2/2006	$2,964	$2,884	$80	145%
200 Corning Inc.	6/9/2006	6/7/2006	$4,516	$4,407	$109	451%
100 Nike Inc.	6/12/2006	6/5/2006	$8,173	$8,118	$55	35%
600 Ahold NV	6/12/2006	6/6/2006	$4,957	$4,823	$134	169%
100 Morgan Stanley	6/12/2006	6/12/2006	$5,883	$5,837	$46	288%

Stock	Date Sold	Date Purchased	Proceeds	Cost	Profit	Percent Profit Annualized
200 Bristol-Myers Squibb	6/13/2006	6/12/2006	$4,972	$4,921	$51	378%
100 Nike Inc.	6/13/2006	6/13/2006	$8,156	$8,111	$45	203%
100 Constellation Energy	6/14/2006	6/5/2006	$5,364	$5,295	$69	53%
200 Corning Inc.	6/14/2006	6/12/2006	$4,273	$4,195	$78	339%
100 ConocoPhillips	6/14/2006	6/13/2006	$5,902	$5,846	$56	350%
100 Procter & Gamble	6/14/2006	6/14/2006	$5,441	$5,399	$42	284%
100 St. Jude Medical Inc.	6/15/2006	5/30/2006	$3,484	$3,433	$51	34%
100 Peabody Energy Corp.	6/15/2006	6/12/2006	$5,116	$5,038	$78	188%
100 Avery Dennison	6/15/2006	6/12/2006	$5,680	$5,525	$155	341%
600 Ahold NV	6/15/2006	6/13/2006	$4,872	$4,773	$99	379%
100 Procter & Gamble	6/15/2006	6/15/2006	$5,457	$5,417	$40	270%
100 Baxter International Inc.	6/16/2006	5/12/2006	$3,857	$3,805	$52	14%
100 Morgan Stanley	6/19/2006	6/16/2006	$5,723	$5,669	$54	116%
100 Morgan Stanley	6/20/2006	6/19/2006	$5,721	$5,664	$57	367%
100 Johnson & Johnson	6/21/2006	1/20/2006	$6,178	$6,127	$51	2%
200 Microsoft	6/21/2006	6/5/2006	$4,561	$4,509	$52	26%
100 Morgan Stanley	6/21/2006	6/12/2006	$5,919	$5,835	$84	58%
100 iStar Financial	6/21/2006	6/16/2006	$3,730	$3,678	$52	103%
100 Suncor Energy	6/21/2006	6/19/2006	$7,016	$6,965	$51	134%
100 UnitedHealth Group	6/22/2006	6/19/2006	$4,465	$4,416	$49	135%
100 Cadbury Schweppes Plc	6/22/2006	6/9/2006	$3,829	$3,768	$61	45%
100 Nike Inc.	6/23/2006	4/7/2006	$8,452	$8,400	$52	3%
200 Tyco International	6/23/2006	6/9/2006	$5,425	$5,369	$56	27%
100 Peabody Energy Corp.	6/23/2006	6/19/2006	$5,187	$5,038	$149	270%
100 Univision	6/23/2006	6/22/2006	$3,322	$3,270	$52	580%
200 Repsol YPF	6/26/2006	6/9/2006	$5,405	$5,351	$54	22%
200 Corning Inc.	6/26/2006	6/19/2006	$4,445	$4,391	$54	64%
100 Univision	6/27/2006	6/23/2006	$3,412	$3,311	$101	278%
100 Peabody Energy Corp.	6/27/2006	6/23/2006	$5,147	$5,061	$86	155%
100 Peabody Energy Corp.	6/27/2006	6/27/2006	$5,134	$5,073	$61	439%
100 Bausch & Lomb Inc.	6/28/2006	6/22/2006	$4,936	$4,857	$79	99%
100 Anadarko Petroleum	6/28/2006	6/26/2006	$4,451	$4,396	$55	228%
200 Corning Inc.	6/28/2006	6/27/2006	$4,467	$4,375	$92	768%
100 Procter & Gamble	6/29/2006	5/11/2006	$5,620	$5,570	$50	7%
200 Unilever Plc	6/29/2006	6/9/2006	$4,349	$4,289	$60	26%
100 Commerce Bancorp	6/29/2006	6/19/2006	$3,523	$3,462	$61	64%
100 ADP	6/29/2006	6/19/2006	$4,498	$4,447	$51	42%
200 Vodafone Group Plc	6/29/2006	6/20/2006	$4,243	$4,193	$50	48%
100 Bank of Montreal	6/29/2006	6/22/2006	$5,339	$5,283	$56	55%
200 Tyco International	6/29/2006	6/23/2006	$5,421	$5,367	$54	61%
200 Cisco Systems	6/29/2006	6/26/2006	$3,975	$3,913	$62	193%
100 General Motors Corp.	6/30/2006	10/18/2005	$3,010	$2,955	$55	3%
100 Eli Lilly	6/30/2006	4/6/2006	$5,538	$5,486	$52	4%
200 Unilever Plc	6/30/2006	6/6/2006	$4,476	$4,426	$50	17%
100 Reuters	6/30/2006	6/6/2006	$4,223	$4,178	$45	16%
100 Genentech	6/30/2006	6/6/2006	$8,165	$7,996	$169	32%
200 Dell	6/30/2006	6/16/2006	$4,947	$4,879	$68	36%
100 Cadbury Schweppes Plc	6/30/2006	6/23/2006	$3,843	$3,791	$52	72%

(Continues)

Stock	Date Sold	Date Purchased	Proceeds	Cost	Profit	Percent Profit Annualized
100 Nike Inc.	6/30/2006	6/28/2006	$8,127	$8,062	$65	147%
200 Dell	6/30/2006	6/30/2006	$4,903	$4,861	$42	315%
100 UnitedHealth Group	6/30/2006	6/30/2006	$4,475	$4,435	$40	329%
				Subtotal	**$4,701**	
100 Nike Inc.	7/5/2006	7/5/2006	$8,040	$7,983	$57	261%
100 Commerce Bancorp	7/5/2006	7/5/2006	$3,296	$3,252	$44	494%
100 Fortune Brands Inc.	7/5/2006	7/5/2006	$6,993	$6,952	$41	215%
100 Abbott Laboratories	7/7/2006	3/27/2006	$4,392	$4,338	$54	4%
100 Bank of Montreal	7/7/2006	6/13/2006	$5,464	$5,410	$54	15%
100 Johnson & Johnson	7/7/2006	6/27/2006	$6,058	$6,007	$51	31%
100 UBS	7/11/2006	7/11/2006	$5,324	$5,276	$48	332%
100 DuPont	7/11/2006	7/11/2006	$4,070	$4,023	$47	426%
200 Advanced Micro Devices	7/12/2006	7/12/2006	$4,583	$4,541	$42	338%
100 Baxter International Inc.	7/17/2006	6/27/2006	$3,788	$3,661	$127	63%
200 Corning Inc.	7/17/2006	7/10/2006	$4,397	$4,345	$52	62%
200 Corning Inc.	7/17/2006	7/17/2006	$4,392	$4,347	$45	378%
200 Unilever Plc	7/18/2006	7/14/2006	$4,480	$4,403	$77	160%
100 Anadarko Petroleum	7/18/2006	7/17/2006	$4,435	$4,380	$55	458%
100 United Technologies	7/18/2006	7/17/2006	$5,932	$5,843	$89	556%
100 Baxter International Inc.	7/19/2006	6/16/2006	$3,859	$3,803	$56	16%
100 Bausch & Lomb Inc.	7/19/2006	7/5/2006	$4,905	$4,854	$51	27%
100 Commerce Bancorp	7/19/2006	7/6/2006	$3,315	$3,259	$56	48%
200 Philips Electronics NV	7/19/2006	7/12/2006	$5,969	$5,915	$54	48%
100 DuPont	7/19/2006	7/14/2006	$4,019	$3,964	$55	101%
100 Bank of Montreal	7/19/2006	7/17/2006	$5,465	$5,409	$56	189%
100 Eli Lilly	7/19/2006	7/18/2006	$5,570	$5,475	$95	633%
100 Procter & Gamble	7/19/2006	7/18/2006	$5,621	$5,569	$52	341%
100 Repsol YPF	7/19/2006	7/18/2006	$2,776	$2,723	$53	710%
200 Bristol-Myers Squibb	7/19/2006	7/18/2006	$4,941	$4,890	$51	381%
200 Corning Inc.	7/19/2006	7/18/2006	$4,411	$4,350	$61	512%
100 Anheuser-Busch	7/20/2006	6/15/2005	$4,682	$4,660	$22	0%
100 Johnson & Johnson	7/21/2006	6/22/2006	$6,183	$6,117	$66	14%
100 Eli Lilly	7/21/2006	7/21/2006	$5,509	$5,463	$46	307%
100 Anheuser-Busch	7/24/2006	6/15/2005	$4,712	$4,662	$50	1%
100 Nike Inc.	7/24/2006	7/6/2006	$8,041	$7,990	$51	13%
100 Wal-Mart Stores	7/24/2006	7/14/2006	$4,448	$4,396	$52	43%
200 Vodafone Group Plc	7/24/2006	7/14/2006	$4,243	$4,163	$80	70%
100 Genentech	7/24/2006	7/17/2006	$8,065	$7,987	$78	51%
100 DuPont	7/24/2006	7/20/2006	$4,069	$4,009	$60	137%
100 CIT Group	7/24/2006	7/21/2006	$4,513	$4,456	$57	156%
100 Eli Lilly	7/24/2006	7/21/2006	$5,537	$5,475	$62	138%
100 Genentech	7/24/2006	7/24/2006	$8,028	$7,985	$43	197%
100 Peabody Energy Corp.	7/25/2006	7/21/2006	$4,595	$4,507	$88	178%
100 Wm Wrigley Jr Co.	7/25/2006	7/25/2006	$4,366	$4,315	$51	431%
200 Microsoft	7/26/2006	5/2/2006	$4,859	$4,807	$52	5%
200 Pfizer Inc.	7/26/2006	5/11/2006	$5,030	$4,968	$62	6%
100 St. Jude Medical Inc.	7/26/2006	6/19/2006	$3,602	$3,435	$167	48%
100 Reuters	7/26/2006	7/5/2006	$4,378	$4,176	$202	84%
100 Anadarko Petroleum	7/26/2006	7/18/2006	$4,436	$4,376	$60	63%
100 DuPont	7/26/2006	7/25/2006	$4,056	$4,014	$42	382%
100 Teva Pharmaceutical	7/27/2006	7/5/2006	$3,320	$3,247	$73	37%
100 UBS	7/27/2006	7/12/2006	$5,340	$5,279	$61	28%

Stock	Date Sold	Date Purchased	Proceeds	Cost	Profit	Percent Profit Annualized
100 Nike Inc.	7/27/2006	7/25/2006	$8,103	$7,981	$122	279%
100 Wm Wrigley Jr Co.	7/27/2006	7/26/2006	$4,524	$4,424	$100	825%
100 Johnson & Johnson	7/28/2006	1/11/2006	$6,283	$6,232	$51	2%
100 Johnson & Johnson	7/28/2006	1/11/2006	$6,286	$6,235	$51	2%
100 AIG	7/28/2006	6/7/2006	$6,094	$6,036	$58	7%
100 Wal-Mart Stores	7/28/2006	7/26/2006	$4,443	$4,385	$58	241%
100 FedEx Corp.	7/28/2006	7/27/2006	$10,278	$10,194	$84	301%
200 Bristol-Myers Squibb	7/28/2006	7/27/2006	$4,899	$4,817	$82	621%
100 Peabody Energy Corp.	7/31/2006	7/20/2006	$5,001	$4,898	$103	70%
100 Teva Pharmaceutical	7/31/2006	7/27/2006	$3,293	$3,240	$53	149%
100 Genentech	7/31/2006	7/31/2006	$8,046	$8,001	$45	205%
				Subtotal	**$3,855**	
100 Genentech	8/1/2006	8/1/2006	$8,041	$7,999	$42	192%
100 FedEx Corp.	8/1/2006	8/1/2006	$10,274	$10,229	$45	161%
100 Electronic Arts	8/2/2006	5/4/2006	$4,977	$4,914	$63	5%
100 Adobe Systems	8/2/2006	5/17/2006	$3,217	$3,162	$55	8%
100 ADP	8/2/2006	7/7/2006	$4,525	$4,456	$69	22%
100 Procter & Gamble	8/2/2006	7/31/2006	$5,794	$5,623	$171	555%
100 Molson Coors Brewing	8/2/2006	8/1/2006	$6,737	$6,686	$51	278%
100 Wm Wrigley Jr Co.	8/2/2006	8/1/2006	$4,597	$4,525	$72	581%
100 Procter & Gamble	8/2/2006	8/1/2006	$5,776	$5,588	$188	1228%
100 Wal-Mart Stores	8/3/2006	8/1/2006	$4,444	$4,388	$56	233%
100 Genentech	8/3/2006	8/2/2006	$8,056	$8,004	$52	237%
100 Peabody Energy Corp.	8/4/2006	8/4/2006	$4,925	$4,877	$48	359%
100 FedEx Corp.	8/4/2006	8/4/2006	$10,457	$10,384	$73	257%
200 Adobe Systems	8/4/2006	8/4/2006	$6,351	$6,311	$40	231%
100 Peabody Energy Corp.	8/4/2006	8/4/2006	$4,913	$4,866	$47	353%
100 FedEx Corp.	8/7/2006	8/7/2006	$10,400	$10,347	$53	187%
100 FedEx Corp.	8/7/2006	8/7/2006	$10,409	$10,372	$37	130%
100 Peabody Energy Corp.	8/7/2006	8/7/2006	$4,914	$4,869	$45	337%
200 Adobe Systems	8/7/2006	8/7/2006	$6,353	$6,313	$40	231%
100 Peabody Energy Corp.	8/7/2006	8/7/2006	$4,923	$4,871	$52	390%
100 Genentech	8/8/2006	8/7/2006	$8,067	$7,998	$69	315%
100 Clear Channel Comms.	8/8/2006	8/7/2006	$2,895	$2,861	$34	434%
100 Clear Channel Comms.	8/8/2006	8/7/2006	$2,894	$2,847	$47	603%
100 BP Plc	8/8/2006	8/8/2006	$7,012	$6,969	$43	225%
100 BP Plc	8/8/2006	8/8/2006	$7,018	$6,977	$41	214%
200 Bristol-Myers Squibb	8/8/2006	8/8/2006	$4,271	$4,203	$68	591%
200 Cisco Systems Inc.	8/9/2006	7/6/2006	$3,972	$3,916	$56	15%
100 Molson Coors Brewing	8/9/2006	8/3/2006	$6,747	$6,680	$67	61%
100 Peabody Energy Corp.	8/9/2006	8/8/2006	$4,920	$4,861	$59	443%
100 Genentech	8/9/2006	8/8/2006	$8,078	$7,999	$79	360%
200 Bristol-Myers Squibb	8/9/2006	8/8/2006	$4,283	$4,229	$54	466%
100 Wm Wrigley Jr Co.	8/10/2006	8/9/2006	$4,645	$4,588	$57	453%
200 Adobe Systems Inc.	8/10/2006	8/9/2006	$6,387	$6,317	$70	404%

(Continues)

Stock	Date Sold	Date Purchased	Proceeds	Cost	Profit	Percent Profit Annualized
100 AIG	8/11/2006	8/1/2006	$6,138	$6,043	$95	57%
100 United Technologies	8/14/2006	8/11/2006	$6,060	$6,002	$58	118%
200 Adobe Systems	8/14/2006	8/11/2006	$6,420	$6,315	$105	202%
100 Eli Lilly	8/14/2006	8/11/2006	$5,441	$5,400	$41	92%
100 St. Jude Medical Inc.	8/15/2006	8/3/2006	$3,455	$3,381	$74	67%
100 Eli Lilly	8/15/2006	8/11/2006	$5,509	$5,417	$92	155%
200 Vodafone Group Plc	8/15/2006	8/11/2006	$4,194	$4,146	$48	106%
100 UBS	8/15/2006	8/11/2006	$5,537	$5,278	$259	448%
100 Electronic Arts	8/15/2006	8/14/2006	$5,032	$4,911	$121	899%
200 Microsoft	8/16/2006	4/28/2006	$4,935	$4,873	$62	4%
200 Microsoft	8/16/2006	4/28/2006	$4,933	$4,887	$46	3%
95 CIT Group	8/16/2006	8/9/2006	$4,152	$4,111	$41	52%
200 Advanced Micro Devices	8/17/2006	7/14/2006	$4,639	$4,393	$246	60%
100 DuPont	8/17/2006	7/27/2006	$4,047	$3,974	$73	32%
200 Tyson Foods Inc.	8/17/2006	8/1/2006	$2,821	$2,763	$58	48%
100 FedEx Corp.	8/17/2006	8/7/2006	$10,450	$10,382	$68	24%
100 CIT Group	8/17/2006	8/9/2006	$4,490	$4,421	$69	71%
100 CIT Group	8/17/2006	8/9/2006	$4,491	$4,371	$120	125%
200 Bristol-Myers Squibb	8/17/2006	8/9/2006	$4,303	$4,229	$74	80%
100 Genentech	8/17/2006	8/10/2006	$8,175	$8,007	$168	109%
100 Peabody Energy Corp.	8/17/2006	8/14/2006	$4,833	$4,442	$391	1071%
200 Adobe Systems	8/18/2006	5/8/2006	$6,895	$6,795	$100	5%
100 Peabody Energy Corp.	8/18/2006	8/17/2006	$4,737	$4,687	$50	389%
200 Vodafone Group Plc	8/18/2006	8/18/2006	$4,171	$4,129	$42	371%
200 Vodafone Group Plc	8/18/2006	8/18/2006	$4,169	$4,127	$42	371%
100 FedEx Corp.	8/18/2006	8/18/2006	$10,399	$10,340	$59	208%
100 Eli Lilly	8/18/2006	8/18/2006	$5,482	$5,444	$38	255%
200 Adobe Systems	8/18/2006	8/18/2006	$6,823	$6,775	$48	259%
100 BP Plc	8/21/2006	8/10/2006	$7,027	$6,945	$82	39%
100 Constellation Brands	8/23/2006	7/7/2006	$2,545	$2,501	$44	14%
100 iStar Financial	8/24/2006	9/19/2005	$4,142	$4,085	$57	2%
200 Vodafone Group Plc	8/24/2006	8/22/2006	$4,207	$4,137	$70	309%
100 Peabody Energy Corp.	8/25/2006	8/23/2006	$4,738	$4,677	$61	238%
100 Wal-Mart Stores	8/28/2006	8/23/2006	$4,442	$4,389	$53	88%
100 CIT Group	8/28/2006	8/25/2006	$4,492	$4,426	$66	181%
100 Boeing Co.	8/28/2006	8/28/2006	$7,389	$7,343	$46	229%
300 Intel	8/29/2006	5/11/2006	$5,882	$5,824	$58	3%
200 Corning Inc.	8/29/2006	7/25/2006	$4,387	$4,339	$48	12%
100 Genentech	8/29/2006	8/24/2006	$8,070	$8,004	$66	60%
300 Intel	8/30/2006	5/10/2006	$5,932	$5,861	$71	4%
100 Bausch & Lomb Inc.	8/30/2006	7/20/2006	$4,885	$4,823	$62	11%
100 Electronic Arts	8/30/2006	8/23/2006	$5,051	$4,996	$55	57%
100 BP Plc	8/30/2006	8/29/2006	$6,798	$6,736	$62	336%
100 Boeing Co.	8/30/2006	8/29/2006	$7,398	$7,341	$57	283%
100 Nike Inc.	8/31/2006	7/27/2006	$8,040	$7,975	$65	8%
100 Ingersoll-Rand Co.	8/31/2006	8/30/2006	$3,778	$3,730	$48	470%
100 BP Plc	8/31/2006	8/30/2006	$6,809	$6,736	$73	396%
100 Caterpillar	8/31/2006	8/30/2006	$6,559	$6,496	$63	354%
				Subtotal	**$5,938**	
100 Verizon Communications	9/1/2006	6/23/2005	$3,554	$3,504	$50	1%
200 Pfizer Inc.	9/1/2006	6/30/2005	$5,570	$5,520	$50	1%

Stock	Date Sold	Date Purchased	Proceeds	Cost	Profit	Percent Profit Annualized
100 Univision	9/1/2006	6/27/2006	$3,457	$3,403	$54	9%
100 Clear Channel Comms.	9/1/2006	8/8/2006	$2,914	$2,862	$52	28%
100 DuPont	9/1/2006	8/21/2006	$4,064	$4,018	$46	38%
100 Washington Mutual	9/5/2006	9/1/2006	$4,224	$4,172	$52	114%
200 Corning Inc.	9/5/2006	9/5/2006	$4,397	$4,341	$56	471%
100 Suncor Energy	9/7/2006	9/6/2006	$7,639	$7,576	$63	304%
100 Suncor Energy	9/7/2006	9/7/2006	$7,543	$7,487	$56	273%
100 Bausch & Lomb Inc.	9/8/2006	9/6/2006	$4,976	$4,832	$144	544%
200 Corning Inc.	9/8/2006	9/7/2006	$4,361	$4,311	$50	423%
200 Corning Inc.	9/8/2006	9/8/2006	$4,345	$4,291	$54	459%
200 Pfizer Inc.	9/11/2006	9/7/2006	$5,564	$5,510	$54	89%
100 Genentech	9/11/2006	9/11/2006	$7,879	$7,836	$43	200%
200 Corning Inc.	9/11/2006	9/11/2006	$4,365	$4,309	$56	474%
100 Verizon	9/12/2006	5/2/2005	$3,575	$3,511	$64	1%
300 Goodyear Tire	9/12/2006	5/15/2006	$4,444	$4,337	$107	8%
300 Applied Materials Inc.	9/12/2006	5/18/2006	$5,251	$5,135	$116	7%
100 General Electric	9/12/2006	6/12/2006	$3,446	$3,395	$51	6%
100 FedEx Corp.	9/12/2006	8/21/2006	$10,348	$10,294	$54	9%
300 Intel	9/12/2006	9/6/2006	$5,893	$5,840	$53	55%
300 Intel	9/12/2006	9/6/2006	$5,882	$5,824	$58	61%
100 Boeing Co.	9/12/2006	9/7/2006	$7,397	$7,343	$54	54%
100 CIT Group	9/12/2006	9/11/2006	$4,494	$4,443	$51	419%
200 Bristol-Myers Squibb	9/13/2006	7/31/2006	$4,927	$4,817	$110	19%
100 Commerce Bancorp	9/13/2006	8/29/2006	$3,366	$3,312	$54	40%
100 Washington Mutual	9/13/2006	9/7/2006	$4,219	$4,168	$51	74%
100 Ingersoll-Rand Co.	9/13/2006	9/11/2006	$3,783	$3,731	$52	254%
100 Anadarko Petroleum	9/13/2006	9/12/2006	$4,465	$4,391	$74	615%
100 DuPont	9/14/2006	8/21/2006	$4,084	$4,021	$63	24%
100 Genentech	9/14/2006	9/11/2006	$7,899	$7,840	$59	92%
100 3M Co.	9/15/2006	7/10/2006	$7,427	$7,317	$110	8%
200 Adobe Systems	9/15/2006	8/21/2006	$7,398	$6,747	$651	141%
100 Genentech	9/15/2006	9/14/2006	$7,940	$7,867	$73	339%
300 Time Warner	9/18/2006	7/7/2006	$5,129	$5,074	$55	5%
100 Anadarko Petroleum	9/18/2006	9/14/2006	$4,475	$4,405	$70	145%
100 Genentech	9/19/2006	9/18/2006	$7,954	$7,868	$86	399%
300 Goodyear Tire	9/19/2006	9/18/2006	$4,318	$4,253	$65	558%
300 Goodyear Tire	9/19/2006	9/19/2006	$4,321	$4,277	$44	375%
200 Tyco International	9/20/2006	7/14/2006	$5,375	$5,323	$52	5%
300 Intel	9/20/2006	9/19/2006	$5,881	$5,831	$50	313%
100 ConocoPhillips	9/21/2006	9/20/2006	$5,854	$5,793	$61	384%
100 Nike Inc.	9/22/2006	4/3/2006	$8,553	$8,488	$65	2%
100 Nike Inc.	9/22/2006	6/27/2006	$8,553	$8,372	$181	9%
100 Molson Coors Brewing	9/22/2006	9/22/2006	$6,714	$6,669	$45	246%
100 Boeing Co.	9/25/2006	8/18/2006	$7,801	$7,737	$64	8%
100 Weyerhaeuser	9/25/2006	9/21/2006	$6,045	$5,962	$83	127%
100 Weyerhaeuser	9/25/2006	9/21/2006	$5,983	$5,942	$41	63%
300 Applied Materials Inc.	9/25/2006	9/21/2006	$5,191	$5,105	$86	154%
300 Goodyear Tire	9/25/2006	9/21/2006	$4,321	$4,271	$50	107%
100 3M Co.	9/25/2006	9/22/2006	$7,362	$7,306	$56	93%
200 Alcoa	9/25/2006	9/25/2006	$5,421	$5,367	$54	367%
100 GlaxoSmithKline Plc	9/25/2006	9/25/2006	$5,432	$5,382	$50	339%
100 General Electric	9/26/2006	1/17/2006	$3,534	$3,494	$40	2%
300 Time Warner	9/26/2006	2/15/2006	$5,503	$5,405	$98	3%

(Continues)

Stock	Date Sold	Date Purchased	Proceeds	Cost	Profit	Percent Profit Annualized
100 Genentech	9/26/2006	9/19/2006	$7,971	$7,909	$62	41%
300 El Paso Corp.	9/26/2006	9/20/2006	$3,991	$3,923	$68	105%
300 Intel	9/26/2006	9/21/2006	$5,881	$5,801	$80	101%
100 Caterpillar	9/26/2006	9/21/2006	$6,551	$6,496	$55	62%
100 Ingersoll-Rand Co.	9/26/2006	9/21/2006	$3,788	$3,697	$91	180%
100 ConocoPhillips	9/26/2006	9/22/2006	$5,838	$5,781	$57	90%
100 Suncor Energy	9/26/2006	9/22/2006	$6,789	$6,726	$63	85%
100 General Electric	9/27/2006	1/17/2006	$3,552	$3,502	$50	2%
300 Time Warner	9/27/2006	2/7/2006	$5,578	$5,528	$50	1%
200 Repsol YPF	9/27/2006	9/6/2006	$5,781	$5,649	$132	41%
100 Anadarko Petroleum	9/27/2006	9/20/2006	$4,344	$4,273	$71	87%
100 Anadarko Petroleum	9/27/2006	9/27/2006	$4,330	$4,271	$59	504%
100 Anadarko Petroleum	9/28/2006	9/19/2006	$4,440	$4,394	$46	42%
				Subtotal	**$5,065**	
100 GlaxoSmithKline Plc	10/2/2006	9/28/2006	$5,415	$5,354	$61	104%
300 Goodyear Tire	10/2/2006	10/2/2006	$4,306	$4,262	$44	377%
300 Goodyear Tire	10/3/2006	10/3/2006	$4,300	$4,259	$41	351%
100 Caterpillar	10/3/2006	10/3/2006	$6,513	$6,471	$42	237%
200 Cisco Systems Inc.	10/4/2006	7/1/2004	$4,710	$4,641	$69	1%
100 General Electric	10/4/2006	12/27/2005	$3,591	$3,530	$61	2%
100 CKX Inc.	10/4/2006	7/26/2004	$1,266	$1,213	$53	23%
100 Suncor Energy	10/4/2006	10/3/2006	$6,652	$6,587	$65	360%
300 Goodyear Tire	10/4/2006	10/4/2006	$4,279	$4,232	$47	405%
300 Goodyear Tire	10/4/2006	10/4/2006	$4,301	$4,253	$48	412%
100 Suncor Energy	10/4/2006	10/4/2006	$6,557	$6,499	$58	326%
200 Alcoa	10/4/2006	10/4/2006	$5,412	$5,368	$44	299%
100 Juniper Networks	10/5/2006	5/11/2006	$1,795	$1,742	$53	8%
100 ConocoPhillips	10/5/2006	10/3/2006	$5,785	$5,735	$50	159%
300 Goodyear Tire	10/5/2006	10/5/2006	$4,276	$4,217	$59	511%
300 Goodyear Tire	10/5/2006	10/5/2006	$4,269	$4,224	$45	389%
300 Goodyear Tire	10/6/2006	10/6/2006	$4,246	$4,193	$53	461%
300 Goodyear Tire	10/6/2006	10/6/2006	$4,265	$4,223	$42	363%
100 ConocoPhillips	10/6/2006	10/6/2006	$5,785	$5,735	$50	318%
100 Anheuser-Busch	10/10/2006	10/10/2006	$4,771	$4,661	$110	861%
100 Anadarko Petroleum	10/10/2006	10/3/2006	$4,309	$4,214	$95	118%
100 Molson Coors Brewing	10/12/2006	10/5/2006	$6,623	$6,565	$58	46%
200 Alcoa	10/12/2006	10/11/2006	$5,405	$5,351	$54	368%
100 Legg Mason Inc.	10/12/2006	10/12/2006	$8,799	$8,741	$58	242%
100 Legg Mason Inc.	10/12/2006	10/12/2006	$8,810	$8,760	$50	208%
200 Sara Lee Corp.	10/13/2006	9/13/2005	$3,294	$3,254	$40	1%
25 Hanesbrands Inc.	10/13/2006	9/13/2005	$573	$566	$7	1%
200 Intel	10/13/2006	2/2/2006	$4,307	$4,249	$58	2%
100 Weyerhaeuser	10/13/2006	6/5/2006	$6,458	$6,344	$114	5%
200 Dell	10/16/2006	7/5/2006	$4,915	$4,859	$56	4%
100 Suncor Energy	10/16/2006	9/8/2006	$7,528	$7,476	$52	7%
100 ConocoPhillips	10/16/2006	9/8/2006	$6,099	$6,054	$45	7%
100 Anadarko Petroleum	10/16/2006	9/19/2006	$4,458	$4,406	$52	16%
200 Pfizer Inc.	10/16/2006	10/10/2006	$5,534	$5,482	$52	58%
200 Alcoa	10/16/2006	10/12/2006	$5,413	$5,357	$56	95%
100 IBM	10/18/2006	4/1/2005	$9,140	$9,046	$94	1%
100 3M Co.	10/19/2006	7/7/2006	$7,615	$7,546	$69	3%
100 BP Plc	10/19/2006	9/6/2006	$6,782	$6,731	$51	6%
300 Goodyear Tire	10/19/2006	10/17/2006	$4,324	$4,259	$65	279%
100 Suncor Energy	10/19/2006	10/18/2006	$7,443	$7,372	$71	352%
100 Wm. Wrigley Jr. Co.	10/20/2006	9/6/2006	$4,658	$4,605	$53	10%

Stock	Date Sold	Date Purchased	Proceeds	Cost	Profit	Percent Profit Annualized
100 ConocoPhillips	10/20/2006	9/8/2006	$6,146	$6,071	$75	11%
200 Pfizer Inc.	10/20/2006	10/20/2006	$5,515	$5,475	$40	267%
100 Wm. Wrigley Jr. Co.	10/23/2006	8/23/2006	$5,065	$4,647	$418	54%
100 BP Plc	10/23/2006	10/23/2006	$6,729	$6,666	$63	345%
100 Suncor Energy	10/23/2006	10/23/2006	$7,535	$7,490	$45	219%
100 ConocoPhillips	10/24/2006	10/20/2006	$6,126	$6,065	$61	92%
100 Schlumberger	10/24/2006	10/20/2006	$6,143	$6,056	$87	131%
100 Suncor Energy	10/24/2006	10/23/2006	$7,566	$7,480	$86	420%
100 Cheesecake Factory	10/25/2006	6/12/2006	$2,951	$2,872	$79	7%
100 ConocoPhillips	10/25/2006	10/20/2006	$6,124	$6,060	$64	77%
100 Caterpillar	10/25/2006	10/20/2006	$6,138	$6,060	$78	94%
100 Anheuser-Busch	10/25/2006	10/25/2006	$4,692	$4,648	$44	346%
100 Dow Jones & Co.	10/26/2006	9/13/2006	$3,528	$3,458	$70	17%
100 Legg Mason Inc.	10/26/2006	10/12/2006	$8,825	$8,771	$54	16%
100 Suncor Energy	10/31/2006	10/30/2006	$7,562	$7,490	$72	351%
100 Suncor Energy	10/31/2006	10/31/2006	$7,537	$7,485	$52	254%
				Subtotal	**$3,733**	
100 ConocoPhillips	11/1/2006	10/30/2006	$6,052	$6,007	$45	137%
100 BP Plc	11/1/2006	10/31/2006	$6,739	$6,665	$74	405%
100 Weyerhaeuser	11/1/2006	10/31/2006	$6,403	$6,333	$70	403%
100 Suncor Energy	11/1/2006	11/1/2006	$7,496	$7,425	$71	349%
100 Suncor Energy	11/1/2006	11/1/2006	$7,545	$7,443	$102	500%
100 GlaxoSmithKline Plc	11/2/2006	10/27/2006	$5,388	$5,336	$52	59%
100 Caterpillar	11/2/2006	10/31/2006	$6,106	$6,046	$60	181%
100 Suncor Energy	11/2/2006	11/1/2006	$7,546	$7,495	$51	248%
100 Weyerhaeuser	11/2/2006	11/1/2006	$6,388	$6,345	$43	247%
100 ConocoPhillips	11/3/2006	10/30/2006	$6,099	$6,033	$66	100%
100 Suncor Energy	11/3/2006	11/2/2006	$7,615	$7,478	$137	669%
100 Teva Pharmaceutical	11/6/2006	11/1/2006	$3,301	$3,244	$57	128%
100 St. Jude Medical Inc.	11/6/2006	11/2/2006	$3,416	$3,346	$70	191%
100 CVS Corp.	11/6/2006	11/3/2006	$2,950	$2,898	$52	218%
300 Applied Materials Inc.	11/6/2006	11/3/2006	$5,188	$5,105	$83	198%
200 Advanced Micro Devices	11/7/2006	10/19/2006	$4,365	$4,307	$58	26%
100 GlaxoSmithKline Plc	11/7/2006	11/3/2006	$5,423	$5,338	$85	145%
100 Fortune Brands Inc.	11/8/2006	5/15/2006	$7,892	$7,814	$78	2%
100 Public Service Enterprise Gp.	11/8/2006	9/15/2006	$6,299	$6,248	$51	6%
100 Ingersoll-Rand Co.	11/8/2006	10/30/2006	$3,735	$3,684	$51	56%
100 Ingersoll-Rand Co.	11/8/2006	10/30/2006	$3,724	$3,683	$41	45%
100 Teva Pharmaceutical	11/8/2006	11/7/2006	$3,286	$3,232	$54	610%
100 Weyerhaeuser	11/9/2006	11/1/2006	$6,400	$6,348	$52	37%
100 CVS Corp.	11/13/2006	11/9/2006	$2,916	$2,865	$51	162%
100 Weyerhaeuser	11/13/2006	11/10/2006	$6,399	$6,339	$60	115%
100 Catalina Marketing	11/14/2006	11/11/2006	$2,525	$2,475	$50	57%
100 St. Jude Medical Inc.	11/14/2006	11/9/2006	$3,406	$3,332	$74	162%
100 Caterpillar	11/15/2006	11/3/2006	$6,107	$6,037	$70	35%
200 Advanced Micro Devices	11/15/2006	11/8/2006	$4,329	$4,277	$52	63%
100 Eli Lilly	11/15/2006	11/13/2006	$5,450	$5,399	$51	172%
100 Genentech	11/15/2006	11/14/2006	$8,062	$7,999	$63	287%
200 Corning Inc.	11/16/2006	10/26/2006	$4,319	$4,265	$54	22%
100 SLM Corp.	11/16/2006	11/9/2006	$4,784	$4,723	$61	67%
100 CVS Corp.	11/16/2006	11/9/2006	$2,948	$2,899	$49	88%
100 Eli Lilly	11/16/2006	11/16/2006	$5,429	$5,387	$42	285%

(Continues)

Stock	Date Sold	Date Purchased	Proceeds	Cost	Profit	Percent Profit Annualized
100 Suncor Energy	11/17/2006	11/17/2006	$7,532	$7,471	$61	298%
100 Suncor Energy	11/17/2006	11/17/2006	$7,518	$7,450	$68	333%
100 Home Depot Inc.	11/20/2006	6/2/2006	$3,854	$3,803	$51	3%
200 Advanced Micro Devices	11/20/2006	11/20/2006	$4,299	$4,253	$46	395%
100 Bausch & Lomb Inc.	11/21/2006	11/17/2006	$4,958	$4,889	$69	129%
100 BP Plc	11/21/2006	11/17/2006	$6,665	$6,611	$54	75%
200 Advanced Micro Devices	11/21/2006	11/21/2006	$4,259	$4,219	$40	346%
100 Time Warner Inc.	11/22/2006	4/22/2002	$2,071	$2,021	$50	1%
100 Carnival Corp.	11/22/2006	3/21/2006	$5,051	$4,998	$53	2%
200 Corning Inc.	11/22/2006	11/20/2006	$4,279	$4,211	$68	295%
100 Teva Pharmaceutical	11/24/2006	11/9/2006	$3,289	$3,232	$57	43%
100 BP Plc	11/24/2006	11/24/2006	$6,654	$6,607	$47	260%
100 Anheuser-Busch	11/28/2006	11/21/2006	$4,675	$4,627	$48	54%
100 Genentech	11/28/2006	11/27/2006	$8,053	$8,001	$52	237%
100 Weyerhaeuser	11/28/2006	11/27/2006	$6,389	$6,334	$55	317%
100 GlaxoSmithKline Plc	11/29/2006	11/15/2006	$5,336	$5,151	$185	94%
100 CVS Corp.	11/29/2006	11/27/2006	$2,825	$2,775	$50	329%
200 Corning Inc.	11/29/2006	11/27/2006	$4,253	$4,199	$54	235%
100 CVS Corp.	11/29/2006	11/27/2006	$2,787	$2,737	$50	333%
100 Teva Pharmaceutical	11/29/2006	11/28/2006	$3,280	$3,228	$52	588%
200 Pfizer Inc.	11/30/2006	10/24/2006	$5,509	$5,449	$60	11%
200 Advanced Micro Devices	11/30/2006	11/30/2006	$4,277	$4,235	$42	362%
				Subtotal	**$3,492**	
100 Home Depot Inc.	12/1/2006	6/2/2006	$3,967	$3,852	$115	6%
100 Caterpillar	12/1/2006	12/1/2006	$6,098	$6,057	$41	247%
200 Pfizer Inc.	12/4/2006	12/4/2006	$4,795	$4,709	$86	667%
300 Micron Technology	12/4/2006	12/4/2006	$4,351	$4,304	$47	399%
100 Peabody Energy Corp.	12/5/2006	8/25/2006	$4,784	$4,675	$109	8%
100 CVS Corp.	12/5/2006	11/17/2006	$2,947	$2,891	$56	39%
100 SLM Corp.	12/5/2006	11/20/2006	$4,781	$4,723	$58	30%
100 Eli Lilly	12/5/2006	11/21/2006	$5,438	$5,378	$60	29%
100 Eli Lilly	12/5/2006	11/21/2006	$5,428	$5,378	$50	24%
200 Advanced Micro Devices	12/5/2006	12/1/2006	$4,271	$4,207	$64	139%
200 Corning Inc.	12/5/2006	12/1/2006	$4,259	$4,207	$52	113%
100 Bausch & Lomb Inc.	12/7/2006	11/30/2006	$4,922	$4,872	$50	54%
100 Peabody Energy Corp.	12/7/2006	12/7/2006	$4,722	$4,677	$45	351%
100 Catalina Marketing	12/8/2006	11/27/2006	$2,801	$2,470	$331	445%
100 Dow Jones & Co. Inc.	12/13/2006	5/10/2006	$3,833	$3,718	$115	5%
100 General Electric	12/13/2006	12/1/2006	$3,572	$3,519	$53	46%
100 Electronic Arts	12/13/2006	12/12/2006	$5,264	$5,205	$59	414%
200 Advanced Micro Devices	12/14/2006	12/7/2006	$4,339	$4,221	$118	146%
100 Black & Decker Corp.	12/18/2006	12/18/2006	$7,871	$7,798	$73	339%
200 Statoil ASA	12/19/2006	12/19/2006	$5,315	$5,271	$44	305%
100 CVS Corp.	12/21/2006	12/18/2006	$3,060	$2,999	$61	247%
200 Catalina Marketing	12/21/2006	12/20/2006	$5,621	$5,563	$58	381%
100 BP Plc	12/22/2006	12/21/2006	$6,720	$6,650	$70	384%
100 Caterpillar	12/26/2006	12/21/2006	$6,099	$6,046	$53	64%
200 Catalina Marketing	12/26/2006	12/21/2006	$5,609	$5,557	$52	68%
100 Black & Decker Corp.	12/27/2006	12/18/2006	$7,895	$7,845	$50	26%

Stock	Date Sold	Date Purchased	Proceeds	Cost	Profit	Percent Profit Annualized
100 FedEx Corp.	12/27/2006	12/22/2006	$10,850	$10,793	$57	39%
100 BP Plc	12/27/2006	12/22/2006	$6,720	$6,673	$47	51%
100 Anadarko Petroleum	12/27/2006	12/22/2006	$4,308	$4,248	$60	103%
100 FedEx Corp.	12/28/2006	12/27/2006	$10,833	$10,782	$51	173%
100 Wal-Mart Stores	12/29/2006	12/19/2006	$4,655	$4,605	$50	40%
100 FedEx Corp.	12/29/2006	12/28/2006	$10,852	$10,793	$59	200%
				Subtotal	$2,294	
				Total	$45,350	

Trading Record for 2007, January–February (Net of All Commissions)

Stock	Date Sold	Date Purchased	Proceeds	Cost	Profit	Percent Profit Annualized
100 GlaxoSmithKline Plc	1/3/2007	11/8/2006	$5,387	$5,333	$54	7%
100 GlaxoSmithKline Plc	1/3/2007	11/8/2006	$5,368	$5,324	$44	5%
100 GlaxoSmithKline Plc	1/3/2007	12/5/2006	$5,386	$5,277	$109	26%
100 AstraZeneca	1/3/2007	12/20/2006	$5,426	$5,376	$50	24%
100 Electronic Arts	1/3/2007	12/20/2006	$5,251	$5,197	$54	27%
200 Catalina Marketing	1/3/2007	12/29/2006	$5,605	$5,545	$60	79%
100 Electronic Arts	1/3/2007	1/3/2007	$5,103	$5,060	$43	310%
100 Genentech	1/4/2007	12/14/2006	$8,218	$8,154	$64	14%
100 FedEx Corp.	1/5/2007	1/5/2007	$10,839	$10,783	$56	190%
100 Freeport-McMoRan	1/5/2007	1/5/2007	$5,055	$5,003	$52	379%
100 Teva Pharmaceutical	1/8/2007	11/30/2006	$3,273	$3,216	$57	17%
100 FedEx Corp.	1/9/2007	1/5/2007	$10,909	$10,792	$117	99%
100 FedEx Corp.	1/9/2007	1/9/2007	$10,842	$10,770	$72	244%
200 Catalina Marketing	1/11/2007	1/3/2007	$5,601	$5,537	$64	53%
100 Suncor Energy	1/11/2007	1/10/2007	$7,134	$7,078	$56	289%
300 Corning Inc.	1/12/2007	12/12/2006	$5,998	$5,945	$53	10%
100 GlaxoSmithKline Plc	1/12/2007	1/8/2007	$5,355	$5,293	$62	107%
100 FedEx Corp.	1/12/2007	1/10/2007	$10,857	$10,765	$92	156%
200 Statoil ASA	1/12/2007	1/10/2007	$4,867	$4,809	$58	220%
100 Suncor Energy	1/12/2007	1/11/2007	$7,093	$7,029	$64	332%
100 ConocoPhillips	1/12/2007	1/11/2007	$6,259	$6,201	$58	341%
200 Statoil ASA	1/17/2007	1/17/2007	$4,853	$4,797	$56	426%
100 Carnival Corp.	1/18/2007	3/6/2006	$5,231	$5,146	$85	3%
100 Carnival Corp.	1/18/2007	3/6/2006	$5,177	$5,141	$36	1%
100 CKX Inc.	1/19/2007	11/28/2006	$1,260	$1,210	$50	29%
100 Motorola	1/19/2007	1/8/2007	$1,923	$1,865	$58	103%
100 Electronic Arts	1/19/2007	1/17/2007	$5,123	$5,063	$60	216%
100 Anadarko Petroleum	1/22/2007	1/3/2007	$4,319	$4,268	$51	23%
100 Schlumberger	1/22/2007	1/3/2007	$6,123	$6,081	$42	13%

(Continues)

Stock	Date Sold	Date Purchased	Proceeds	Cost	Profit	Percent Profit Annualized
100 Schlumberger	1/22/2007	1/3/2007	$6,143	$6,066	$77	24%
100 Archer Daniels Midland	1/22/2007	1/18/2007	$3,171	$3,099	$72	212%
100 Schlumberger	1/22/2007	1/22/2007	$6,119	$6,077	$42	252%
100 Suncor Energy	1/23/2007	1/3/2007	$7,593	$7,539	$54	13%
200 Catalina Marketing	1/23/2007	1/18/2007	$5,625	$5,559	$66	87%
100 Anadarko Petroleum	1/23/2007	1/22/2007	$4,318	$4,268	$50	428%
300 Corning Inc.	1/24/2007	1/17/2007	$6,082	$5,903	$179	158%
100 Suncor Energy	1/24/2007	1/24/2007	$7,542	$7,494	$48	234%
200 Corning Inc.	1/25/2007	12/7/2006	$4,333	$4,205	$128	23%
100 Suncor Energy	1/25/2007	1/25/2007	$7,527	$7,472	$55	269%
100 Caterpillar	1/26/2007	1/5/2007	$6,102	$6,047	$55	16%
100 Suncor Energy	1/26/2007	1/25/2007	$7,600	$7,478	$122	595%
200 Statoil ASA	1/31/2007	12/20/2006	$5,397	$5,341	$56	9%
100 Commerce Bancorp	1/31/2007	1/16/2007	$3,356	$3,293	$63	47%
100 Motorola	1/31/2007	1/22/2007	$1,941	$1,865	$76	165%
100 Anadarko Petroleum	1/31/2007	1/25/2007	$4,325	$4,257	$68	97%
				Subtotal	**$2,988**	
100 Eli Lilly	2/1/2007	12/7/2006	$5,452	$5,398	$54	7%
100 Electronic Arts	2/2/2007	1/19/2007	$5,399	$5,063	$336	173%
100 Eli Lilly	2/5/2007	12/7/2006	$5,446	$5,395	$51	6%
200 Corning Inc.	2/5/2007	1/25/2007	$4,269	$4,215	$54	43%
100 Anadarko Petroleum	2/7/2007	2/6/2007	$4,278	$4,219	$59	510%
200 Statoil ASA	2/8/2007	2/8/2007	$5,195	$5,153	$42	297%
100 Sanofi-Aventis	2/12/2007	2/9/2007	$4,426	$4,367	$59	164%
100 Washington Mutual	2/12/2007	2/9/2007	$4,394	$4,342	$52	146%
200 Catalina Marketing	2/12/2007	2/9/2007	$5,631	$5,581	$50	109%
200 Statoil ASA	2/13/2007	2/12/2007	$5,201	$5,149	$52	369%
100 General Electric	2/14/2007	2/9/2007	$3,612	$3,556	$56	115%
200 Dell	2/14/2007	2/12/2007	$4,779	$4,709	$70	271%
200 Catalina Marketing	2/14/2007	2/14/2007	$5,523	$5,473	$50	333%
100 Sanofi-Aventis	2/15/2007	2/13/2007	$4,384	$4,326	$58	245%
100 SLM Corp.	2/16/2007	2/5/2007	$4,372	$4,301	$71	55%
100 SLM Corp.	2/16/2007	2/5/2007	$4,377	$4,252	$125	98%
100 Electronic Arts	2/20/2007	2/5/2007	$5,151	$5,047	$104	50%
200 Statoil ASA	2/21/2007	2/20/2007	$5,151	$5,099	$52	372%
100 Carnival Corp.	2/21/2007	2/21/2007	$4,867	$4,817	$50	379%
100 Weatherford Intl. Ltd.	2/26/2007	12/26/2006	$4,247	$4,185	$62	9%
200 Motorola	2/26/2007	2/21/2007	$3,849	$3,791	$58	112%
100 Eli Lilly	2/26/2007	2/23/2007	$5,453	$5,388	$65	147%
100 Weatherford Intl. Ltd.	2/27/2007	2/27/2007	$4,148	$4,087	$61	545%
100 Suncor Energy	2/28/2007	2/28/2007	$7,106	$7,051	$55	285%
				Subtotal	**$1,746**	
				Total	**$4,734**	

Stocks Purchased During 2005, 2006, and 2007 and Not Sold as of February 28, 2007

	Closing Price as of 2/28/2007
100 Fannie Mae (FNM) Bought 1/19/05 at $67.74	$56.76
100 Wal-Mart Stores (WMT) Bought 3/10/05 at $52.29	$48.31
100 Wal-Mart Stores (WMT) Bought 3/10/05 at $52.29	$48.31
100 Viacom Class A (VIA) Bought 3/17/05 at $37.39	
Company was restructured December 31, 2005	
Holdings are now:	
50 CBS Corporation (CBS) Sold 5/22/07 at $32.81	$30.37
50 Viacom (VIA) Sold 5/22/07 at $43.92	$39.56
100 Viacom Class A (VIA) Bought 3/18/05 at $36.99	
Company was restructured December 31, 2005	
Holdings are now:	
50 CBS Corporation (CBS) Sold 5/22/07 at $32.76	$30.37
50 Viacom (VIA) Sold 5/22/07 at $43.50	$39.56
100 Tyco International (TYC) Bought 4/14/05 at $33.58	$30.83
300 Ford Motor Co. (F) Bought 9/15/05 at $9.87	$7.91
100 Fifth Third Bancorp (FITB) Bought 11/29/05 at $41.36 Sold 5/23/07 at $41.97	$40.28
100 Juniper Networks (JNPR) Bought 12/6/05 at $23.02 Sold 5/8/07 at $23.63	$18.91
1,000 Gateway (GTW) Bought 12/12/05 at $2.95	$2.06
200 Intel Corp. (INTC) Bought 1/18/06 at $22.79 Sold 5/23/07 at $23.09	$19.86
100 Yahoo! Inc. (YHOO) Bought 1/18/06 at $35.48	$30.86
100 Yahoo! Inc. (YHOO) Bought 2/2/06 at $34.37	$30.86
100 Cheesecake Factory (CAKE) Bought 5/31/06 at $29.27	$27.29
100 Qualcomm Inc. (QCOM) Bought 6/2/06 at $46.80	$40.30
100 Peabody Energy (BTU) Bought 8/9/06 at $48.71 Sold 4/23/07 at $49.65	$40.42
100 BP Plc (BP) Bought 8/23/06 at $69.36	$61.54
100 BP Plc (BP) Bought 8/23/06 at $69.33	$61.54
100 Cheesecake Factory (CAKE) Bought 11/27/06 at $28.61 Sold 4/26/07 at $29.49	$27.29
100 Electronic Arts (ERTS) Bought 12/6/06 at $54.40	$50.42

(Continues)

	Closing Price as of 2/28/2007
200 Motorola (MOT) Bought 12/7/06 at $21.79	$18.52
100 Peabody Energy (BTU) Bought 12/11/06 at $46.57 Sold 4/16/07 at $47.52	$40.42
300 Micron Technology (MU) Bought 12/11/06 at $14.33	$11.86
100 Anadarko Petroleum Corp. (APC) Bought 12/18/06 at $43.91 Sold 4/9/07 at $44.57	$40.29
200 Advanced Micro Devices (AMD) Bought 12/21/06 at $21.12	$15.07
100 BP Plc (BP) Bought 1/3/07 at $66.72 Sold 4/13/07 at $68.14	$61.54
200 Constellation Brands (STZ) Bought 1/4/07 at $25.37	$23.46
100 Commerce Bancorp (CBH) Bought 1/8/07 at $34.61 Sold 5/30/07 at $35.38	$33.38
200 Advanced Micro Devices (AMD) Bought 1/16/07 at $18.09	$15.07
100 SLM Corporation (SLM) Bought 1/18/07 at $46.47 Sold 4/16/07 at $55.31	$42.65
200 Advanced Micro Devices (AMD) Bought 1/24/07 at $15.99	$15.07
100 Suncor Energy (SU) Bought 1/26/07 at $74.85 Sold 3/28/07 at $75.99	$71.13
100 Anadarko Petroleum Corp. (APC) Bought 2/7/07 at $42.09 Sold 3/26/07 at $42.80	$40.29
100 Johnson & Johnson (JNJ) Bought 2/21/07 at $65.00	$62.93
100 Johnson & Johnson (JNJ) Bought 2/22/07 at $64.89	$62.93
100 Sanofi-Aventis (SNY) Bought 2/22/07 at $43.56 Sold 4/11/07 at $44.20	$42.41
100 General Electric (GE) Bought 2/22/07 at $35.51 Sold 4/27/07 at $36.18	$34.91
200 Pfizer Inc. (PFE) Bought 2/22/07 at $25.89 Sold 4/12/07 at $26.33	$24.96
100 Carnival Corp. (CCL) Bought 2/23/07 at $47.81 Sold 4/25/07 at $48.41	$46.44
100 Washington Mutual (WM) Bought 2/26/07 at $43.33 Sold 5/22/07 at $44.01	$43.08
200 Motorola (MOT) Bought 2/27/07 at $18.92	$18.52
200 Dell (DELL) Bought 2/27/07 at $23.46 Sold 3/27/07 at $23.82	$22.85
200 Corning Inc. (GLW) Bought 2/27/07 at $20.85 Sold 3/7/07 at $21.16	$20.63
100 SLM Corp. (SLM) Bought 2/27/07 at $42.76 Sold 4/13/07 at $45.32	$42.65
100 Eli Lilly (LLY) Bought 2/27/07 at $53.81 Sold 4/2/07 at $54.40	$52.59
100 Weatherford Intl. (WFT) Bought 2/27/07 at $40.89 Sold 3/7/07 at $41.54	$40.10
200 Statoil ASA (STO) Bought 2/27/07 at $25.41 Sold 3/1/07 at $25.72	$25.56
100 Texas Instruments (TXN) Bought 2/27/07 at $30.69 Sold 3/6/07 at $31.65	$30.96

Stock sale updates as of 5/31/07

Notes

PREFACE

1. Martha A. Brożyna, Gender and Sexuality in the Middle Ages: A Medieval Source Documents Reader (Jefferson, NC: McFarland, 2005).
2. The trading results that Martha achieves with her family's money are not included in the appendixes, which provide details of Martha and Aidan's personal trading for their own account only.

CHAPTER 1

1. Steve Fraser, *Every Man a Speculator* (New York: HarperCollins, 2005), 391.
2. Ibid., 389.
3. Staff, "Saving Graces for your 401K Plan," *Fortune Special Sections*, 12 May 2003. <http://www.timeinc.net/fortune/services/sections/fortune/finc/2003_05saving.html>.
4. Investment Company Institute, "Frequently Asked Questions about Stock Mutual Funds," August 2006. <http://www.ici.org/funds/abt/faqs_mf_stock_funds.html>.
5. Investment Company Institute, "401(k) Plan Asset Allocation, Account Balances, and Loan Activity in 2005," *Research Perspective* 12, no. 1 (August 2006), 00. <http://www.ici.org/stats/res/per12-01.pdf>.
6. Garry Emmons, "Where Main Street Meets Wall Street," *Harvard Business School Working Knowledge for Business Leaders*, 12 October 1999. <http://hbswk.hbs.edu/item/2583.html>.
7. Jeremy J. Siegel, *Stocks for the Long Run* (New York: McGraw-Hill, 2002), 13.

CHAPTER 2

1. Michael Maiello, "Day Trading Eldorado," *Forbes*, 12 June 2000.
2. Peter Lynch, *Beating the Street* (New York: Simon & Schuster, 1993), 284.
3. James J. Cramer, *Jim Cramer's Real Money: Sane Investing in an Insane World* (New York: Simon & Schuster, 2005), 164–165.
4. Toni Turner, *A Beginner's Guide to Day Trading Online* (Holbrook, MA: Adams Media, 2000), 76.

CHAPTER 3

1. Robert Rhea, *The Story of the Averages* (Colorado Springs, CO: Rhea-Greiner & Co., 1934), 12.
2. Ibid.
3. Robert Rhea, *The Dow Theory: An Explanation of its Development and an Attempt to Define its Usefulness as an Aid in Speculation* (New York: Barron's, 1932), 13, 35.
4. Rhea, *The Story of the Averages*, 57.
5. Rhea, *The Dow Theory*, 32.
6. Rhea, *The Story of the Averages*, 12.
7. Rhea, *The Dow Theory*, 86.
8. Rhea, *The Story of the Averages*, 57.

CHAPTER 4

1. David Dreman, *Contrarian Investment Strategy* (New York: Random House, 1980); and David Dreman, *Contrarian Investing Strategies: The Next Generation* (New York: Simon & Schuster, 1998).
2. Anthony M. Gallea and William Patalon III, *Contrarian Investing* (New York: New York Institute of Finance, 1998).
3. Peter Lynch, *One Up on Wall Street: How to Use What You Already Know to Make Money in the Market* (New York: Simon and Schuster, 1989), 55.
4. Ibid., 59.

CHAPTER 5

1. Peter Lynch, *One Up on Wall Street: How to Use What You Already Know to Make Money in the Market* (New York: Simon and Schuster, 1989); Peter Lynch, *Beating the Street* (New York: Simon & Schuster, 1993); and Peter Lynch, *Learn to Earn: A Beginner's Guide to the Basics of Investing and Business* (New York: Simon and Schuster, 1995).
2. Li Yuan and Christopher Rhoads, "Icahn Bid Adds to Woes Dogging Motorola's CEO," *Wall Street Journal*, 31 January 2007.

CHAPTER 6

1. Jonathan Charkham, *Keeping Good Company: A Study of Corporate Governance in Five Countries* (Oxford: Clarendon Press, 1994), 76.
2. Ibid., 95.

CHAPTER 7

1. Charles Forelle and James Bandler, "The Perfect Payday," *Wall Street Journal*, 18 March 2006.

CHAPTER 8

1. Robert G. Hagstrom Jr., *The Warren Buffett Way: Investment Strategies of the World's Greatest Investor* (New York: John Wiley & Sons, 1994), 52.

Bibliography

Charkham, Jonathan. *Keeping Good Company: A Study of Corporate Governance in Five Countries*. Oxford: Clarendon Press, 1994

Cramer, James J. *Jim Cramer's Real Money: Sane Investing in an Insane World*. New York: Simon & Schuster, 2005.

Dreman, David. *Contrarian Investment Strategy*. New York: Random House, 1980.

_____. *Contrarian Investing Strategies: The Next Generation*. New York: Simon & Schuster, 1998.

Emmons, Garry. "Where Main Street Meets Wall Street." *HBS Working Knowledge*, 12 October 1999.

Forelle, Charles, and James Bandler. "The Perfect Payday." *Wall Street Journal*, 18 March 2006.

Fortune Staff. "Saving Graces for your 401K Plan." *Fortune*, 12 May 2003.

Fraser, Steve. *Every Man a Speculator*. New York: HarperCollins, 2005.

Frost, A. J., and Robert R. Prechter. *Elliott Wave Principle*. Chappaqua, NY: New Classics Library, 1995.

Gallea, Anthony M., and William Patalon III. *Contrarian Investing*. New York: New York Institute of Finance, 1998.

Hagstrom, Jr., Robert G. *The Warren Buffett Way: Investment Strategies of the World's Greatest Investor*. New York: John Wiley & Sons, 1994.

Investment Company Institute. "401(k) Plan Asset Allocation, Account Balances, and Loan Activity in 2005." *Research Perspective* **12**, no. 1 (August 2006).

_____. "Frequently Asked Questions About Stock Mutual Funds," August 2006. <http://www.ici.org/funds/abt/faqs_mf_stock_funds.html>.

Lynch, Peter. *Beating the Street*. New York: Simon & Schuster, 1993.

_____. *Learn to Earn: A Beginner's Guide to the Basics of Investing and Business*. New York: Simon and Schuster, 1995.

_____. *One Up on Wall Street: How to Use What You Already Know to Make Money in the Market*. New York: Simon and Schuster, 1989.

Maiello, Michael. "Day Trading Eldorado." *Forbes*, June 12, 2000.

Rhea, Robert. *The Dow Theory: An Explanation of its Development and an Attempt to Define its Usefulness as an Aid in Speculation*. New York: Barron's, 1932.

_____. *The Story of the Averages.* Colorado Springs, CO: Rhea-Greiner & Co., 1934.

Siegel, Jeremy J. *Stocks for the Long Run.* New York: McGraw-Hill, 2002.

Turner, Toni. *A Beginner's Guide to Day Trading Online.* Holbrook, MA: Adams Media Corp., 2000.

Yuan, Li and Christopher Rhoads. "Icahn Bid Adds to Woes Dogging Motorola's CEO." *Wall Street Journal,* 31 January 2007.

About the Authors

Aidan J. McNamara is associate publisher at The Deal, LLC in New York, publisher of the weekly financial magazine *The Deal* as well as *The Daily Deal* and TheDeal.com. He holds an MA (with distinction) in Area Studies (Eastern Europe and Russia) from the University of London, a joint degree of the School of Slavonic and East European Studies and the London School of Economics awarded in 1981. He also has a BA in German from the University of Manchester, England (1980). He has worked in financial publishing in New York City since 1996, initially with *Institutional Investor* magazine and then with *The Deal*. For the previous 14 years he held various international banking positions with the U.K.-based Lloyds Bank Group, (now Lloyds TSB Group), including at the bank's London head office as well as short-term assignments at a number of international branches around the world. This period also included multiyear postings to Portugal, Germany, and the United States. From 1992 to 1995 he was the sole New York representative of The National Bank of New Zealand, at that time a subsidiary of Lloyds Bank.

Martha A. Brożyna received a PhD in history from the University of Southern California in 2005 and a BA in history and political science from Rutgers University, where she graduated Phi Beta Kappa in 1995. She also studied at the Polish Academy of Arts and Sciences, Institute of History in Warsaw, Poland in 1998–1999, with funding from a Fulbright grant. She has taught courses in Latin and World and Western Civilization at Rutgers University and Essex County College, New Jersey. She has authored numerous articles in books and journals and presented at several conferences on topics related to her specialty field of medieval history with particular focus on women's history and the history of sexuality. She published *Gender and Sexuality in the Middle Ages: A Medieval Source Documents Reader* in 2005 (Jefferson, NC: McFarland & Co.).

Robert Teitelman is the founding editor-in-chief of The Deal, LLC, which includes the weekly *Deal, Daily Deal* and TheDeal.com. Previous to *The*

Deal, he had been the editor of *Institutional Investor* magazine and had worked at *Forbes* and *Financial World* magazines. He is a graduate of the College of William and Mary in 1976 and holds graduate degrees in international affairs and journalism from Columbia University (1978, 1981). He is also the author of two books, *Gene Dreams: Wall Street, Academia and the Rise of Biotechnology* (1989) and *Profits of Science: The American Marriage of Science and Technology* (1994).

Index